Essays and st

Reading Leslie Marmon Silko

Critical Perspectives through
Gardens in the Dunes

Edited by
Laura Coltelli

EDIZIONI
plūs
pisa university
press

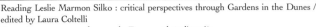

Reading Leslie Marmon Silko : critical perspectives through Gardens in the Dunes /
edited by Laura Coltelli
(Learning resources and research. Essays and studies ; 1)

813.54 (21.)
1. Silko, Leslie Marmon   I. Coltelli, Laura

CIP a cura del Sistema bibliotecario dell'Università di Pisa

© Copyright 2007 by Edizioni Plus - Pisa University Press
Lungarno Pacinotti, 43
56126 Pisa
Tel. 050 2212056 – Fax 050 2212945
info-plus@edizioniplus.it
www.edizioniplus.it

Member of

Page layout
David Nieri

Cover
Jacopo Ligozzi, *Papavera Somniferum fl. pleno* (28x46), 1926 Orn. (GDSU - Gabinetto Disegni e Stampe,
Galleria degli Uffizi, Firenze). Under licence from the Ministero dei Beni e delle Attività Culturali.
Any further reproduction shall not be allowed.

ISBN 978-88-8492-432-2

CONTENTS

ACKNOWLEDGMENTS

The initial idea of this collection of essays on *Gardens in the Dunes* (1999) by Leslie Marmon Silko arose from a workshop at the Mystic Lake Symposium on Native American literature that was held in Minnesota in 2004, splendidly organized by Gwen Griffin.

The group of participants present on that occasion (Deborah Miranda, Barbara Robins, Kim Roppolo, Annette Van Dyke) has over the past months increased to include other colleagues, both European and American, who enthusiastically accepted my invitation to create this work.

The resulting variety of approaches to the novel offers a vast interpretive range, highlighting specific aspects or focusing on the historical context, how the characters are built up, the clash/meeting between cultures and civilizations, intertextuality, language peculiarities. Some of the most evident themes that characterize *Gardens* — such as that of the garden conceived within a wide-ranging metaphorical framework, or that of a feminine principle linking characters and events throughout the unfolding story, have aroused a common interest, as is natural, thereby contributing to confirmation of an interpretive framework or providing further insight into such a vast and complex novel.

Special thanks to all the contributors who have shown great helpfulness and goodwill and in overcoming the occasional drawbacks and delays that derived from working at a distance, exacerbated at times by the quirks of technology. Undaunted, their spirits have been constantly buoyed by a sense of closeness transmitted through unfailing enthusiasm and the desire to provide as exhaustive a reading as possible of this developmental path through various worlds that Leslie Silko once again invites us to explore.

I would also like to express sincere thanks to the University of Pisa Press (the only Italian University Press to be a member of the American University Presses) for accepting this work, and deeply felt gratefulness to Rachele Avagliano — a Ph.D. candidate in American Literature — for painstaking and meticulous work on the copy-editing stage of the collection, which she performed with great devotion, precision and infinite patience. A similar word of gratitude to Dr. Rachel Barritt Costa who has given generously of her time, interest, encouragement and expertise to make this book possible.

Finally, heartfelt thanks to Leslie Marmon Silko for showing us that flowers, plants and gardens, in their colors, in their intimate essence, preserve and transmit history and culture, differences and affinities, sense of belonging and an ever-present potential of fruitful exchange.

LESLIE MARMON SILKO'S
GARDENS IN THE DUNES:
CONTACT ZONES AND CROSS CURRENTS

A. LaVonne Brown Ruoff

As more and more contemporary Indian authors have visited or studied abroad, several of them have incorporated their experiences into their writing. Among these is Leslie Marmon Silko (Laguna, b. 1949).[1] The fact that these writers have expanded the subject of their writing beyond narratives about their tribes and Native American experience in the United States raises for some critics the extent to which their work is Native American literature. Elizabeth Cook-Lynn (Lakota) argues, for example,

> authority lies in *nationalism*, not *cosmopolitanism*. The persistent political questions that plague the study of the literatures of indigenous populations in America can be put aside only if the intellect of a people expressed in literary art is examined as the fabric holding people together, not as the fundamental difference or similarity that either embraces or denies its colonization, or as a danger or threat to or collaborator in the eminence and aesthetic autonomy of American canonical thought.
>
> ("Literary and Political Questions" 41–42)

Elsewhere Cook-Lynn laments that "few significant works are being produced today by the currently popular American Indian fiction writers who examine the meaningfulness of indigenous or tribal sovereignty in the twenty-first century" ("The American Indian Fiction Writers" 85).

In *Gardens in the Dunes*, Silko challenges this concept of Native American literature by locating part of her novel in Europe and South America.[2] She uses the age-old literary device of placing a naïve protagonist in the midst of an alien and unfamiliar country in order to portray her reactions to these strange civilizations.

Silko focuses on issues arising from the encounters between people from different cultures—how concepts of power determine relations between American Indians and non-Indians from the United States and Europe. As Michel Foucault points out, power is "the process which, through ceaseless struggles and confrontations, transforms, strengthens, or reverses them" (92–93). Mary Louise Pratt calls the intersections of such encounters the "'contact zones,' social spaces where disparate cultures meet, clash, and grapple with each other, often in highly asymmetrical relations of domination and subordination" (4). For Pratt, the contact perspective emphasizes "how subjects are constituted in and by their relations to each other" (7). *Gardens* also incorporates what Pratt calls the "transcultural" process that occurs during the colonial encounter (6). Such encounters include as well the concept of hybridity. Homi Bhabha stresses that the language of the critique of colonialism can bridge the polarity of colonizer/colonized by creating a space of place of "hybridity," a "third-space," where communication, negotiation and, by implication, translation can occur and where the construction of a "a political object that is new, <u>neither the one nor the other</u>, properly alienates our political expectations, and changes, as it must, the very forms of our recognition of the moment of politics" (25).

To illustrate the strength of the response of her protagonist, Indigo, to Euro-American and European cultures, Silko devotes sections of her novel to delineating the young girl's traditional tribal culture, either through descriptions of events as they happen or through memory. Silko also depicts Indigo's assimilation and the kind of changes she must endure in order to live within a non-Indian environment. Indigo wears a psychological mask to hide her true identity and feelings from non-Indians. Arnold Krupat notes that for all the "complex relations with white Americans and Europeans," Sister Salt and Indigo are "entirely secure in their Indian identities." He also points out that the girls need to go home to continue to be who they are (113; 141; note 29). The author also uses multiple-voiced and multicultural discourse to enable her protagonist to express her true self. Critic and novelist Louis Owens (Cherokee/Choctaw) comments that "for Native Americans the only burden of expectation is that he or she put on the constructed mask provided by the colonizer, and the mask is not merely a mirror but more crucially a static death mask, fashioned beforehand, to which the living person is expected to conform" (218).

Gardens is a complex mix of locations and themes. Even more than she did in *Almanac of the Dead*, Silko adopts here a global perspective on the relationship that human kind developed with nature and religion. Her own experiences in Europe influenced this global perspective because her visits there connected her to her European ancestors. In a 1998 interview with Ellen Arnold, Silko emphasizes that while she was on book tours in Zurich and Germany, she strongly felt the spirits of her German ancestors. She also emphasizes her that her ancestors and her love of old stones linked her to Scotland: "I knew there was something of what's alive there [Europe], that there's a kind of continuity . . . Europe is not completely Christianized. . . . There is a pagan heart there, and the old spirits are right there" (166). In the same interview, Silko strongly contradicts Cook-Lynn's emphasis on American Indian nationalism and regionalism when she states that "the Pueblo people, the indigenous people of the Americas, we're not only Indian nations and sovereign nations and people, but we are citizens of the world" (165). As an author, Silko says she tries to "get rid of this idea of nationality, borderlines and drawing lines in terms of time and saying, oh well, that was back then." Those who "would make the boundary lines and try to separate them [people in Europe and the Indigenous peoples in the Americas] those are the manipulators. Those are the Gunadeeyah, the destroyers, the exploiters" (170).

In the "Author's Note" in the "Scribner Paperback Fiction Reading Group Guide," Silko describes how she combined the story of two young sisters with her interest in Old Europe.[3] She also stresses her love of gardens, which, in the novel, represent unity with nature. Gardening and oneness with nature are major themes in the novel. As Angelika Köhler perceptively comments, the gardens "function as images or historical paradigms, of cultural systems; they symbolize values of beauty and concepts of thinking; the represent social hierarchies, among others, the dichotomies of man versus nature or man and nature, respectively" (239).

Silko's love of gardening dates back to her childhood, when all the households at Laguna had vegetable gardens and she used to help her great-grandmother water her flowers:

> Nearly all human cultures plant gardens, and the Garden itself has ancient religious connections. For a long time I've been interested in pre-Christian European beliefs, and the pagan devotions to sacred groves of trees and sacred springs. My German translator gave me a fascinating book on the archaeology of Old Europe, and in it I discovered ancient artifacts that showed the Old European cultures once revered snakes, just as we Pueblo Indian people still do. So I decided to take all these elements orchids, gladiolus, ancient gardens, Victorian gardens, Native American gardens, Old European figures of Snake-bird Goddesses and write a novel about two young sisters at the turn of the century. (Author's note)

Gardens is an epic-like novel, which centers on the lives of two sisters, Salt Sister and Indigo, who live with their mother and Grandmother Fleet. Although Silko depicts Salt Sister as a member of a Colorado River tribe, she undoubtedly bases the name on Old Salt Woman, a spirit figure in Pueblo and Navajo religion.[4] Salt is also the name of the protagonist of D'Arcy McNickle's *The Runner in the Sun*, in which the young Pueblo saves his people by journeying to Mexico to bring back maize.

The young girls, mother, and grandmother are the only members of the fictional Sand Lizard people still inhabiting the old gardens of the desert near the lower Colorado River.[5] Silko bases the gardens on those on her family's property near Laguna (Arnold 173). She depicts the Sand Lizards as a nation of desert dwellers who lived in harmony with their natural environment. For hundreds of years before the Euro-American invaders came, the Sand Lizard people lived in the "old gardens" in the desert, gathering foods and planting crops. The Sand Lizard people trust rain clouds to water their crops rather than depend either on the Colorado River, which divides Arizona and California, or on food distributed at reservations, as many Colorado River tribes did. In an interview with Arnold, Silko says that the groups from this area were Uto-Aztecan mixed with Yuman: "So many of the cultures along the Colorado River were completely wiped out. There's no trace of them left. And it was done by gold miners and ranchers" (163). Silko created a fictional tribe because

> I wanted them to be from a group that was completely obliterated. But also I wanted the artistic and ethical freedom to imagine them any way I wanted. . . . I did do lots and lots of reading about the Colorado River area and the tribes and the people, and then I tried to imagine a people who had characteristics that made others remark they were different.   (Arnold 172–73)

One aspect of the group's strangeness is its attitude toward its enemies. After the Sand Lizard people fiercely fought the Apaches, they freed their enemies when they realized their opponents were defeated. Unlike other tribes, the Sand Lizard people valued "sex with strangers for alliances and friendships that might be made" (202). Also unlike other tribes, they did not smother their "half-breed babies because they were afraid of them" (202). Sand Lizard mothers were so powerful that their bodies changed everything in their fetuses to Sand Lizard. Consequently, this group did not distinguish between full and half-bloods. For example, Sister Salt is the half-blood child of a Sand Lizard mother and the white preacher who raped her. Creating a tribe, describing the interactions between the surviving Lizard people and other tribes, and incorporating events that affected Indian sovereignty during the 1890s and early twentieth century, Silko grounds her novel's characters in their tribal world before she introduces the South American and European segments.

The novel begins during the period of the Ghost Dance Movement, led by Wovoka or Jack Wilson (Paiute, 1858–1932). From 1889, the movement spread from the Paiutes through the Plains Indians. In the novel, the mother and sisters take part in a Ghost Dance at Needles, California, which Silko told

Arnold she based on one held in 1893 at Kingman, Arizona (167). Silko also uses the fictional Ghost Dance to introduce the theme of the Messiah or Jesus, who is a unifying figure in the novel. As Lee Schweninger comments, the Messiah "speaks across cultures, as well as across continents" (69).

Silko may refer to the Ghost Dance that the Walapai or Pai held in 1889 in Kingman. While Silko stresses Paiute dominance in the novel's Ghost Dance, Henry F. Dobyns and Robert C. Euler emphasize Walapai participation in the Kingman ceremony. The Walapai "borrowed" the dance from their Southern Paiute neighbors to the north. Dobyns and Euler describe the ritual as "a response to a group trauma resulting from the Pai's demoralizing contact with Anglo Americans" (vii-viii). Although the Ghost Dance contained numerous formal similarities to traditional Pai rituals, its emphasis on resurrection and a messiah-like figure similar to Jesus differed from the Pai's native religion. The ritual and its concepts fractured Pai religious unity, which was never restored. Dobyns and Euler conclude that the Ghost Dance offered the Pai both fantasy compensation and a substitute for political action (1–2). Sometime between September, 1889, and June, 1890, a large Ghost Dance may have been held near Kingman, which was not reported in the local newspaper. According to Dobyns and Euler, "'all the Walapais from all parts of their country got together for the biggest dance they ever had after the white people came'." The authors conclude that the Ghost Dance movement among the Walapai passed its peak and began to lose adherents in the spring of 1891 (21; 34).[6]

In *Gardens*, the Ghost Dance at Needles marks a turning point in the family's life together because shortly thereafter the Indian police take away the sisters' mother. Grandmother Fleet subsequently dies and the two girls are captured trying to find their mother. Sister Salt is sent to the agency at Parker, Arizona, now the Colorado Reservation, while Indigo is sent to the Sherman Institute, Riverside California.[7] Although Sister Salt escapes the reservation school, she remains near Parker, where she becomes a laundry entrepreneur and sometime prostitute to the men who arrive to build the Parker Canyon dam. Sister Salt works and lives with Big Candy, whose baby she bears. Candy, who is African American and part Muscogee-Creek, is a gourmet cook for and business partner of a white man. Candy's partner runs most of the operations in Parker. When the army takes over the town, Sister Salt returns with her baby to the old gardens.

Most of the novel is devoted to the physical, psychological, and spiritual journey that Indigo must take before she gains the knowledge of plants necessary for survival and has the opportunity to return to the old gardens to be reunited with her sister. Indigo is a naïve, affectionate observer whose responses link her experiences in the white world with those of her Indian culture. To some extent, she plays the role of the "wise fool" because as a child, her responses are instinctive and are not corrupted by being reared in a corrupt society. She perceives things that her older, non-Indian companions miss.

After Indigo escapes from Riverside, she hides in the orchards of Edward and Hattie Palmer, who persuade the school to let the child stay with them in order to learn how to be a servant. Indigo brings impulsiveness, affection, and a deep love of animals and nature to a couple primarily motivated by cold intellectuality. Indigo's loving companions are Edward's monkey, Linnaeus, and later the parrot, Rainbow, a gift from the amateur scientist's sister.[8] Edward's unsuccessful schemes take him to Brazil and Corsica, where he attempts to find plants he can sell or a farm to make money. In the end, this would-be capitalist is defeated by his own greed. Before her marriage, Hattie Abbott was educated at home in Oyster Bay, Massachusetts, and graduated from Vassar. She defies her mother's wishes by taking a reading program at Harvard in preparation for applying for admission to its graduate program. Silko bases Hattie on Margaret Fuller (1810–50), a critic, journalist, and social reformer, who, Silko says, was a "great hero of mine" (Arnold 179). After the thesis committee turns down Hattie's unorthodox proposal to write her master's thesis on "The Female Principle in the Early Church," a male student she trusted tries to force himself upon her. Hattie subsequently has a mental breakdown and her doctor advises her not to immerse herself further in intellectual pursuits. Hattie's marriage to Edward Palmer removes her from the difficult status of being a failed student and unmarried woman. For Hattie, the relationship with Indigo brings out maternal longings and a capacity for love, of which she was unaware. *Gardens* recounts Hattie's journey to find herself and her place as an independent woman. By the end of the novel, Hattie leaves Edward, who dies shortly thereafter. Hattie fulfills her earlier promise to help Indigo rejoin her sister and then moves abroad to join Aunt Bronwyn and their mutual friend, *professoressa* Laura.

One of the major themes in the novel is Europeans' and Euro-Americans' unending desire to renovate and desire in order to introduce something new, which they replace with something even newer. This theme and the influence of Old Europe on Americans is portrayed in the conflict over the family gardens between Edward Palmer and his sister, Susan Palmer James. Edward cherishes the Italian Renaissance gardens now reaching their maturity and decorated with statuary. Susan destroys all this to create an English landscape garden. Ironically English gardens are already out of fashion. The artificiality of Susan's management of nature is exemplified by her elaborate attempts to create a blue garden, even though some of her hot-house plants wilt before her annual Blue Garden Masque, an event designed to show off her gardens.

In the sections on the Palmer's and Indigo's visit to England and Italy, Silko introduces Aunt Bronwyn and *professoressa* Laura. These two strong, sympathetic, and knowledgeable women are excellent guides for the group and kind mentors to Hattie and Indigo. Aunt Bronwyn and Laura are American and European equivalents of Grandmother Fleet. Both are deeply committed to nature and antiquities, which differentiates them from most other people. Further, both are accomplished storytellers, steeped in the mythology and lore of the regions where they reside. Sensitive to Hattie's and Indigo's feelings, Aunt Bronwyn and Laura provide them with needed emotional support. In order to focus more intensely on the environment and antiquities of England and Italy, Silko does not include extended characterizations of other people from these countries. Very minor characters appear, perform their functions, and disappear very quickly.

Aunt Bronwyn's grandfather was an Englishman who revered and collected old stones. After her English husband died, Aunt Bronwyn remained in England and resided on the estate inherited from her grandfather. How different Aunt Bronwyn is from her neighbors is exemplified by her participation in the Antiquity Rescue Committee, which protects an ancient grove of oaks and yews near a stone circle as well as migrating toads. Aunt Bronwyn emphasizes the danger of tampering with ancient stones because they and the groves housed the spirits of the dead. She claims that the Potato Famine of 1846 and European wars were caused by crimes against the stones and groves.[9] Her grandfather tried to find fragments of the old stones. This, Aunt Bronwyn says, is "the land of the stones that dance and wake after midnight" (237). Her stories and Laura's remind us of the universal interrelationship between belief and ancient stories. Silko's use of myth in the novel recalls Mircea Eliade's description of such stories as "an extremely complex cultural reality . . . . Myth narrates a sacred history; it relates an event that took place in primordial time, the fabled time of the 'beginnings'" (5).

Aunt Bronwyn's strong link to nature is exemplified by her close relationship to her white cattle, which she feeds and calls in song-like tones. Descended from an old Celtic breed, the cattle have the shape of a crescent moon on their horns. According to Aunt Bronwyn, this mark means the cattle belong to the moon. Her great passion is restoring the old gardens of her estate. Formerly a Norman abbey, only the cloister and its walled garden remain. Aunt Bronwyn is an avid follower of the theories of "Gustav Fechner, who believed plants have souls and human beings exist only to be consumed by plans and transformed into glorious new plant life."[10] "If a garden wasn't loved," Bronwyn tells Hattie, "it could not properly grow!" (240).

Silko contrasts the beauty of the English countryside with the crassness of Bristol and Bath. When the Palmers land in the bustling, smoky port city of Bristol, Aunt Bronwyn meets them. As they cross the city, they pass the Old Slave Market, a reminder of the consequences of capitalist greed and the days when Bristol was one of the "golden triangle of world trade."[11] Although Aunt Bronwyn and Hattie talk of slavery as being in the past, Indigo reminds the adults that the threat of slavery still exists for the Sand Lizard people: "My sister and I know how to hide from the slave catchers" (231). Indigo has seen them. The Palmers dismiss her comment as exaggeration, though Aunt Bronwyn believes her. The brief Slave Market episode introduces what Lela Gandhi describes as "the troubling reciprocity between the metropolitan centre and the colonial periphery," which is sounded through the "knowledge that the metropolis is not safe from the cultural contagion of its own 'peripheral' practices" (134).

Most of the section on England is set in and around the old walled city of Bath, located on the River Avon's old flood plain. In its hills are stands of ancient oaks preserved since the time of the Celtic kings. The Romans built over an "old Celtic settlement near three thermal springs, sacred to the ancient Celtic god Sulis" (234). Because they could not permit Sulis to rule supreme, they built a temple "with a great pool over the springs, dedicated to Sulis and to Minerva as well" (234). Excavations in and around Bath reveal its occupation by the Celts, Romans, Normans, Tudors, and Elizabethans. Bath is now the refuge of "business tycoons from London and Bristol," who cut down ancient oaks on the hills to make way for gigantic mansions (235). This history underscores Silko's theme of the drive of Europeans and Euro-Americans to destroy the remnants of earlier civilizations in order to reshape the land according to their own vision or greed. The serenity of Aunt Bronwyn's gardens contrasts starkly with the hubbub and crowdedness of Bath. Her gardens are a history of many cultures that existed in England or that the English visited, such as a wild grove containing the remains of the Norman baptistery; indigenous plants of England; and those brought from Italy, the Americas, Africa, and Asia.

In the English section, Silko reintroduces her continuing theme of the clergy's endless wars against the old religions. She links the suppression of the Ghost Dance religion with earlier persecutions of non-Christians. For Silko, England is a "contact zone," in which opposing religions fought for supremacy. Aunt Bronwyn describes how the Catholic Church suppressed the Druid religion, excommunicated tree worshipers, and ordered that the ancient stones be dug up and hid. Silko reminds us that "the wisest Christians were respectful of the pagan spirits" (261). She emphasizes that this suppression was not limited to Europe. Indigo links the suppression of early religions to the whites' attempts to wipe out the Ghost Dance religion. Indigo gives a unique account of Jesus's betrayal and flight that combines Christian and Ghost Dance beliefs: After Jesus was betrayed and the Pharisees tried to have him killed, he returned to the mountains beyond Walker Lake. Although he has gone to the East, Jesus will return with the first snow. The stone circles and the stone ring at the remains of Christ Church convince Indigo that the Messiah may have stopped here. For her, Jesus is a living God who had dwelt among Indians and who will return.[12]

Also in this part of the novel, Silko establishes the interrelationship between civilizations and religions, themes she elaborates further in the segment on Italy. Much of the Italian section describes the Palmer's and Indigo's visit with *professoressa* Laura at her villa in Lucca, near Pisa.[13]

Laura is a kindly scholar, antiquities collector, and divorcee, whom Indigo immediately likes. Her reverential attitude toward artifacts contrasts with Edward's scientific beliefs. While Edward believes that the artifacts of stone and terra cotta in Laura's gardens belong in the care of scientists, she regards them as creative objects that "must have fresh air and sunshine, not burial in a museum" (294). Laura does, however, bring them inside during the winter.

A horticulturist, Laura has successfully hybridized gorgeous gladioluses.[14] Her elegant home in the hills, cooled by breezes off the mountains, and beautiful gardens are an enchanted setting, to which the Palmers and Indigo respond. The delicious food, fragrant gardens create an atmosphere reminiscent of Shakespeare's *A Midsummer Night's Dream*. The beauty of the surroundings, a sumptuous lunch, and good Italian wine relax Edward and Hattie so that "in the glow of the wine they forgot themselves and the awkward moments and embarrassments of their previous attempts at sexual intimacy. This session took them quite far indeed, although they stopped short of the act" (292). The sensuality of the moment makes Hattie realize that she wants to conceive a child. The splendid villa and its delightful surroundings seem far removed from rumors of Italian unrest after Humbert I was assassinated on 19 July, 1900.[15]

Much of this section is devoted to vivid descriptions of Laura's gardens, which, like Aunt Bronwyn's, reflect many civilizations. They include a formal Italian garden; an old woods; a black garden filled with black hybrid gladioluses, whose color symbolized fertility, birth, and the Great Mother; and a rain garden designed to be seen in the light of the moon. One of the themes of this section is the naturalness of Old Europeans' attitude toward sex. That Indigo understands such open sexual references disturbs the Palmers. The black garden's sensuality is revealed not only in its beauty and fragrance but also in its many snake and fertility symbols of creatures that are part human and part animal or are closely linked to animals. Among these are a huge head of Medusa and the figure of the Minotaur; a bold, naked fat man astride a tortoise; and a carving of a human vulva made in Macedonia in the fourth millennium; a terracotta, snake-headed figure with human arms and breasts, holding a baby snake; a mother bear holding her cub that expresses her affection for her offspring; and a snake-headed figure cradling a baby snake to her breast.[16] In Greek culture, sacred serpents regularly accompanied heroes. According to the fictional Laura, rural villages of the Black and Adriatic Seas still practice snake worship because people believed "black or green snakes bore guardian spirits that protected their cattle an their homes" (298). A white, crowned snake was the guardian of life water and life milk. Because of their association with water, snakes were also important to the fictional Sand Lizard people and to the Pueblos.

After the Palmers and Indigo leave Lucca, they travel to Corsica. There Edward illegally makes some citron cuttings to take back to California and plant on his ranch. Unfortunately for Edward, the officials arrest him and confiscate his cuttings. In the Corsica section, Silko contrasts the lush life at the villa in Lucca with the hardscrabble poverty the Corsican peasants endure. This is dramatized in the scene in which the group visits their driver's family, all of whom live in one room. The simple but abundant lunch that the peasants feed their visitors contrasts with the sumptuous feast and elegant table service at Laura's villa. In the Corsica episode, Silko moves from emphasizing the survival of the worship of ancient idols and snakes to stressing the Catholic Church's bureaucratic suppression of popular religious belief. The Corsican family takes the Palmers and Indigo to see the image of the Madonna that appears on the wall of their local abbey school. The abbey had been built to house a beautiful picture of the Madonna, made of hammered silver on gold. After the picture lost its power to heal, the image of the Virgin began to appear on the whitewashed walls of the school. This scene represents a "contact zone," in Pratt's words, or a cultural battleground in which two Corsican groups present opposing opinions. According to Silko, the attempt by angry monks carrying crucifixes to stop the group from visiting the image represents "this fight against the corporate church that tries to tell people what is holy. And yet there's the persistence of the Virgin to appear on schoolhouse walls and not stay with the silver."[17] After the monks leave, the Madonna appears because the people, whose lives were a constant struggle, needed her. Through Indigo's responses, Silko links the religion of the people to the American Indian Ghost Dance movement:

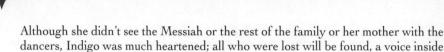

Although she didn't see the Messiah or the rest of the family or her mother with the dancers, Indigo was much heartened; all who were lost will be found, a voice inside her said; the voice came from the Messiah, Indigo was certain.   (320)

Indigo's and Hattie's travels in England and Italy provide each with a greater knowledge of Old European religion, culture, agriculture, and horticulture. Indigo learns about the existence of new plants and methods of agriculture unknown to her people. When she reunites with Sister Salt, Indigo brings with her a precious collection of seeds and knowledge that she uses to restore the old gardens in the dunes. Hattie's contacts with Indigo, Aunt Bronwyn, and Laura awaken a dormant affection in the young woman. Hattie has learned from Aunt Bronwyn and Laura lessons about independence, natural religions, gardening, and preservation of ancient trees and artifacts. These lessons and her own growing pleasure in natural beauty give Hattie an understanding of nature and of human love that transform her from a frigid woman willing to accept being ruled by a selfish, greedy, and unsuccessful husband to a loving foster mother who leaves her husband and, after his death, moves to England to live with her aunt.

Gardens is an unexpected combination of an account of Indian survival in the late nineteenth and early twentieth centuries, the role of independent women in this period, and humankind's changing religions and relationships to the land. Silko has written a compelling novel about the challenges Native people faced in the contact zone, where they interacted with Europeans and Euro-Americans. By locating the action of her novel on two continents, Silko expands the range of Native American literature.

NOTES

1. This essay is a revised version of the Silko section in "Images of Europe in Leslie Marmon Silko's *Gardens in the Dunes* and James Welch's *The Heartsong of Charging Elk*."

2. The novel is an interesting example of travel literature written from a Native point of view, although space limitations do not permit discussion here.

3. The author's note is unpaged. All references to *Gardens* are to the paperback edition (2000).

4. Elsie Parsons states that among the Laguna, Tewa, Isleta, and Zuni, the spirit is called Salt Old Woman; the Acoma equate her with Thought Woman. In the Laguna (Keres language) story, Old Salt Woman is the grandmother of the Hero Twins, Maseewi and Uyuyewe. When people refuse to feed them, the War Twins transform the humans into birds and stones. Later, the twins settle with Salt Woman at the Salt Lake of Zuni. In the Laguna "Salt-Woman" story, she and the boys enter the house of the Parrot clan but are not fed. Salt Woman prepares soup, dipping her hand into the soup to salt it. She puts into the soup scabs removed from her arms, which are salt. Her grandsons, the Hero

Twins, go outside to play shuttle cock, which they throw at the children, turning them into jays, and at the Parrot clan people, transforming them into stones. Salt Woman and the Hero Twins first go to Laguna and then south to the salt lake south of Zuni. Salt Woman tells them that they will stay in the lake and that the Zuni Parrot clan people, who carry prayer sticks, beads and down, will be in charge of the salt. Salt Woman enters the lake, shakes the water, and salt forms all around it. The Hero Twins go to live in the mountains, where they can watch over the lake. The Acoma (Keres language) story is similar (Parsons 1:196; 1:208–09 Table 1). For the story, see Franz Boas (1:17–18; 1:285–86).

5. There was a Lizard clan in Old Laguna. Around 1879, thirty or forty immigrants from Laguna were allowed to settle at Oraibi at Hopi. The Lagunas intermarried, became bilingual, and joined Hopi Corn groups, equating their clans with these groups. The Lizard clan joined Yellow Corn or Earth people. Earth or Sand are another name for the Laguna Lizard clan. See Parsons 1:925. Silko may derive the Sand Lizard's tolerance for children from mixed marriages from the intermarriage of the immigrant Lagunas with the Hopi. By the early twentieth century, people at Laguna sometimes intermarried with whites and Mexicans. Silko's own ancestry reflects this pattern.

6. See also A. L. Kroeber, ed.

7. Silko's grandfather, Henry Marmon, attended this Indian school (Arnold 163).

8. Linnaeus is named after Carolus Linnaeus (Carl Von Linné, 1707–78). The parrot is a figure that recalls both the native cultures of South America and the Southwest.

9. Silko alludes to the Irish Potato Famine (1845–49). A fungus destroyed the potatoes, which were the primary food source for most of the Irish people. Between 500,000 and 1,100,000 died during the famine. See "Irish Potato Famine."

10. Fechner (1802–87) was a German scientist and philosopher best known for his *Elemente de Psychophysic* (1860), which suggests that mind and body appear to be separate entities but are only different sides of one reality.

11. David Richardson points out that between 1730 and 1745, Bristol was "the premiere British port trading with Africa." The decline of Bristol's slave trade after 1745 was due largely to the outbreak of war with Spain in 1739 and its extension to France in 1743 (2.vii: xiii-xvi).

12. Silko began to realize "that there are lots of different Jesus Christs, and the Jesus or the Messiah of the Ghost Dance and some of the other sightings of the Holy Family in the Americas were just as valid and powerful as other sightings and versions of Jesus." Also influential was Elaine Pagel's *The Gnostic Gospels*. The two were MacArthur fellows at the same time (Arnold 164).

13. Silko has made many visits to Italy and Lucca, where her good friend, Laura Coltelli, lives. Silko dedicated *Gardens* to her. A generous hostess, Coltelli, however, is not the *professoressa* of the novel, as I suggested in an earlier version of this essay. A treasured friend of mine, Coltelli, however, has been a major force in introducing Native American literature in Italy through three issues of *Native American Literatures*, *Winged Words: American Indian Writers Speak*, and other works.

14. Silko wrote an early sketch about a gladiolus man who learned to cultivate the flower when he was at Sherman Institute. When he planted gladioluses on the family land back home, the clans people got angry because it was not a food crop. This represents a conflict between "the needs for food and economy. And so for years and years, I've intended to write this short story called "The Gladiolus Man" (Arnold 163).

15. The Palmer's awkward romantic moment may also be a deliberate contrast with the passionate scene between the lovers in Keats's *The Eve of St. Agnes*. The full name of Humbert I is Umberto Ranieri Carlo-Emanuele Giovanni-Maria Gerdinando Eugenio (b. 1844).

16. Also known as Gorgo, Medusa had a round, ugly face; snakes instead of hair; huge wings; and the teeth of a boar. Her eyes could transform people into stone. At the moment of her death, she gave birth to Pegasus and Chrysor. She may originally have been an independent earth goddess. Half man and half bull, the Minotaur is the offspring of a handsome bull and Pasiphae, whom Daedalaus disguised as a cow so that she could have sex with the bull. Minotaur is doomed to wander in a labyrinth that Daedalus created. Paul Beekman Taylor notes that in the *Aeneid* (6.24–26), Virgil referred to the Minotaur as the first mixed breed. Taylor suggests that the Minotaur "figures the violence and mixed heritage that engenders cultural change" (37).

17. According to Silko, a similar incident occurred in Yaqui country (Arnold 186).

WORKS CITED

Arnold, Ellen L. "Listening to the Spirits. An Interview with Leslie Marmon Silko." *Conversations with Leslie Marmon Silko*. Ed. Ellen L. Arnold. Literary Conversations Ser. Jackson: UP of Mississippi, 2000. 162–95.

Bhabha, Homi K. *The Location of Culture*. London: Routlege, 1994.

Boas, Franz. *Keresan Texts*. 8 vols. New York: Amer. Ethnological Soc., 1928; New York: AMS, 1974.

Coltelli, Laura. *Native American Literatures*. Pisa: 1989; 1990–91; 1992–93.

———. *Winged Words: American Indian Writers Speak*. Lincoln: U of Nebraska P, 1990.

Cook-Lynn, Elizabeth. "Literary and Political Questions of Transformation: American Indian Fiction Writer." *Anti-Indianism in Modern America: A Voice from Tatekeya's Earth*. Urbana: U of Illinois P, 2001. 34–44.

———. "Literary Criticism: What is the Future of the Native American Novel." *Ikce Wicasta: The Common People Journal* 4.12 (Winter 2001): 6–9.

———. "The American Indian Fiction Writers: Cosmopolitanism, Nationalism, the Third World, and First National Sovereignty." *Why I Can't Read Wallace Stegner and Other Essays*. Madison: U of Wisconsin P, 1997. 78–96.

Dobyns, Henry F., and Robert C. Euler. *The Ghost Dance of 1889 Among the Pai Indians of Northwestern Arizona*. Prescott Coll. Studies in Anthropology 1. Prescott, AZ: Prescott Coll. P, 1967.

Eliade, Mircea. *Myths, Dreams, and Mysteries: The Encounter Between Contemporary Faiths and Archaic Realities*. 1957. Library of Religion and Culture. 2nd ed. New York: Harper, 1967.

Fitz, Brewster E. "Chapter 7, Tolle, Lege." *Silko: Writing Storyteller and Medicine Woman*. American Indian Literature and Critical Studies Ser. 47. Norman: U of Oklahoma P, 2004. 101–232.

Foucault, Michel. *The History of Sexuality: An Introduction*. Trans. Robert Hurley. New York: Vintage, 1978.

Gandhi, Leela. *Postcolonial Theory: A Critical Introduction*. New York: Columbia, 1998.

"Irish Potato Famine." *Encyclopaedia Britannica*. 2005. Encyclopædia Britannica Premium Service 19 Dec. 2005 <http://search.eb.com.proxy.cc.uic.edu/ eb/article-9003032>.

Köhler, Angelika. "'Our human nature, our human spirit, wants no boundaries': Leslie Marmon Silko's *Gardens in the Dunes* and the Concept of Global Fiction." *Amerikastudien* 47.2 (2002): 237–44.

Kroeber, Alfred L., ed. *Walapai Ethnography*. Memoir 42. Menasha, WI: Amer. Anthropological Assn., 1935.

Krupat, Arnold. *Red Matters: Native American Studies. Rethinking the Americas*. Philadelphia: U of Pennsylvania P, 2002.

Mooney, James. *The Ghost Dance Religion and the Sioux Outbreak of 1890*. Washington: Bureau of Amer. Ethnology. 14th Annual Report (1892–93). Pt. 2. Ed. Anthony F. C. Wallace. Abr. Chicago: U of Chicago P, 1965.

Owens, Louis. *I Hear the Train: Reflections, Inventions, Refractions*. American Indian Literature and Critical Studies Ser. 40. Norman: U of Oklahoma P, 2001.

Pagel, Elaine. *The Gnostic Gospels: A Startling Account of the Meaning of Jesus and the Origin of Christianity Based on Gnostic Gospels and Other Secret Texts*. New York: Random, 2004.

Parsons, Elsie C. *Pueblo Indian Religion*. Vol. 1. 1939. Lincoln: U of Nebraska P, 1996.

Pratt, Mary Louise. *Imperial Eyes: Travel Writing and Transculturation*. London: Routledge, 1992.

Reichard, Gladys A. *Navaho Religion: A Study of Symbolism*. Bollingen Ser. 18. New York: Bollingen Foundation, 1963. Princeton: Princeton UP, 1974.

Richardson, David, ed. "The Years of Ascendancy, 1730–1745." *Bristol, Africa and the Eighteenth Century Slave Trade to America*. Vol. 2. Bristol: Bristol Rec. Soc., 1987.

Ruoff, A. LaVonne Brown. "Images of Europe in Leslie Marmon Silko's *Gardens in the Dunes* and James Welch's *The Heartsong of Charging Elk*." *Sites of Ethnicity: Europe and the Americas*. Ed. William Boelhower, Rocio Davis and Carmen Birkle. Heidelberg: Universitätsverlag, 2004. 179–98.

Schweninger, Lee. "Claiming Europe: Native American Literary Responses to the Old World." *American Indian Culture and Research Journal* 27.2 (2003): 61–76.

Silko, Leslie Marmon. *Garden in the Dunes*. New York: Scribner, 2000.

———. *Almanac of the Dead*. New York: Penguin, 1992.

Taylor, Paul Beekman. "Silko's Reappropriation of Secrecy." *Leslie Marmon Silko: A Collection of Critical Essays*. Ed. Louise K. Barnett and James L. Thorson. Albuquerque: U of New Mexico P, 1999. 23–62.

Womack, Craig. *Red on Red: Native American Literary Separatism*. Minneapolis: U of Minnesota P, 1999.

LANDSCAPES OF MIRACLES
AND MATRIARCHY IN SILKO'S
GARDENS IN THE DUNES

Mary Magoulick

The topics of matriarchy and women in religion have long interested feminists and have enjoyed unusual general popularity since the success of Dan Brown's novel *The Da Vinci Code* (2003). Yet probably the greatest attention this work has received has been to question, disprove, and discredit the content (which is admittedly speculative, i.e. fictional). Women and female centered figures or themes in most religions around the world and throughout history have long been belittled, ignored, or relegated to the margins. Yet the narratives, images, and metaphors persist, sometimes in fictional accounts. Leslie Marmon Silko's *Gardens in the Dunes* (1999) — from four years before Brown's bestseller — offers a complex and hopeful treatment of matriarchal themes that incorporates an awareness of the second-class, often despised status of women in religion. Silko's work traces the interconnections and relationships among women in a variety of religious contexts, referencing mystical women like the Virgin of Guadalupe, a Mayan blue woman, and European pagan images of the Great Mother, none of whom emerges as a primary focus, but all of whom provide an inspirational backdrop for the story. In Silko's work, all the women characters survive and thrive through vital and affirmative connections to the land and gardens, which unite and inspire her characters in communities that, given this history, emerge as miraculous just by persisting.

Silko sets her work in 1900 and employs the style and subject matter of Victorian novels in this story of a Native American orphan. The characters' adventures take them around the world in consideration of various religious and gardening practices, but always with an underlying emphasis on building community and family. Using a typical quest motif, in fact a typically Victorian one (Dickensian even, given the orphan story), Silko nevertheless rhetorically undermines the Victorian trope by using it to create fictional communities of women who challenge the patriarchy and its typical misuse of the environment. Silko subverts the patriarchal story mode with matriarchal content and messages. The term matriarchy is usually employed to indicate a society where women control politics, economy, and/or culture. Thus matriarchy cannot fully exist within a patriarchy (where men are in control). But one function of art is to explore and reconcile us to paradox. A duality where patriarchy and matriarchy coexist might seem impossible, as miraculous indeed as gardens in sand dunes. Paradox, most obviously one of landscape, is a controlling metaphor of the novel reflected in the title. Silko's women do not rule society and in fact suffer under the oppressive patriarchy. Still, they find and support each other to build communities that constitute matrices of matriarchy within the patriarchy. That their communities (and gardens) thrive *is* the miracle, at least from within the perspective of the dominant patriarchy.

Silko's women help each other and the land to survive. Nature emerges as a source that may be shaped in various ways, but (at least in this novel) only flourishes with the care women provide, even while it heals and helps them in turn. As some critics have noted, Silko's exquisite prose is infused with dream sequences and "consummately beautiful sentences" (Aldama 458). The lyrical style is especially evident in descriptions of nature: "The huge night-blooming Victoria lily dominated the center of the pool with perfumed white blossoms as big as teapots; it was early enough that the flowers were still open, crowding the smaller blue water lilies that required full sun to blossom" (161). It is appropriate that the style sparkles in descriptions of nature, since she draws profound connections between the environment, women, and their ability to build their communities through caring for the land and its fruits. The controlling metaphor of the novel is that nature is beautiful and good.

Working with nature through gardening is one of the primary means for Silko's characters to survive the patriarchal system that controls, harasses, and seduces them and to build and maintain communities of women. Gardening has long been metaphorically connected to both women and concepts of paradise in Western religions. Demeter or Ceres from Greco-Roman mythology bears the titles Goddess of the Earth, Agriculture, and Fertility (Bell). Many other cultures also link these characteristics in females deities, for instance Isis, Inanna, and Cybele are powerful women goddesses from the ancient Near East associated with fertility and agriculture: "Like Inanna, Isis and Demeter, she [Cybele] was regarded as the founder of agriculture and law" (Baring and Cashford 295). All of these women were also either punished (for instance Demeter's daughter is stolen from her) or they die or suffer in some way (for instance Inanna's descent into the underworld and Gilgamesh's mocking denial of Ishtar) (Baring and Cashford). In fact, Cynthia Eller's analysis of what she calls *"The Myth of the Matriarchal Prehistory"* reveals the improbability of a glorious past where women ruled—a true matriarchy. Instead, all the actual stories we have of such women, she points out, show women who are no longer in power, who are subjugated, controlled, domesticated, punished, or killed: "myths of women's former dominance, whether from ancient Greece or contemporary New Guinea, are used to keep women down" (178). She also reveals that there are no proven cases of exclusively female rule or dominance, whether socially or in religion. There are always male gods and heroes who exist alongside (and typically dominate) powerful women. In the long run, then, such stories support the status quo of men in power, according to Eller. But she resists pessimism as a result of such insights. Rather, Eller hopes feminists today will work toward a better future regardless of the existence or prominence of matriarchies in our past. It is such a vision of possibility and survival, written for contemporary readers, upon which Silko builds in her narrative.

The premiere woman in the Judeo-Christian tradition, Eve, fits the patterns of women as inferior to men and of women "goddesses" or heroes connected to gardening and fertility. As the first sinner, Eve is despised for causing our ejection from Eden—a perfect garden. As a result of her actions women become bearers of children (fertile) outside of "paradise" and humans are simultaneously made into tillers of soil. In this Western vision of man's relationship with nature, Adam and Eve must struggle against the land outside Eden, scratching at the soil in toil, with goals of controlling and taming the wilderness. Specifically, God tells Adam and Eve in Genesis: "Cursed you are . . . dust you shall eat . . . cursed is the ground because of you; in toil you shall eat of it all the days of your life; thorns and thistles it shall bring forth to you" (*Holy Bible*, Gen. 3.14). The "curse" toward man and the land, along with the expulsion of people from the lovely, verdant nature of paradise (now guarded against all humans by an angel), and the negative descriptions by God himself of post-Edenic nature—with "dust," "thorns," and "thistles"—all reveal much about the Western worldview in regard to gardens and nature.

Our very metaphors contain notions of "taming" or "conquering" "the wilderness," which has not been a positive image until quite recently. In addition to conceiving of nature as something to battle, we also have a Western tradition of considering nature as beneath us, something that exists for our use (and abuse). In fact this Christian attitude is believed to have overturned previous, pagan attitudes regarding nature (a perspective Silko embraces): "By destroying pagan animism, Christianity made it possible to exploit nature in a mood of indifference to the feelings of natural objects" (White 10). Our Western sense of disconnection from and superiority to nature surfaces in the actions and mindsets of most of the male characters in Silko's work.

Yet the recovery of Eden is also a powerful metaphor in the Judeo-Christian tradition. Eve's improper tasting of fruit leads to the fall from a perfect relationship with nature in an ideal garden. But the concept of redemption comes to fruition in the womb of another woman, Mary, the savior Christ's mother. According to Catholic theology, the Virgin Mary's womb is the enclosed garden (the new Eden) that bears fruit (Jesus) that according to Christian faith returns believers miraculously to paradise. Carolyn Merchant explains: "The Virgin Mary's womb becomes a metaphor for the garden into which the Holy Ghost cast his special blessing, producing Christ as mankind's savior. The enclosed garden symbolized the womb of the virgin. Mary was a garden of sweetness, blossoming with the fullness of life. She offered hope for recovering heaven" (53). Mary is arguably a goddess figure, still revered around the world by Catholics, who see her in visions and visitations, build shrines to her, wear and adorn their homes with images of her, and, most significantly, often put statues of her in their gardens. In fact the concept of the womb as garden inspires, according to Merchant, "medieval enclosed gardens" that are intricately connected in the medieval worldview to the "mysteries of womanhood" (54). Women and gardens are both associated with the hope for the reinvention of spiritual and earthly paradise.

Silko opens her novel in an Eden-like homeland to which her main character Indigo hopes relentlessly to return, a desert landscape that holds miraculous, ancient, terraced gardens: "Grandma Fleet told them the old gardens had always been there. The old-time people found the gardens already growing, planted by the Sand Lizard, a relative of Grandfather Snake, who invited his niece to settle there and cultivate her seeds" (14). Typically, dunes evoke images of an inhospitable, probably barren landscape like that to which Adam and Eve are banished. Yet contrary to both our assumptions and the instructions of God to Adam, Silko's dunes *are* the garden, the paradise that shapes and binds her community of women. Here the snake in the garden is not evil, but the progenitor and guardian, who passes his knowledge on to a woman ("his niece"). Thus from the opening of the novel, we find many motifs of the Judeo-Christian tradition — a heavenly garden, a snake that gives fruit and knowledge to a primeval woman, the establishment of gardening, and a paradise that is temporarily lost. Unlike the Eden myth, however, gardening here takes place by current humans in the original site, which exists in this world. This Sand Lizard garden is described as, "heavenly," "blossoming," "fragrant," "magical," "refreshing," "wonderful," "delicious," and "intoxicating" (all in the first paragraph), and this place evokes in the sisters, who are naked and rolling down the dunes in the opening scene, feelings of effortlessness, "ease," warmth, laughter, and belonging (13).

Such a heavenly, wonderful, magical place is a "miraculous" paradise, yet unlike Eden, it is neither lost nor entirely the work of god. In the Western tradition, a post-Edenic garden reflects inherently man's control of nature, which, as Merchant explains reflects the "'will of civilization to overcome nature and achieve unconditional human mastery over the earth'" (Merchant 50). Silko's garden results from a blend of nature and nurture; it is terraced and reflective of generations who have tended it since the first woman "cultivate[d] seeds" there. One of the lessons taught to the Indian women who tend the gardens in the dunes is to leave some fruits to seed themselves each harvest (15). Throughout the book there is a sense that women gardeners cooperate with rather than control or use nature. This cooperation with and care of nature is the means to matriarchy—a place like paradise from within this feminist rhetoric. Similarly, in many places within the text, we see Indigo at her happiest when she is in gardens. Even in the throes of homesickness, she finds comfort from nature, as in this scene: "The dawn flooded the porch with golden green light that lifted as she stepped into its radiance and pulled her toward it. She bounded down the front steps and felt the dampness of the grass through her slippers. She ran into the light pouring between the giant trees near the house along the vast lawns. To run and run over the soft earth while breathing the golden fresh air felt glorious" (160). Nature soothes and inspires Indigo, especially when she can share it with her family (as in the novel's opening scene). We find many such scenes of the women experiencing nature as soothing and inspiring throughout the novel.

Gardens involves three primary women characters, two Native sisters from the Sand Lizard people named Sister Salt and Indigo (discussed previously), and Hattie, a white, would-be scholar of religion and a proto-feminist from a prominent East Coast family. Hattie's proposed thesis topic on the "female spiritual principle in the early church," plans to examine evidence from Gnostic texts of "high status for women and the feminine influence in early Christianity," but is rejected by the patriarchal university system at Harvard's Divinity School (Silko 100–01; Ross 35). Hattie is devastated by this utter rejection of her research, "Hattie felt she had been dismissed as a suffragist" (101). Hattie suffers deep depression, diagnosed as "female hysteria, precipitated by over stimulation," that she is expected to overcome by marriage to horticulturalist Edward Palmer, whose involvement with forces destroying nature is finally his undoing (229). While Edward is in the Amazon chasing his dreams of orchid cultivation and fortune (for very male, Western goals of profit and fame), Hattie turns her attention to Indigo, whom she all but adopts when she finds the young Indian girl in her husband's greenhouse one day. It is Indigo, rather than Edward, who helps to "cure" Hattie. Indigo, the younger of the Sand Lizard sisters, hides in the garden to escape the abusive boarding school where she was placed nearby. It is significant that throughout the novel, including in this case, the women meet in gardens. The key women characters from all cultures that these two subsequently visit are also consistently connected with gardens and their cultivation.

Hattie's harsh treatment by the patriarchy threatens to destroy her; in fact toward the end of the novel she is assaulted, raped, robbed, left for dead, and then considered shamed. But Hattie survives and gets some revenge by burning the town where her attacker lives and where the White people disapprove of her as an independent woman who helps Indians. Hattie then staggers to the camp where Indigo and her community of Indian women are dancing and singing rituals of the Ghost Dance. Though Hattie seems close to death, the Indian women promise to dedicate their ritual to her. When they return from a night of dancing, Hattie is awake and tells them "how she woke feeling so much better and then noticed the beautiful glow outside the lean-to, so much like the strange light she saw before" (469). A previous view of this supernatural light (to be discussed below) comes during a strangely prophetic dream she has in England. Her vision and her cure are "miraculously" healing.

When Hattie's father arrives to the scene of her healing and vision, to "save" her, he disrupts the harmonious community of women, evident in the outrageous noise his visit provokes, "the parrot squawked loudly and the monkey screamed; the baby woke and began to cry. Hattie burst into tears" (470). Hattie in fact finds the healing light that has soothed her throughout the novel in the humble Indian camp. But her father cannot conceive that she is in her right mind to want to stay there. When Hattie refuses to accompany her parents home and instead begs them to intercede on behalf of the Indian ceremony about to be shut down, her family concludes that she is crazy and forces her to accompany them: "Hattie managed to break free of her father and left the lawyer holding the empty coat; but the soldiers dismounted and helped them subdue her. . . . Hattie struggled with her captors," but she is removed, leaving Indigo weeping for her (471). Still Hattie emerges from this removal to a happy ending, at least from Silko's point of view, by rejoining her Aunt Bronwyn, the eccentric woman in England who tends gardens, eschews the popular culture of her time, and instead uses her money to support archeological digs that investigate pre-Christian (presumably matriarchal) pagan cultures in Europe. Since, as we will see, these gardens of her aunt brought Hattie joy and "enlightenment," this is a happy ending for her. Hattie also stays in contact with Indigo and her family, sending letters, cash, and promises of continued support and love. These women so disdained and considered misfits by society at large build a firm community of love and support that seems capable of enduring even the worst assaults.

Like Hattie's struggle against patriarchy, Indigo and Sister Salt's encounters with the white world are full of exploitation, often senseless violence, and misunderstanding. The sisters are raised by their mother and grandmother in the gardens in the dunes but must travel to nearby Needles, California during winter months to meet with others, sell goods, collect seeds, and participate in messianic religious gatherings—presumably Ghost Dance gatherings (where their mother is lost one year when the government raids the event). When the grandmother dies the subsequent winter at the gardens, the girls leave the dunes in search of their mother, but are quickly seized by white men and put into the system. Sister Salt is deemed too old for the boarding school and gets shipped to a reservation-like ghetto, where she is exploited—doing laundry for the dam workers and prostituting herself (though she doesn't think of this as shameful). Although her money is eventually stolen, she is less concerned with that than with maintaining the community of women she belongs to at the camp and with caring for herself and the son she bears there. Meanwhile, upon her seizure, Indigo is placed in a harsh environment of assimilation—at boarding school—until she escapes to Hattie.

While Hattie loves and nurtures Indigo, many others in her privileged, White world, including her husband Edward, often find Indigo annoying, or at least an improper object of Hattie's attention. They indulge Hattie, and suffer Indigo, but never quite welcome her. While Hattie finds in Indigo a daughter to love, Indigo never relinquishes thoughts of home or the gardens and the lessons of her grandmother about tending them. Indigo's feelings for Hattie are strong, but as a builder of community, she is loyal to her first family and consistently dreams of a reunion: "She missed Sister and Mama; were they together now? Hattie was very kind to her but she missed her sister and mother so much" (283). Sister Salt is similarly focused on their ultimate reunion. And once she has toured the world, seen gardens by other women, and learned to listen to Indigo, even Hattie finally realizes the need to help Indigo rebuild her community: "suddenly she realized they must help the Indian child return to her sister and mother! This was all wrong! How foolish she had been!" (249). The use of exclamation points to emphasize each point here shows that Hattie has come to believe sincerely in the significance of community. We will see that Hattie's encounters with the strange, exciting light have helped her literally "see the light" of the importance of community (the light metaphor is discussed more below).

But before they return to the dessert, the makeshift family travels from New England to England, then Italy, both to visit family (Aunt Bronwyn) and for Edward to seek means to begin a citrus farm to save his floundering finances. Like so many women in the novel, Aunt Bronwyn cultivates her garden in England passionately, with "plants from all over the world" and stones from pagan times that Bronwyn claims still hold power (240). For Indigo, the adventure yields one primary result: "a wonderful opportunity for gardening ideas — Indigo had a small valise full of carefully folded wax paper packets with the seeds she'd gathered" (240). She also expands her "family," not only by deepening her relationship with Hattie, but by gathering animals as well. Bronwyn sends the group to her Italian friend Laura, a professor whose interests overlap Bronwyn's.

Even while Hattie and Indigo come to understand and deepen their commitment to community and gardens during the voyage, the dominant male, Edward, seems annoyed by their efforts and realizations. Indigo receives gifts of seeds and instructions everywhere she travels. But Edward, who wants to take from foreign gardens secretly, rather than being happy with the seeds and cuttings he too is offered, is constantly annoyed at what he thinks of as a pretense of the child's commitment to both her "family" and gardening. He bristles at the attention "the child" receives: "He found himself a bit irritated at the *professoressa*'s attention to the child, especially her generous gifts of packets of seeds and corms from her hybrids, although he could see that she made an identical bundle for him and Hattie. It seemed a bit ludicrous for Laura to pretend the Indian child would ever plant the corms or seeds, much less perform the pollination process for hybrids, even if she did take notes on all the necessary steps. Of course, Laura could not be expected to know anything about American Indians" (303). Edward's condescension is misplaced, for it is his schemes for gardening for profit that prove to be illegal, ludicrous, and even dangerous, whereas Indigo's efforts yield multiple blessings back home. In the end Edward's horticultural efforts all fail, and he has only a chimera of any human community, and that finally kills him. Meanwhile both Hattie and Indigo survive in the communities and gardens they cultivate.

In fact, several of the men in the novel strive for fame and riches, in plots typical of the genre of Victorian novels, where men survive and thrive as heroes through their industry, ingenuity, aspirations, and partly by lucky birth or circumstance. Such characters' efforts typically win riches and glory, which equal success as the patriarchy defines it. Edward fails at all such quests: to make a name for himself finding flowers, to avenge his name by becoming wealthy and famous, and then simply to survive. Interestingly all his failures seem presaged by an encounter he has early in his career with a mythical "blue woman" in Mexico. He finally dies in humiliation, still chasing gold, fame, and health, at the hands of a charlatan doctor whom Hattie warns him not to trust. Even on his deathbed, he is convinced his plans would have worked if not for bad luck: "Oh the burn of regret lest someone knowledgeable see the neat pyramid stacks of the irons and buy them before he did! He drifted off on the Pará River once more, his head rested on gardenia blossoms in the big Negress's lap in the canoe; when he looked up at her face it was sky blue" (427). While he "burns with regret" over a lost purchase and chance for fame, he remembers the blue faced woman who possibly tried to warn him of the folly of his greed. Here in his final vision of her (or anything) she seems to offer comfort or another attempt at teaching him about the rest and beauty to be found in nature. But it is unclear, with his final thoughts of regret, whether he listens. He is ultimately subsumed into the woman, the sky, in the memory of the beauties of nature he sought to exploit and control. The blue woman has her revenge, one might interpret, or perhaps it is all a simple lesson, one Edward couldn't learn in life, of the futility in trying to control nature and the loss of not realizing how to enjoy its miracles.

Another prominent male character, Sister Salt's boyfriend Big Candy, works hard at the camp where the dam workers live. Sister Salt "thought Candy's kindness to women was his best quality" (218). But in spite of his life spent mainly among Mexicans and Indians, Big Candy's main goal is very Western, to save enough hard-earned money to buy independence and his own restaurant. When his money is stolen by an interesting Mexican woman, we see his transformation: "he wasn't the man [Sister Salt] knew; he was someone different. . . . Big Candy was half crazy, frantic to recover the money. Sister Salt could tell by the expression in his eyes he blamed her and the twins because they were friendly with the woman. She pointed out she had lost everything too, but Big Candy's face was rigid with anger" (385). Following his obsession, Big Candy wanders out of the central story to chase after the Mexican woman because he cannot let go of his male dreams or his money. His quest is diminished the more we learn of the Mexican woman (Delena), who seeks to bring life and hope back to her village that was devastated by white greed and violence. She steals for the life of her community, not out of personal greed. In the end Big Candy loses his most valued sense—his taste—and becomes a literally "smaller" version of himself: "his passions . . . were gone" (461). Unlike Edward, Candy seems to realize at the end that he "'took a wrong turn'" (460). In fact he may be on the road to illumination. There is a hint that his plan to serve as a driver of a wagon going to the very place Delena is going may lead him to encounter her again. We are left wondering about Candy's future.

Virtually all men in the narrative are inadequate heroes, far less effectual and interesting than the women. Thus in Silko's version of Victorian storytelling, we find our heroes among the women. While their struggles (being separated from family, struggling against oppressive forces, going on long, arduous quests) are superficially similar to their male counterparts, their narratives challenge the primacy of male heroic quest narratives. The women's rewards are not to achieve riches or fame in the Western sense; rather their quests are to be allowed to exist outside the patriarchal system, to tend their gardens, build their communities, and live according to their own visions.

By allowing these women to find each other and build communities, Silko creates a subversive, virtually miraculous matriarchy. Her women remain strong-minded, adventurous, intelligent, caring, and loyal even in the face of dismissive attitudes, exploitation, assault, and rape. And as we have seen, all of the key female characters share a passionate devotion to gardening. Tending their gardens becomes a mundane yet miraculous conduit for survival. For instance, the dam Sister Salt observes being built finally floods most of the nearby land, making the previously arid land the Indians had been granted the most desired. "Maytha joked their land would become prime irrigated farmland soon. . . . Vedna said this must be what the Bible meant about the least shall be first" (431). The food and flowers Indigo and Sister Salt grow (partly from Indigo's worldly collection), like the gladiolus from Laura, raise the whole town's spirits, and thus make the town folk more tolerant of the Indians, as Indigo realizes: "so those flowers turned out to be quite valuable after all" (475). She also realizes their practical benefits, "Those gladiolus weren't only beautiful; they were tasty!" as the women have been eating the bulbs (476). But these makeshift gardens aren't enough for Indigo, who "had been thinking of the old gardens more and more" showing her ongoing devotion to the original gardens and to building a truly strong community there (448). So the sisters finally return home, fulfilling Indigo's dreams and the promise of the novel's opening scene.

Throughout the novel we see gardening as a fundamental means for building community and learning life's most important lessons, especially among and from the point of view of women. Through their devotion to their gardens, the women build worlds that endure to nurture body and soul—as food and as sources of beauty. Indigo thinks to herself at the end of the novel, "How strange to think these small plants traveled so far with so many hazards, yet still thrived while Edward died. Grandma Fleet was right—compared to plants and trees, humans were weak creatures" (447). Edward, the Victorian gentleman who considers his horticultural knowledge far above Indigo's, dies miserably and without success at any of his horticultural or other dreams. But though Edward mocks the very thought of Indigo gardening, she succeeds at it while also re-building a community. Hattie likewise becomes a devotee of gardens, dreaming of them often and writing to her father: "'I wish you had been with me to see the *professoressa's* black gladiolus garden with the "madonnas" in their niches,' she wrote. 'The rain garden serpent goddesses were quite wonderful. They won me over entirely'" (424). The women's successes underscore the men's failures at gardening, community, and life. Gardens grow from and help maintain matriarchies that are miraculous when viewed in light of the arrogant assumptions of the patriarchy.

More obviously miraculous events connected to landscape also occur in the novel, primarily in the form of visionary dreams. For instance, the mysterious, miraculous "shining light" soothes and helps the women characters—especially Indigo and Hattie. Indigo experiences the light during her participation in Ghost Dance ceremonies. She sees the messiah as "white" and "shining" and thinks, "No wonder he called himself the morning star!" (31). Throughout the novel this light is especially important to Hattie, for whom it represents revelation and comfort. In fact she first reads of it in the Gnostic gospels she studies, where illumination is a key tenant. The greeting, "'May you be illumined by the light'" and other references to light surface throughout her studies of the feminine element in early Christianity (97). Her studies become real when Hattie sleepwalks to a pagan stone in Aunt Bronwyn's garden that she previously dreamed of, and where she is "illumined:"

> She saw something luminous white move through the foliage of the corn plants and the tall sunflowers. Her heart beat faster as she heard the soft rhythmic sound of breathing approach her. She felt a strange stir of excitement and dread at what she would see when she stepped through the gateway. The luminosity of the light was astonishing: was she awake or asleep? How beautiful the light was! Her apprehension and dread receded; now a prismatic aura surrounded the light. It was as if starlight and moonlight converged over her as a warm current of air enveloped her; for an instant Hattie felt such joy she wept.   (248)

This great joy also gives inspiration, for it is at this point that Hattie decides to return Indigo to her family (249).

Hattie gets various tantalizing pieces of information that explain her vision of the mysterious light throughout her journey, and each mention quickens her heart. The light seems connected with an ancient mask, animal figures, other objects from the matriarchal gardens of Aunt Bronwyn and Laura, and with Christ and his mother, the Virgin Mary. In fact it is while looking at an apparition of Mary in Corsica that Hattie realizes the light as specifically *miraculous*: "So this was what was called a miracle—she felt wonder and excitement, though she saw the flow of colored light on the wall for only an instant" (320). Whenever she dreams of, recalls, or hears mention of the light, she feels "peace" (327), "well-being and love" and "happiness" (406). "The glowing light" is "more real now than her manuscript or her marriage" (372), making it the real reason for her healing, not only from her attack, but from her brutalization in general at the hands of the patriarchy which dismisses her. Hattie feels bliss when she experiences the light during her convalescence at the Ghost Dance after her attack. In fact it seems responsible for her healing: "The crushing pain was gone and her head felt clear; all her senses were alert for the first time since the assault . . . the light outside became brighter and more luminous—she recognized it at once and felt a thrill sweep over her. How soothing the light was, how joyously serene she felt" (469). Here the illumination seems most complete, though we are left assuming she will learn more about her light when she lives with Aunt Bronwyn after the novel ends.

Notably, Edward also experiences a sharp, supernatural light. But for him it is "blinding" and causes headaches and other great pain (90). He in fact becomes addicted to laudanum and slides into his downfall and ultimately his death as a result, partly, of the torment he perceives this light and things associated with it to be. But to Hattie and Indigo, and presumably anyone who is open to it (though in this novel that only includes women), the light is comforting, inspiring, healing, and miraculous. Throughout, the light is directly connected to religion and nature, especially matriarchal religious traditions, like those Aunt Bronwyn and Laura study and revive, and the traditions that Indigo and Sister Salt were raised upon. Dreams are key events in the novel in a variety of ways. While Edward's dreams torment him, Indigo and Hattie have prophetic and healing dreams, usually. In one case Indigo's mother sings to her in "the Sand Lizard language she'd never heard before. . . [to reassure her that she is] snug and warm. . . . She felt so much love she wept; she knew then where Mama was and always would be. Dance, little clouds, dance! Play in the wind!" (468). This "miraculous" ability to understand her mother even though she is speaking in a language Indigo doesn't know, shows the power of these dreams. Both women's visions conceive of nature as a consistently good, nurturing, healing force, messages and "illumination" partly communicated to them in dreams.

There are also miraculous stones and figurines of all sorts in the European gardens. But one of the more intriguing specific symbols that connect the pagan tradition from which Hattie's vision flows and the Sand Lizard tradition is the snake who is connected to gardening and nurturing women. In Laura's gardens especially, there are "masks and terra-cotta figures of goddesses that were half snake or half bird" (284) as well as "concentric circles . . . the all-seeing eyes of the Great Goddess; and the big triangles represented the pubic triangle, another emblem of the Great Goddess" (291). There are many animal figures, including snakes, among the many ancient figures they see, and they are usually explicitly connected to women. There is even mention in the stories of these objects (that Laura tells) of a traditional luminous glow. The *professoressa* explains it all as best she can to the curious Indigo, who is especially intrigued by the snakes so similar to her own culture's traditions: "Laura said when she was a girl her grandmother always kept a black snake in the storeroom to protect it from mice and rats. Indigo smiled; yes, Grandma Fleet always thanked the snakes for their protection—not just from rodents but from those who would do you harm. At the spring above the dunes lived the biggest snake, very old—the water was his" (299).

The fact that the snake retains positive attributes in Europe is intriguing in light of the obviously contrary view of snakes among the dominant (Christian) culture, where they are Satanic, an evil force in paradise that helped separate man from it. In contrast, this female, matriarchal view of the snake sees it as a protective, positive force. This contradiction is addressed by Silko in considering the figure of the Virgin of Guadalupe, who "crushes the snake," under her feet in most popular images of her. The word Guadalupe translates (from Náhuatl and Spanish) as "she crushes the serpent," who needs crushing as both the devil (from the Christian point of view) *and* a representative of the Aztec hero "Quetzalcoatl, the Plumed Serpent" (Demarest and Taylor 78). Hattie appears to have learned some of this lore: "Hattie drifted off to sleep recalling the pictures and statues of the Blessed Virgin Mary standing on a snake. Catechism classes taught Mary was killing the snake, but after seeing the figures in the rain garden, she thought perhaps the Virgin with the snake was based on a figure from earlier times" (304). When she later dreams of gardens, Hattie connects all these themes: "Perhaps she would return to England or Italy—she dreamed about the gardens often. Aunt Bronwyn's old stones danced in one of her dreams, and in another dream, Laura's figures of the snake and bird women sang a song so lovely she woke in tears" (392). The positive potential of snakes has miraculously survived in spite of the more negative, popular attitude of snakes as demonic.

This positive view is ultimately more real to Hattie than the traditional one, and it is all connected to the Gnostic gospels, illumination, and the Great Mother (450), confirming as well Grandma Fleet's wisdom, "Grandma Fleet always said snake girls and bird mothers were everywhere in the world, not just here!" (455). The snake has for many cultures been a figure of eternal life and resurrection. One more miracle in the novel is the unlikely restoration of the sisters to the garden, provoking the happy tumble through the "paradise" of their home in the first paragraph of the novel. The sisters return revitalized, with a baby, many new plants, new animals, and a strong extended family. And a new snake welcomes them home: "Early the other morning when she came alone to wash at the spring, a big rattlesnake was drinking at the pool. The snake dipped her mouth daintily into the water, and her throat moved with such delicacy as she swallowed. She stopped drinking briefly to look at Sister, then turned back to the water; then she gracefully turned from the pool across the white sand to a nook of bright shade. Old Snake's beautiful daughter moved back home" (477). The sisters leave the gardens in despair, experience violence, greed, and hardships of all kinds in the outside world, and return against all the odds to health and beauty. Like the eternal rhythms of gardens returning to bloom, or snakes returning to life, these women survive and persist, to build communities, new, hybridized, and changed, but persistent, well, and promising.

The Victorians epitomize the hubris of "civilized" men who believe that nature exists to be "tamed," "harnessed," "controlled," and used, preferably for profit. This attitude of controlling the landscape leads to the devastation of the environment that continues in our society today and that resulted in the subjugation of Native Americans. The ingenious, productive, world-changing gardens of Native Americans were often considered and described as "messy" by Europeans—evidence of their savagery (Wessel). In fact Native people were very efficient, successful gardeners, giving the world many of our most important crops today—corn, tomatoes, potatoes, peppers, and chocolate, among many others (Weatherford). In Silko's novel, the destructive potential of the Western mindset is evident in the effect it has on women and on Native Americans, including those removed from their land and forced to work for whites. One sign of the Western attitude toward nature in this novel is the dam that changes and harms the earth for men's profit and "progress." This dam attracts mostly trouble, destruction, and competition.

Yet by opening and closing the novel with views of a traditional garden tended by Native women, a garden and women who flourish miraculously in spite of all the odds and forces against them, Silko offers a hopeful vision. The novel suggests that women's connection to the landscape, in terms of understanding it, cultivating it, and preserving it, is far more profound than any other force in their lives, including the patriarchy. Women survive and endure by gardening and by remembering the lore of their matriarchies.

Silko's characters of Hattie, Bronwyn, and Laura do not find (or reveal) all the mysteries of a matriarchal prehistory. Hattie will not be allowed to complete her thesis on the role of women in religion. Yet from another perspective (in another light) the novel offers a metaphorical realization of Hattie's thesis topic.

Silko imagines how the rhetoric of gardens, snakes, goddesses, and matriarchy can inspire community and life in the women whose lives she creates. Given that this novel is written for us, a contemporary audience, Silko thereby also confirms myth scholar Cynthia Eller's position, that a matriarchal past is rhetorically reflective of contemporary women rather than of our ancestors. In other words, it doesn't matter if a matriarchy existed or exactly what it looked like. We can build our future from the seeds we have, from this novel's perspective, by tending gardens and building communities. Writing from a Native American perspective, in an interesting, pseudo-Victorian, postmodern context, Silko weaves a tapestry of women and landscape of luminous potential. Nature gives us all life; even in the most difficult circumstances it is within our grasp as women to embrace that miracle of life and potential. We can all "see the light" and like the sisters, Hattie, and the old snake, "move back home," however we rebuild or envision that home (477).

WORKS CITED

Aldama, Frederick Luis. "Leslie Marmon Silko. *Gardens in the Dunes.*" *World Literature Today* 74.2 (Spring 2000): 457–58.

Baring, Anne, and Jules Cashford. *The Myth of the Goddess: Evolution of an Image.* London: Arkana (Penguin Books), 1993.

Bell, Robert E. *Women of Classical Mythology: A Biographical Dictionary.* New York: Oxford UP, 1991.

Demarest, Donald, and Coley Taylor, eds. *The Dark Virgin: The Book of Our Lady of Guadalupe.* 1956. *The Heath Anthology of American Literature: Concise Edition.* Gen. ed. Paul Lauter. New York: Houghton Mifflin, 2004. 72–80.

Eller, Cynthia. *The Myth of Matriarchal Prehistory: Why an Invented Past Won't Give Women a Future.* Boston: Beacon, 2000.

May, Herbert G., and Bruce M. Metzger, eds. *The New Oxford Annotated Bible with the Apocrypha, revised standard version.* New York: Oxford UP, 1977.

Merchant, Carolyn. *Reinventing Eden: The Fate of Nature in Western Culture.* New York: Routledge, 2003.

Ross, Jacquelyn. "Books. Review of *Gardens in the Dunes.*" *News from Native California* 15 (Winter 2001): 34–35.

Silko, Leslie Marmon. *Gardens in the Dunes.* New York: Scribner Paperback Fiction, 1999.

Weatherford, Jack. *Indian Givers: How the Indians of the Americas Transformed the World.* New York: Ballantine Books, 1989.

Wessel, Thomas R. "Agriculture, Indians, and American History." *Agricultural History* 50 (January 1976): 9–20.

White, Lynn, Jr. "The Historical Roots of Our Ecological Crisis." *The Ecocriticism Reader*. Ed. Cheryll Glotfelty and Harold Fromm. Athens: U of Georgia P, 1996. 3–14.

TIPS FOR NURTURING THE HOME GARDEN

Barbara K. Robins

Do we know what or where "home" is? It seems we frequently use the word home to represent a wide range of our attitudes towards place. The complexity of our relationships to place, to others, to environmental forces, to our physical selves and our spiritual selves, all gets embraced in that single word whether we are leaving it, returning to it, or finding ourselves firmly attached to it in all present and future tenses. There are no certainties in this relationship, yet it means everything. In Leslie Marmon Silko's *Gardens in the Dunes*, the garden is the ultimate metaphor of home. Regardless of its size, productivity of its plants, the skills of its stones, or the varieties of its residents, the garden holds the keys to our wholeness.

That a novel with a title, which so clearly suggests one distinct place, should almost immediately require its characters to undertake several journeys is surprising and even ironic. But *Gardens* offers a complex narrative with deeply human concerns at its heart. It is far more than the struggle of Sister Salt and Indigo to return to each other and their ancestral place or a travel narrative with exotic adventures. A host of dualities is explored here, not the least of which is the fixed nature of gardens and the moveable nature of home.

Gardens in the Dunes, Silko's third novel, is set in a non-specific time during the late 1890s, a time of dramatic adjustments for Native Americans. Sister Salt and Indigo are sisters being raised by a mother and grandmother.[1] As dislocated members of a small group of people who call themselves Sand Lizard, the loss of male relatives and the loss of security resulting from white encroachments and violence against the indigenous residents are both historically and emotionally accurate. Silko's persistent interests in social decay and history are present here as well as her gardener's sensibility and eye for the multitude of plants described throughout. From amaranth to black gladiolas, the visual impact of many scenes in the novel is painterly. Every garden has its own style and colors, a point many painters have been well aware of, including Claude Monet,[2] who was cultivating gardens purposefully for their inspiration during the same general period as Silko's *Gardens*.

Silko engages this novel as a Trickster/Artist. She freely employs the techniques of tricksters to subvert reader expectations concerning indigenous peoples, history[3] — especially where global trade and influence is concerned — and human relationships to so-called non-sentient beings. As artist, Silko juxtaposes images of historical and contemporary social relevance. Silko maintains two narrative threads throughout — one that is historical mimesis, and another extra-diegetic narrative that is contemporary and ironic. Silko participates in her narratives in several forms. She is the narrator of her novel and appears as the character Delena who arrives late in the novel as the entrepreneurial and radical leader of a traveling dog circus.[4] As narrator and character, Silko introduces chance as one element of dramatic change. As social critic, Silko embeds historical elements that require our contemporary perspective as readers to fully understand. Silko's layering of images creates a text that is visually complex as well as consciousness-raising.

Using tricksters as a creative model offers a wide variety of playful approaches in the writing, even if the underlying message is a serious one. In writing about another Trickster/Artist, Morris-Carlsten offers a succinct list of effects when the trickster is applied as a theoretical construct. Sculptor Bob Haozous considers himself a mixed-blood Apache artist who refers to certain trickster attitudes in his visual works: "Conceptual attributes of the Trickster or Trickster signs include: irony; humor; multiple meanings; subversions of meaning; transgression of cultural boundaries; hybrid or syncretic acts; controversial images; ambiguous meanings; absurd or grotesque meanings; acts of play; teasing or satire; double images that mean two things at once or double acts . . ." (Morris-Carlsten 81).

In her mimetic narrative, Silko begins simply by fragmenting a small family and dispersing them to places unknown to each other. "Home" comes under attack by foreigners with startlingly different experiences for each of the Sand Lizard sisters. This variation on "double images" reveals some of the duplicity Americans exhibited regarding Indians and Indian issues of this time period. Sister Salt remains in her home region where she must witness the encroachment of the foreigners' political power and environmental destruction. Indigo is set into motion traveling west to east and then from New World to Old. Silko places a child in a sort of "Reverse Migration"[5] that calls attention to the previous migrations of colonial forces and the displacement of indigenous peoples. Indigo longs for home and family, but unlike an adult in a similar situation, she carries little "baggage." While she does long to be reunited with her family, she remains open to the experiences of travel. In one typical moment of self-aware confidence, she calls attention to the trickster quality of her own actions: "She had to laugh at her dark Sand Lizard face in the gilded oval mirror; now a Sand

Lizard girl was loose in the white people's world" (160). The most immediate reading of this scenario is that the "captured and institutionalized" Indian girl has been "set free" away from the confining boundaries of either a reservation or boarding school. This freedom is elusive, however, as Indigo is under the guardianship of the Palmers who have agreed to school her in the basics of reading (in English), math, and geography. There is disagreement between Hattie and Edward regarding Indigo's education. Edward is comfortable with a "training program" that would leave Indigo little choice but that of a domestic servant. Hattie rejects this future for Indigo, but despite her liberal leanings concerning education, she has no clear vision for either Indigo or herself.

Human behavior is sometimes erratic, irresponsible, thoughtless, and even dangerous, but direct comment and corrections are too easily ignored. The trickster draws in with wile and with foolishness but eventually "springs the trap" to reveal the problem behaviors and engage the imagination for more suitable responses. Haozous' visual approach is to create images that juxtapose historical icons and symbols with mundane scenes of contemporary life. The effects are confusing, shocking, and disorienting but cause viewers to consider the means by which those same images were kept separate from each other. His work raises the question, "What rules of historical representation are being broken here?" Those rules are a product of colonialism, a point Vizenor addresses in "Trickster Discourse: Comic Holotropes and Language Games." For Haozous and Vizenor, tricksterism is essential to survival: "The stoic 'savage' survived in literature and emulsion; invented, painted and photographed by postcolonial adventurers; the modern individual was then interpreted as the structural opposition to bourgeois democracies" (*Narrative Chance* 193).

Silko also relies on tricksterism for social commentary and for calling attention to the manner in which we simultaneously torment and neglect the earth. We torment Mother Earth via our lack of commitment, awareness, and respect. Haozous represents our behaviors symbolically through the multiple forms of automobiles, airplanes, pollution clouds, the corporate logos of American big business. Silko's verbal imagery includes many of the same objects. The frequent mention of trains and boats recalls a time of indiscriminate environmental destruction for the sake of "progress." The Lizards' old gardens become a subversion of the biblical Garden of Eden story. In Silko's version, the Sand Lizard people are expelled from their desert home and forced to witness the environmental degradations, particularly the devastation caused by the dam building project on the Colorado River.

Against the backdrop of leisurely pleasurable travel, global trade is a quiet but serious subtext in this novel. Silko is especially interested in the trading of natural resources that requires ecological destruction in one area to promote fashionable trends of another area. Every port scene in *Gardens* includes a description of the huge stacks of lumber, cotton, orchids, marble slabs, all living beings converted into commodities for trade. Aunt Bronwyn recalls to Hattie and Edward the history of trading in human slaves, a recollection that produces discomfort and could be read as Silko invoking the socially corrective form of teasing,[6] but the most painful image of this commodity-driven market is the cage of recently-captured parrots that upsets Indigo and her pet Rainbow upon their arrival in Genoa (278). These brief images become reminiscent of scenes from *Almanac of the Dead*, in which contemporary societies have degraded into patterns of mindless consumption of all living beings.

To literally set this adventure in motion, Silko stretches probability. By elaborating on Indigo's basic characteristics of smart, plucky, and dislocated child, she adds a pair of wealthy newlyweds willing to take an Indian child into their home and on their travels. They have expensive clothes made for her, instruct her, buy her books, and give her pets. Consider this image of Indianness as a dark girl wearing blue satin ribbons, a monkey on one arm, a brightly colored parrot on her shoulder,[7] and carrying a valise of fine papers and colored pencils. Further, she has a talent for gardening, engaging in all opportunities to collect seeds which she saved "in scraps of paper with her nightgown and clothes in the valise so she could grow them when she got home" (187).

All along the journey from west coast to east, Silko mentions prevailing assumptions concerning gardening as pastime, the decorative placement of flowers, or a nostalgic habit. She contrasts the collective negatives and positives of global trade against small, subsistence communities. Symbolically, the Sand Lizard Old Gardens are the indigenous agricultural practices threatened by the demands of agribusiness and global trade. In the opening sections, local, low-impact, subsistence farming maintains intimate contact with the land. Intimacy is knowledge and closeness, and instructive in the caring that prevents separation of human from place in any real or metaphorical sense. The Sand Lizard characters of Grandma Fleet, Mother, Sister Salt, and Indigo care for each other and, in so doing, reflect what Vine Deloria Jr. states is characteristic of indigenous practice: "When using plants as both medicines and foods, Indians were careful to use the plant appropriately. By maintaining the integrity of the plant within the relationship, Indians discovered many important facts about the natural world that non-Indians only came upon later" (Deloria and Wildcat 24).[8]

Such a relationship requires sophisticated transferal of knowledge and a moral sensibility concerning one's relationship to all other beings within one's

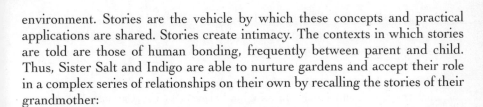

environment. Stories are the vehicle by which these concepts and practical applications are shared. Stories create intimacy. The contexts in which stories are told are those of human bonding, frequently between parent and child. Thus, Sister Salt and Indigo are able to nurture gardens and accept their role in a complex series of relationships on their own by recalling the stories of their grandmother:

> Grandma Fleet told them the old gardens had always been there. The old-time people found the gardens already growing, planted by the Sand Lizard, a relative of Grandfather Snake, who invited his niece to settle there and cultivate her seeds. Sand Lizard warned her children to share: Don't be greedy. The first ripe fruit of each harvest belongs to the spirits of our beloved ancestors, who come to us as rain; the second ripe fruit should go to the birds and wild animals, in gratitude for their restraint in sparing seeds and sprouts earlier in the season. Give the third ripe fruit to the bees, ants, mantises, and others who cared for the plants. A few choice pumpkins, squash, and bean plants were simply left on the sand beneath the mother plants to shrivel dry and return to the earth. (16–17)

Grandma Fleet is parenting both her granddaughters and her plants. By contrast, the different approaches to nurturing plants among the novel's characters make for presumptive comparisons to the treatment of Indigo and other children. Hattie is lenient but loving. Edward is controlling, and his sister Susan, self-absorbed. Her realization that Indigo has seen her and the Scottish gardener engaged in extra-marital relations prompts her to bribery with a gift of the parrot to maintain Indigo's silence on the matter. Aunt Bronwyn and Laura the *professoressa* are patient, interested, and instructive and provide the greatest influence on Indigo's developing abilities to nurture plants.

Silko's construction of garden/home/parents is now complete. If Silko's motives, in part, are to subvert the meanings of fixed and/or mobile,[9] it is stories which are the most fluidly mobile, crossing time and distance. Several characters, including Hattie, Sister Salt, and Indigo, experience moments in which memories of stories make them feel connected to place/parent. The feelings of love and joy that often accompany these memories are not limited to relationships with biological ties. Hattie becomes an adoptive mother to Indigo and nurtures her over storybooks. The emotional and physical bonds created are no less meaningful. Once again, it is worth noting that their opportunities to create intimate, homey spaces are frequently within modes of transportation, namely trains and boats. These movable homes highlight the most important aspects of parenting even while juxtaposed with a more traditional idea of home/garden as fixed place.

In *Power and Place*, Vine Deloria Jr. suggests the land presents "personality" that must be interwoven with the practical matters of teaching and learning and is therefore connected to one's morality:

> [P]ower and place are dominant concepts—power being the living energy that inhabits and/or composes the universe, and place being the relationship of things to each other. It is much easier, in discussing Indian principles, to put these basic ideas into a simple equation: Power and place produce personality. This equation simply means that the universe is alive, but it also contains within it the very important suggestion that the universe is personal and, therefore, must be approached in a personal manner. . . . The broader Indian idea of relationship, in a universe that is very personal and particular, suggests that all relationships have a moral content.   (23)

Direct personal experience with the land is learning and produces knowledge. This alone will not guarantee an intimate connection to place or others. Stories, nurturing, and imagination are also needed to enable individuals and their communities to thrive. Silko demonstrates cultural continuance and the skills of moral relationships through Sister Salt. By the time she and Indigo are separated from their mother and grandmother, Sister Salt has sufficiently internalized the cultural values to draw upon them as a guiding construct when faced with new situations. Given the premise that most learning takes place by age five,[10] Sister Salt has had the longest, least interrupted contact with her mother's and grandmother's culture. To use Deloria's terms, Sister Salt exhibits the "personality" of the Sand Lizard people most clearly, by always relating herself to the power of her place. This is crucial to her becoming a nurturing parent to her own child, which she apparently does so successfully.

With moral behavior at stake, we should recall the Sand Lizard culture is a fictional culture. Silko situates her Sand Lizard tribe/family in the American Southwest to effectively comment on issues that signal loss of moral and nurturing relationships while protecting the cultural and spiritual integrity of the tribes which do live in the region. As decolonizing strategy in and of itself, the similarity to the extant tribes of the southwest enables Silko to make an effective comment on colonial pressures and the will of the U.S. government to establish itself as a political and cultural parent for these tribes.

Silko's personal history includes living within the region of the Southwest, including Laguna Pueblo, but the choice of this region is probably not limited to familiarity. The southwest already occupies a place in the American imagination as exotic, alien, and filled with an "Indian local color." Placing this tiny family, never more than four members for reasons of violence and displacement, in the Southwest enables Silko to comment on tourism, large-scale agricultural practices that require destruction of indigenous eco-systems and the re-routing of water sources, population influxes, displacement of indigenous groups, plight of economic refugees, and various Americanization policies including Indian boarding schools. Silko is not alone in her criticism of these forces. Southwest regional writers are abundant and prolific, prompting Eric Anderson to observe: "These texts sometimes define migration as a resistance or survival strategy rather than as an expansionist inevitability, and they often articulate in some way the problems as well as the possibilities of personal as well as cultural movement" (3). For all the abundance, there exists a profound lack of awareness on the part of American readers for texts by Native American writers, poets, storytellers, and artists that celebrate travel: "This immense indigenous literature of travel and migration has been underappreciated as a body of work; it has also been underestimated as a political strategy, particularly in the Southwest, where Euro-American migratory styles and motives intervene so problematically with Indians in motion" (22).

Silko embraces the possibility of text as both resistance and survival strategy. For both Sister Salt and Indigo, migration becomes necessary to their individual survival but their actual journeys differ dramatically. In short, Indigo represents survival/hybridity, a cross pollinator of cosmopolitanism. The skills and seeds Indigo acquires will become survival through hybridity. She has two opportunities for heterosis, the increased vigor of crossbreeds: the genetic via seeds/plants and the spiritual/cultural via stories.

On the other hand, Sister Salt represents resistance, caution, even isolation. Sister Salt must resist diminishment, outside control, and erasure. Her survival skills are products of self-honesty. She does not keep what is given to her if she finds it hypocritical. This is especially true in her disappointment with the father of her baby, Big Candy. She is clearheaded about her duties as a protective and nurturing mother: "That's what Big Candy didn't seem to understand—doubts weaken tiny babies. Think happily of the baby or stay away!" (359).

Throughout Gardens, Silko is practicing indigenization[11] and decolonization. Ultimately, she is making room for world views denied validity by Western/ Christian culture. Travel enables discovery of "alternative indigenousnesses," and tricksters may even be the ultimate travelers. As "picaresque characters," trickster is "always going along" and going about the business of "insuring that man remains 'unfinished' by fossilized institutions, open and adaptable instead to changing contemporary realities" (Wiget 21).

Travel can precipitate personal regeneration, but it is not universally allowed to Native Americans. William Bevis argued in his 1987 essay "Native American Novels: Homing In" that Silko, Momaday, Welch and McNickle[12] preferred a concept of "homing in" for their respective protagonists. McNickle's Archilde, Momaday's Abel, Silko's Tayo and Welch's Jim Loney return home after having tried the life off the reservation. Bevis states:

> [M]ost Native American novels are not "eccentric," centrifugal, diverging, expanding, but "incentric," centripetal, converging, contracting. The hero comes home. "Contracting" has negative overtones to us, "expanding" a positive ring. These are the cultural choices we are considering. In Native American novels, coming home, staying put, contracting, even what we call "regressing" to a place, a past where one has been before, is not only the primary story, it is a primary mode of knowledge and a primary good.   (582)

In Silko's novels *Almanac of the Dead* and *Gardens in the Dunes*, the notion of "regression" is problematic. Characters leave home for complex reasons and return for equally complex reasons, now with a multitude of experiences and even tangible goods that have the potential to make significant cultural changes. This is not to refute Bevis in his observation that place, "home," is a "primary good" but rather that as a living entity, place is capable of change without losing its essential personality. Particularly in *Gardens*, Indigo returns to her place with tangible goods, experiences, and concepts which become subsumed into her family's Sand Lizard cultural framework. Each novel also emphasizes, to varying degrees, the turmoil of the late nineteenth and early twentieth centuries. The same upheaval that fueled conflicts and wars also created opportunities for travel that Indians, among others, exploited: "James McCarthy[13] traveled to China in about 1918. The First World War seemed to open travel to many rural Americans" (Silko, Letter).

For a variety of good reasons, Bevis selects to focus on the return as represented in literary texts published in the 1970s as part of the Native American Renaissance, but he also overlooks a 1976 lithograph created by Luiseño artist Fritz Scholder titled "Indian in Paris." The image is typical of Sholder's bold graphic design in which an obviously tribal man fills the space and directly faces the viewer. He wears decorated clothing made in the style of the plains tribes with fringed shirt and a blanket wrapped around his torso. He wears red face paint, and holds both a feathered lance and war shield.[14] His stance is posed but at ease. Behind him is a distant landscape marked by what appears to be a miniature Eiffel Tower. The pose is clearly meant to challenge viewer assumptions about Indians. Foremost, this man wearing his native garb in a foreign land is confident of his position. He "towers" over that symbol of European engineering and elegance. Perhaps this man's considerable distance from the predictable throngs at the foot of the Eiffel Tower explains why Bevis and others took no notice of his visit.

It appears that Bevis simply sees travel as a feature of white culture. That many Native American authors did not see this limitation is profoundly clear in the more recent novels by Momaday, Welch and Silko. Even if we disregard Momaday's acclaimed *Way to Rainy Mountain*,[15] his novel *Ancient Child* is a layering of travel and migration myth. The protagonist, Locke Setman, a professional artist, recalls a career which leads him to all the major museums and galleries of Europe and America. Over the course of the novel, he undertakes a spiritual migration, one that leads him to Oklahoma, into the southwest, and ultimately to Devil's Tower in Wyoming. Setman undergoes profound personal changes that connect him to each of these places. Welch's *Heartsong of Charging Elk*, like *Gardens*, is set in the last years of the nineteenth century. Charging Elk becomes a performer in Buffalo Bill's Wild West Show, certainly another author's comment on the relationship between Indians and tourists. Welch offers some interesting exceptions to the premise that Indians travel purposefully as a series of mishaps contribute to Charging Elk being lost in France for years. Ultimately, he makes his decision to marry a Frenchwoman and begin a family in an adopted country.

Closely related to story, learning, and imagination is memory. In *Ceremony*, memory has healing capacity and in *Gardens* takes on global complexities matching the global migrations. This necessitates that Silko send all her characters on migrations with both life threatening and regenerative potential. "[H]ealing involves the right triggering of memory, a health within things, natural to body and mind" (Lincoln 242). There is also a range in the kind and ability of memory from the acutely aware to the completely absent. Several characters in *Gardens* must either navigate personal challenges and painful memories to regenerate or succumb to self-destructive obsessions.

Recalling Laguna rituals of memory, story, and place in her essay "Interior and Exterior Landscapes," Silko writes, "the journey was an interior process of the imagination, a growing awareness that being human is somehow different from all other life — animal, plant, and inanimate. Yet, we are all from the same source: awareness never deteriorated into Cartesian duality, cutting off the human from the natural world" (*Yellow Woman* 37). Early in Indigo's journey she sees Indian women selling pottery to tourists in Albuquerque. She is curious but reticent to speak to them for fear they will see her white girl's clothes and wonder "What kind of Indian are you?" (*Gardens* 126). Over time and distance, Indigo replaces this fear and shame with confidence. Once back at home, Indigo reveals her increased confidence by her dealings with the white trader's wife in the town of Needles. Selling some of her dresses, Indigo is unafraid to deal with the older woman whose racism is palpable. Now the clothing is a practical matter and Indigo doesn't worry about what others might think of an Indian girl wearing or selling a white girl's clothing (417).

However, not every member of Indigo's blended family is ready to undertake an interior passage. Hattie's situation is one requiring healing and recovery of her inner self. The travels to ancestral gardens/lands in Europe re-awaken memories and the stories which in turn heal her spiritually, but not easily. Hattie's vague and poorly considered optimism crumbles after her brutal rape and beating. Until then, she denies the causes of her bouts of melancholy, delaying her journey of spiritual healing that leads her back to England.

On the other hand, Edward is troubled by memories he compartmentalizes and draws upon selectively to further his career. His history is one of collecting adventures, stories of which captivated Hattie during their courtship in which he characterized himself as "the innocent tourist hell-bent on disaster" (81). He is compelled by his obsessions "to discover a new plant species that would bear his name, and he spent twenty years of his life in this pursuit . . ." (80). His Pará River expedition for rare orchid species haunts him physically in the form of a broken leg that healed imperfectly, financially with the loss of the orchid and other plant specimens he collected, and emotionally from the betrayal of his expedition companions. His financial backers paid for his medical care and the fees involved with his arrest and deportation for smuggling plant materials, but Edward still stings with the knowledge his colleague Mr. Eliot was on the journey to destroy the jungle habitat after Edward had collected all the species he needed for clients. Edward does not remember these incidents in a manner that would encourage his personal regeneration. He is controlled by what Vizenor labels "Terminal Creeds," those scientific constructions "which result in misunderstanding, misappropriation, violence, and death" (qtd. in Lundquist 91). Vizenor's observation is correct in every way for Edward, including his death at the hands of the quack Dr. Gates.

The importance of memory and its relationship to healing is not limited to humans. In fact, there is an interdependence of memory among people and plants habitually grown together. In "Killing our Elders," Brenda Peterson explores one relationship with people and the old growth trees of Oregon. Describing the practices of Nez Percé Indians, ancient trees were hollowed out enough to hold the body of a deceased elder. When the bark was replaced, the tree would heal its wound, encasing the elder: "The old trees held our old people for thousands of years. . . . If you cut those ancient trees, you lose all your own ancestors, everyone who came before you. Such loneliness is hard to bear" (Hogan and Peterson 243).

Memory becomes historicism in the hands of colonialism. Vizenor states, "The trick, in seven words, is to *elude historicism, racial representation, and remain historical"* (*Trickster* xi). Remaining historical is a tough trick indeed in the face of marketing practices favored by American business interests. Silko plays with the boundaries limiting Indian travel by incorporating juxtaposed motifs of the Indian as tourist attraction and as tourist. In the late 1890s, Fred Harvey was an already well-established entrepreneur placing dining cars on the trains traveling through the Southwestern states of California, Arizona, New Mexico.[16] With increased travel in automobiles, a similar route through the same states becomes part of Route 66, "The Mother Road" of Depression era migrations. In every era, including the present one, Indians are marketed within the image of the Southwest as destination. Perhaps we have a tolerance for being exploited *as* tourists, but it is unlikely we give little if any thought to the possibility we exploit *by being* tourists. The changes to Indian cultures are described by Rayna Green:

> Like their ancestors who had endured the first invasions, this second group of survivors figured out new ways to evade these new "conquerors." They adapted and transformed much of their plastic and performance art to suit the needs, desires, and market venues of those desirous of consuming their goods, ceremonies, and identities. Some of these artworks and the communities which produced them were forever changed by that adaptive strategy. Most native people who participated in the new market for their goods, however, were never simply mindless and mechanical producers of art for a specific market . . . they also engaged in commentary and resistance while simultaneously participating in the markets that attempted to control what they produced. (201)

Tourism and its associated developments destroy the environment and the indigenous cultures sought out for consumption, all the while assuming that consumption and change are neutral or positive processes to the indigenous peoples and the cultures in which they live. In *Gardens*, Grandma Fleet and Mother watch for the tourists willing to buy their baskets and trinkets made of plant fibers. The pattern continues with Indigo and Hattie observing the Indian women selling pottery and beaded items in Albuquerque and at other stops along the route. Sister Salt continues the practice of souvenir making as economic necessity against the backdrop of environmental destruction that is displacing Indians who have the artistic skills and reducing the area where native materials can be gathered. Among Sonoran Desert cultures, "Baskets, food, and medicinal plants are harvested, pruned, and sometimes transplanted or actively managed by controlled burns" (Nabhan, *Biodiversity* 30). Nabhan describes relationships that are persistent and key to diversification of species. Just as important, the interactions among those species and the assistance of "mutualists," other plants, animals, insects and those people who are harvesting, transplanting, pruning, and generally looking out after the well-being of the plants for mutual benefit: "However, ignorance of such biotic interactions has led to the decline of particular plant species that have lost their mutualists . . ." (Nabhan, *Biodiversity* 31). Perhaps, DNA + experience = Memory.

Creating fictional Indian tourists is both satirical and decolonizing. True to indigenous values of moral relationship to all beings, Indigo is an ideal tourist. Her expansive appreciation for new places, people, stories, and experiences recall traditional reasons for travel that do not merely duplicate white, middle-class tourism as consumption of exotic experiences or upper class "collecting" of artifacts that is associated with imperialistic means to making knowledge.

Counter to the western assumption that the "objects of research do not have a voice and do not contribute to research or science" (Smith 61), Indigo is a fellow traveler for Edward, the novel's representative for western scientific methodology. Beyond his intellectual control, she learns and contributes, and if her voice is not heard, the parrot Rainbow's certainly is!

Another example of Indian travel, Ghost Dancers, along with sympathetic Mormons, travel to locations hoping to intersect with the Holy Family who are themselves moving about the world visiting the believers. Unlike the Christian concept of enclosed sacred space as the place to find God, the Holy Family seeks out the believers:

> Indigo said in England there were a great many Christ Churches but the Messiah and his family seemed to travel most of the time. Sister nodded. That was because so many greedy and cruel people did damage only the Messiah could repair. Trouble was in so many places, he had to travel constantly, and so did the Mother of God, who often went to help alone. (457)

Meanwhile, white citizens seek to disrupt such activities. Disruption occurs at all levels, from the breaking up of camps of people preparing to dance, to destroying entire regions and ecosystems by building dams to support what we now call agribusiness. Railroads, towns, an infrastructure gets built that reveals a way of thinking that overlooks the more subtle relationships between humans, other living beings, and place.

To further decolonize this relationship to Christianity, the Sand Lizard family speaks of the Holy Family as an Indian family, fully cognizant of the challenges Indians were struggling with. Another Trickster/Artist, Jim Logan (Métis) offers a similar image in his 1992 acrylic and mixed media *Jesus Was Not a Whiteman*. The image is borrowed from El Greco's painting *The Savior* and augmented with feathers and bingo chips. Logan states:

I wanted [Native People] to be able to see Christ as an Indian and have the imagery put in their minds that he could be an Indian. He definitely wasn't Spanish. He definitely wasn't German. He didn't look like Salvador Dali's image of Christ. But if they have the licence to do that then I have the licence to make him Indian! So I made him an Aboriginal Jesus.   (qtd. in Ryan 123)

Silko, Trickster/Artist telling a long story to draw us in before the trap is sprung, has one more twist subverting conventional notions concerning the relationships between plants and humans. Just as they exhibit memory, plants have volition and the will to travel. The seeds and plants collected by Edward and Indigo are on their own migrations. Eventually, the plants will interact with others of their species creating new forms, and quite possibly, enter into relationships with us humans, a possibly risky collaboration on many fronts. We can enter this relationship generously. Recall Ts'eh in *Ceremony* who uses transplanted seedlings to improve the rains in certain areas. Typical of oral stories in which Spiritual Beings provide proper roles and behaviors for humans, Ts'eh is a mutualist considerate of all the beings in her place. In *Gardens*, Edward, Grandma Fleet, and Indigo are characters most often seen transporting some kind of plant material. Carrying and even hybridizing plants for purposes of indigenizing is Deloria's "making culture"[17] and is practiced by many characters including Mrs. Wegman, the Scottish gardener in the employ of Susan, Maytha and Vedna, Aunt Bronwyn, Laura and others. Underlying all these examples is the warning to maintain the appropriate relationship: "if a garden was not loved it could not properly grow!" (*Gardens* 242). The evidence of old trade abounds during Indigo's travels. Even in Italy, familiar foods of sweet peppers, yellow squash are integrated into local cuisine: "Indigo's eyes widened at the sight of food she knew, and as she tasted the peppers she thought of them grown so far from their original home; seeds must be the greatest travelers of all!" (293). The experience is charming, "homely" in the way the foods take Indigo, through her memory, back to her indigenous place/family. It is also Silko's way of raising the question that resists Western control over history—"So how DID these plants get here?" Lest we come to the conclusion plants merely follow us on our migrations, are the passive cargo carried by us and our will alone, Silko offers other possibilities. Aunt Bronwyn is said to be interested in the theories of Gustav Fechner wherein plants have souls and human beings exist only to be consumed by plants and be transformed into glorious new plant life (242). Also, several characters, including Edward, Aunt Bronwyn, Laura, and even Indigo, are engaged in hybridizing certain plants. Hybridity, in this novel, is dualistic. In husbandry, crossbreeding can result in either growth or defect, heterosis or infertility, improved adaptability or increased dependence. Silko's exploration of nineteenth century orchid collecting and breeding reveals all of these outcomes but given the obsessions for orchids in our present day suggests we have much to learn. The modern-day orchid hunter story is one such morality tale.

The adventures of John Larouche first appeared as an article for *The New Yorker* by Susan Orlean. An eccentric plant collector and breeder, Larouche was hired by a manager of the Seminole tribe to acquire rare orchid and bromeliad species from the protected state lands of the Fakahatchee Strand State Preserve in Florida.[18] Like Silko's Edward, Orlean describes Larouche as a schemer, "Folding virtue and criminality around profit" (5). Certainly, this obsession with plants and the willingness to convert them as a life form into a commodity is not restricted to time, place or ethnicity. Orlean's observation of the contemporary plant-growing industry is direct: "In Florida, plants are everywhere, like money. Plants are money" (87). The irony in Orlean's experiences is her discovery many people do not want to migrate in order to connect with a new environment, expand their sense of connection to a greater place, or seek regeneration. Orlean struggled to understand the obsession for orchids and other plants and finally reached this conclusion: "I was starting to believe that the reason it matters to care passionately about something is that it whittles the world down to a more manageable size. It makes the world seem not huge and empty but full of possibility" (109). This attitude carried into a place without the appropriate concern for mutual benefit makes that place vulnerable. Orlean elaborates:

> Florida is a wet, warm, tropical place, essentially featureless and infinitely transformable. It is as suggestible as someone under hypnosis. Its essential character can be repeatedly reimagined. The Everglades soil that is being contaminated by intractable Brazilian pepper trees is now being scraped up in order to kill the invader trees, and the sterilized soil is going to be piled high, covered with plastic snow, and turned into a ski resort. Any dank Florida cypress swamp can be drained and remade as a sub-division, and that subdivision can be made to look like a Tuscan village or a New England town, and the imitation Tuscan village or Vermont town can be filled with people from New York or Chicago or Haiti who have remade themselves into Floridians. The flat plainness of Florida doesn't impose itself on you, so you can impose upon it your own kind of dream.   (123–34)

In Silko's lexicon, the destroyer's vision is one of change based on novelty and fashion, like Edward's sister Susan, who rips out mature trees in order to transform her wooded New York estate into an English Meadow. It is apparent that even techniques, such as hybridizing a plant, can be the result of one's loving and imaginative commitment to plant and place or another way of controlling, of distorting, both. In the world of orchid collecting, Larouche instructs Orlean on the popularity of hybridizing: "The only ones (Orchids) with features that have no real purpose are the hybrids, because someone put them together and came up with an unnatural thing. That's the cool thing with hybridizing. You are God. You do the plant sex. It's a man-made hobby" (qtd. in Orlean 94).[19] This degree of manipulation is a far cry from the relationship of the mutualist who is ever mindful of the balance that must be maintained for the mutual and long-term benefit of all beings involved.

"Nothing beats a good rationalization" seems to be the truism in this world of hybridity for fashion. Where there is potential for profit, there is nothing sacred, including the appropriation of stories from peoples, who just minutes ago were the target of ethnic genocide for their assumed savagery and pagan beliefs. In my reading of *Gardens*, Silko challenges us to see the gross negligence that is occurring in our relationships to place and all other beings. She refers directly to stones, meteors, stories, and white cattle. To properly place these white cattle in the overall Trickster's scheme, we may need to juxtapose certain images of contemporary life with those of historical and symbolic importance—namely, White Buffalo Calf Woman.[20] Centuries ago she visited several plains tribes, bringing them ceremonies and the instruction they needed to form appropriate relationships with their buffalo relatives. Her prophecy of returning to the people was manifested with the birth of Miracle in 1994.[21] Sacred to some, this white buffalo was seen as a gold-mine in the making for others.[22] Is it ethical to appropriate an indigenous story, recreate a facsimile sacred being, and then promote the package as tourist destination? Silko does not take this issue head-on but in the manner of subverting expectations, "re-routes" readers to ancestral roots. A personal journey of exploration is given in tantalizing fragments to Indigo complete with epic myths (King Arthur and his Knights of the Round Table), spiritual entities (walking stones, Little People), and a sacred animal whose self-sacrificing companionship with humans has been elevated via ancestral symbols to be the Great Mother herself. The white, horned "Moon-cow" created the universe with her own curdled milk (Walker 181).[23] Aunt Bronwyn knows, "The white cattle belonged to the moon—see the shape of the crescent moon in the cow's horn?" (*Gardens* 240). There are a number of fascinating correlations between this particular breed of cattle and the buffalo herds of North America that came to symbolize "Indianness" and the wildness of the west that became an increasing threat to westward expansion. Buffalo were slaughtered by the thousands in the nineteenth century for profit and for the direct correlation made to the livelihood, physical and spiritual, of the plains peoples: "At one time, the church ordered the slaughter of all herds of white cattle, which were suspected of pagan devotions. . ." (264). This alternative indigenousness gives an image of the Great Mother clearly as important as White Buffalo Calf Woman. Perhaps now we might stop distorting the stories that do not belong to us and learn to live in an appropriate relationship with buffalo, with cattle, with all our relatives, without using hybridization for the purposes of fashion.

If it seems we have moved far from the novel's events, the time has come to reveal the Trickster/Artist's punch line. For all of Western Culture's accomplishments and strengths, stories have been forgotten, fashion, greed and obsessions have taken control, and the newcomers to the place we call Turtle Island[24] are confused about what a nurturing and intimate relationship to this home is. Silko entertains and teases, with increasing persistence, with image after image of unleashed female sexuality as powerful, uncontrollable, and fertile. This subversion challenges male dominance in the family, intellectual development, hierarchal controls within the church. But, the rub is that the majority of the examples encountered on the journey through America, England, and Italy are collected by a small Sand Lizard girl. We have been pulled in—the reverse migration has taken us back to other indigenous homes and jolted our faulty memories back to those times when we knew how to nurture the power/personality of our place.[25] We have been caught demonstrating not only poor nurturing behavior, a loss of cultural memories, but of being hypocritical, of lecturing from positions of terminal creeds and false decorum.

The garden holds the keys to our wholeness, wherever it happens to be: "This is the land of the stones that dance and walk after midnight" (239). Indigo feels the power of the stones and sings a song to them that reconnects her across time and distance to her home/family: "The Black rock, the black rock—the rock is broken and from it pours clear, fresh water, clear, fresh water!" (267). Can we envision a world with "more" spiritual choices? Could diversity of ritual be just as essential to our well-being as diversity of flora and fauna? Silko's novel reassures us that intimacy and nurturing is possible through direct experience with the place in which we live and the places which we visit. Beware of novelty and short-sightedness of fashion. We have responsibilities to be honest to ourselves and respect the power of place, our garden/home with all its incumbent personality. Learn—be willing to regenerate personally through migrations, physical and interior. Imagine—be willing to accept the possibility of incredible things, such as the memory of plants. Nurture—be a good parent, a responsible mutualist to all other beings. Tell good stories—teach, pass on what makes us thrive. With these simple tips, your home garden will be a joy for years to come.

NOTES

1. Leslie Silko was a guest speaker at the NEH Summer Institute, "Working From Community: American Indian Art and Literature," organized by Gail Tremblay at the Evergreen State College in Olympia, Washington, summer 2003. During her presentation, Silko stated she "always wanted to write a story about sisters."

2. Claude Monet was born in Paris, France, in 1840 and died in Giverny, France, in 1926. Among his most famous paintings is *Blue Waterlilies* (c. 1916–19), from the series *Waterlilies*, Musée d'Orsay, Paris.

3. Deloria and Wildcat argue the ". . . most devastating feature of the Western worldview in its general character and practical application . . . [was] that Europeans possessed the Truth and it was their job to make sure all people they met on the planet were shown the Truth. . . . They literally could not understand any other history other than their own because their history became and was understood as The World History" (37).

4. While discussing the inspiration for several characters in *Gardens*, Silko stated in her 2003 NEH "Working from Community" presentation that a series of personal frustrations caused her to fantasize about having a dog circus.

5. My understanding of this concept comes from Lummi artist Jewell James who has transported a total of five totem poles over three different land routes from Bellingham, Washington, to each of the 9/11 Terrorist Attack sites. The poles themselves carry prayers for America's healing. The "reverse migration" concept, however, addresses the historical relationships between tribes and colonial forces. By traveling a "Reverse Trail of Tears," or "Reverse Lewis & Clark Route," the historical event is not magically "undone" but added to the current dialogue regarding violence, cultural and religious conflicts, sovereignty, and the processes of awareness, understanding, and ultimately healing.

6. In *Custer*, Vine Deloria Jr. offers the following explanation: "For centuries before the white invasion, teasing was a method of control of social situations by Indian people" (149).

7. While speaking to the 2003 NEH "Working from Community" participants, Silko stated that she was "uncertain why a monkey appears [in *Gardens*], but knows there must always be parrots."

8. Nabhan's studies with Sonoran Desert peoples have acknowledged that "farmers and hunter-gatherers recognize, name, and in some cases, manage ecological interactions between dozens of rare native plants and animals. . ." (*Biodiversity* 30).

9. Eric Anderson finds the poetry of Wendy Rose particularly articulate on this duality in which "the languages of both the petroglyph and mobile home [come together] . . . as rich metaphors for a rootedness that doubles as a routedness" (19).

10. This premise is discussed by Deloria and Wildcat.

11. I am referring here primarily to the definition of indigenizing as given by Linda Tuhiwai Smith who in turn includes the perspective of M. Annette Jaimes. Indigenism is "being grounded in the alternative conceptions of world view and value systems" (146).

12. Bevis was speaking collectively about the writers who have been given much credit for initiating the Native American Renaissance. He also includes Louise Erdrich's *Love Medicine* as an example of the homing in plot that values tribe and tribalism over individualism.

13. James McCarthy was a Papago who traveled widely abroad, and in America published his memoirs. Silko indicated at the NEH "Working from Community" she knew McCarthy and was inspired by his and other stories of Indians traveling.

14. Biographers of Fritz Scholder note that his high school art education was under the tutelage of Lakota painter Oscar Howe in Pierre, South Dakota. Howe spent time in Paris during WWII.

15. Kimberly Blaeser's essay *"The Way to Rainy Mountain*: Momaday's Work in Motion" is included in Gerald Vizenor's *Narrative Chance*.

16. Marta Weigle's very helpful timeline of the tourism in the Southwest demonstrates the near simultaneous rise of travel to the region, the increasing availability of photography and the photo postcard, innovative advertising efforts and the display of Geronimo at the Trans-Mississippi International Exposition in Omaha, Nebraska, in the years 1893–98.

17. "To indigenize an action or object is the act of making something of a place. The active process of making culture in its broadest sense of a place is called indigenization" (Deloria and Wildcat 32).

18. Larouche saw a legal loophole involving tribal sovereignty, endangered species protection laws and state jurisdiction which backfired after Larouche and his all-Seminole harvesting crew were arrested in 1994 for removing ghost orchids from the swamp.

19. Orlean's non-fiction story about an odd man in a plant-as-commodity world becomes the film "Adaptation." This hybrid storyline tells us ghost orchids are "more than a thing of beauty" and are actually sought after by young Seminole men for a "traditional ceremony" in which the plant is processed into a drug that, once inhaled, helps people "be fascinated" with everyday life. This turn of the colonizer's knife comes after the violent dislocation and dispossession of the Seminoles and other Southeastern tribes and then credits "traditional tribal practices" with a product diametrically opposed to the relationships with power and personality of indigenous place. In this case, the stereotype that Indians are "into" exotic drug ceremonies makes it possible for viewers to rationalize their own fantasies of exploitation.

20. The story of White Buffalo Calf Woman is widely available. I refer primarily to the one recounted by Lame Deer.

21. The first white buffalo calf to be born since 1933, Miracle was born August 20, 1994 on the Heider's Farm in Janesville, Wisconsin. She lived to be ten years old and went through three color changes as was expected by Native American spiritual leaders.

22. Since Miracle's birth, there have been several other births that have been presented to the public as buffalo but have been genetically determined to be frauds, the hybridized crossing of buffalo and breeds of white cattle such as the Charolais.

23. White Park Cattle have a pedigree going back to Celtic times and are currently endangered with approximately 1000 living globally. Herds are maintained in England and America.

24. A 'short-hand' title for the North American continent that relies on knowing the story of how this dry land is being held up by Grandmother Turtle.

25. I do not mean to assume or create certain subsets of audience here based on place of ethnic origin. Silko's message is a very broad one and could apply to anyone whose family origins include a migration to North America.

WORKS CITED

Adaptation. Screenplay by Charlie Kaufman, and Donald Kaufman. Dir. Spike Jonze. Perf. Nicolas Cage, Meryl Streep, and Chris Cooper. Columbia, 2002.

Anderson, Eric G. *American Indian Literature and the Southwest.* Austin: Texas UP, 1999.

Bevis, William. "Native American Novels: Homing In." *Recovering the Word: Essays on Native American Literature.* Ed. Brian Swann and Arnold Krupat. Berkley: California UP, 1987.

Deloria, Vine Jr. *Custer Died For Your Sins: An Indian Manifesto.* New York: Avon, 1969.

Deloria, Vine Jr., and Dan Wildcat. *Power and Place: Indian Education in America.* Golden: Fulcrum Resources, 2001.

Graulich, Melody, ed. *"Yellow Woman:" Leslie Marmon Silko.* New Brunswick: Rutgers UP, 1993.

Green, Rayna. "We Never Saw These Things Before: Southwest Indian Laughter and Resistance to the Invasion of the Tse va ho." *The Great Southwest of the Fred Harvey Company and the Santa Fe Railway.* Ed. Marta Weigle and Barbara A. Babcock. Phoenix: Heard Museum; Tucson: Arizona UP, 1996.

Greymorning, Stephen, ed. *A Will to Survive: Indigenous Essays on the Politics of Culture, Language, and Identity.* New York: McGraw, 2004.

Hogan, Linda, and Brenda Peterson, eds. *The Sweet Breathing of Plants: Women Writing on the Green World.* New York: North Point, 2001.

Lame Deer, John (Fire), and Richard Erdoes. *Lame Deer Seeker of Visions: The Life of a Sioux Medicine Man.* New York: Simon & Schuster, 1972.

Leighton, Ann. *Early American Gardens: "For Meate or Medicine."* Boston: Houghton, 1970.

Lincoln, Kenneth. *Native American Renaissance.* Berkeley: California UP, 1983.

Lippard, Lucy R. *Mixed Blessings: New Art in a Multicultural America.* New York: New P, 1990.

Lundquist, Susanne. *Native American Literatures: An Introduction.* New York: Continuum, 2004.

McCarthy, James. *A Papago Traveler: The Memories of James McCarthy.* Ed. John G. Westover. Sun Tracks 13. Tucson: Arizona UP, 1985.

McNickle, D'Arcy. *The Surrounded.* 1936. Albuquerque: New Mexico UP, 1964.

"Miracle, The Sacred White Buffalo." 30 Dec. 2005 <http://www.homestead.com/WhiteBuffalo Miracle/>.

Momaday, N. Scott. *Ancient Child.* New York: Harper, 1990.

———. *The Way to Rainy Mountain.* Albuquerque: New Mexico UP, 1969.

Morris-Carlsten, Traci L. "Trickster in Contemporary Native American Art and Thought: The Indigenous Cultural Language of Bob Haozous." *American Indian Art Magazine* 30.4 (Autumn 2005): 78–85.

Nabhan, Gary Paul. *Enduring Seeds: Native American Agriculture and Wild Plant Conservation.* San Francisco: North Point, 1989.

———. "Native American Management and Conservation of Biodiversity in the Sonoran Desert Region." *Biodiversity and Native America*. Ed. Paul E. Minnis and Wayne J. Elisens. Norman: Oklahoma UP, 2000.

Orlean, Susan. *The Orchid Thief: A True Story of Beauty of Obsession*. New York: Ballantine, 1998.

Ryan, Allan J. *Trickster Shift: Humor and Irony in Contemporary Native Art*. Vancouver/Toronto: UBC P; Seattle: Washington UP, 1999.

Silko, Leslie M. *Almanac of the Dead*. New York: Simon and Schuster, 1991.

———. *Ceremony*. New York: Signet, 1978.

———. *Gardens in the Dunes*. New York: Simon & Schuster, 1999.

———. Letter to the author. 20 Feb. 2006.

———. *Yellow Woman and a Beauty of the Spirit: Essays on Native American Life Today*. New York: Simon & Schuster, 1996.

Smith, Linda Tuhiwai. *Decolonizing Methodologies: Research and Indigenous Peoples*. London/New York: Zed Books; Dunedin, New Zealand: Otago UP, 1999.

Vizenor, Gerald, ed. *Narrative Chance: Postmodern Discourse on Native American Indian Literatures*. Albuquerque: New Mexico UP, 1989.

———. *The Trickster of Liberty: Native Heirs to a Wild Baronage*. Norman: Oklahoma UP, 2005.

Walker, Barbara G. *The Woman's Encyclopedia of Myths and Secrets*. San Francisco: Harper, 1983.

Weigle, Marta, and Barbara A. Babcock, eds. *The Great Southwest of the Fred Harvey Company and the Santa Fe Railway*. Phoenix: Heard Museum; Tucson: Arizona UP, 1996.

Welch, James. *The Heartsong of Charging Elk*. New York: Anchor, 2000.

Wiget, Andrew. *Native American Literature*. Boston: Twayne, 1985.

Witzel, Michael Karl. *Route 66*. 1996. Ann Arbor: Lowe, 2002.

HISTORY IN *GARDENS IN THE DUNES*

Joy Porter

As Kimberley M. Blaeser has pointed out, history does more than inform Native literature: "in a very real way history *forms* native writing. It provides, of course, much of the real subject and impetus, but beyond that the consciousness of historical continuum is sounded in the voice of native writers, and traced in the form and methods of their literary expression" (37). *Gardens in the Dunes* is an especially rewarding text in this regard, given that the spine of the narrative is a late nineteenth century story describing a series of interconnecting, intercultural and transnational relationships. The reader learns about the resourcefulness of a young native girl called Indigo as she is forced to form a new sort of family with a privileged American non-native couple, and about how that unit alters as it is transplanted across the globe from the desert of the American Southwest, to Riverside (California), to New England, to Lucca in Italy, Bath in England, Corsica and finally, back to where the girl's story began. Although the novel successfully presents a series of contrasting voices and perspectives on the events that unfold, it is the integrity of Indigo's story that carries most weight. It is through Indigo, a child from a culture Silko invented as emblematic of all the small tribes who became remnants, or who ceased to exist, that the reader learns how to survive in spite of vulnerability. We learn, as Silko put it in the Arnold's interview, how one might conquer powerlessness, that is, how to "keep your insides alive, while you do what you can to fight" (184).

Crucially, much of the history presented in *Gardens* subverts conventional understandings of the past. The Ghost Dance is portrayed from a native and positive perspective, not as a doomed and impotent revivalist faith but as a beautiful and spiritually powerful example of Indian syncretism. Rather than an emphasis upon Indian acculturation and Indian boarding schools, in *Gardens* the focus rests with the irrepressible force of native resistance to the imposition of all things non-Indian. The novel voices new and important interconnections between colonisation, empire and the subjugation, classification, exploitation and transportation of plants, animals and peoples. Gender is also examined in depth, as is nineteenth century science and the way in which women have related to the production and perpetuation of knowledge including religious knowledge. Centrally an Indian understanding of the importance of an essential reciprocity between all things is repeatedly contrasted with a profit-centred, scientific and reductive understanding of the world. In many instances, this privileging of alternative ways of comprehending and engaging with the world serves to make dominant thinking seem ridiculous. Therefore, as Silko described it in the interview with Ellen L. Arnold, the whole of *Gardens* is "pretty funny" (184).[1]

Just as significant is the way in which the events within *Gardens* conjure a set of inclusive, interactive truths that are spiritual in nature and transcendent of time. Silko described this aspect of her work in her previous text *Storyteller*, writing, "You should understand / the way it was / back then, because it is the same / even now" (94). *Gardens* invokes a language that connects the animate and inanimate world and that speaks of an eternal, feminine force of violent retribution and ultimate renewal. Above all, it prioritises the spiritual over all other ways of comprehending the world. The way in which each individual in the book relates to gardens and by extension to their interior landscape, to their spiritual self, is the clearest indicator of their worth and character. In sum, *Gardens* encourages its readers to understand the past in new ways, to reimagine place, and to reforge a spiritual relationship to the animate and inanimate world.

One of the most interesting ways in which *Gardens* connects with history is its relationship to a famous figure active in the period in which the book is set, Sigmund Freud. Whilst Silko has acknowledged that both *Gardens* and her previous 1991 book *Almanac of the Dead* are "post-Marxist" in that both novels portray capitalism as an irredeemably negative force, she has also stressed that *Gardens* should be seen as "post-Freudian," indeed, that it should be seen as a tribute to Freud.[2] Silko read all of Freud's work prior to writing the novel as well as works such as H.D.'s *Tribute to Freud*, a book written in 1944 that recalls H.D.'s period as Freud's analysand around 1933-34. H.D.'s book has many correspondences with the main themes of *Gardens*. It concerns itself with how Freud helped Hilda Doolittle explore "that particular field of the unconscious mind that went to prove that the traits and tendencies of obscure aboriginal tribes, as well as the shape and substance of the rituals of vanished civilizations, were still inherent in the human mind—the human psyche" (Barnes qtd. in Arnold 82; H.D. 12–13).[3] Like Silko, H.D. describes another dimension where universal understanding is possible. In the same way that *Gardens* describes an all-inclusive spiritual syncretism that can combine pre-Christian or "pagan" belief with heretical Christianity (a phenomena Brewster E. Fitz has described as Silko yearning for a "written orality" resembling the ultimate "pure language"), *Tribute to Freud* describes translatable dreams whose language and imagery are "common to the whole race, not only of the living but of those ten thousand years dead." "In the dream," H.D. tells us, "man, as at the beginning of time, spoke a universal language, and man, meeting in the universal understanding of the unconscious or the subconscious, would forgo barriers of time and space, and man, understanding man, would save mankind" (Fitz x; H.D. 71).

The same theme connects directly to both books' focus upon snakes and serpents. As Brewster Fitz has pointed out, the grand narrative that emerges in Silko's writings is "the principle of aboriginal serpentine matriarchal spirituality" (193). This is a spirituality that knows no temporal or national boundaries; instead snake spirituality binds disparate cultures together. As Edward (whose orientation the reader quickly learns to distrust) says of Indigo (whom the reader immediately empathises with and admires), "The child was from a culture of snake worshippers and there was no sense in confusing her with the impression the old Europeans were no better than red Indians or black Africans who prayed to snakes" (304). The reader gains precisely this impression as *Gardens* progresses, that a form of serpentine matriarchal spirituality binds peoples across nations and across time. At the end of *Gardens*, the novel's message of positive renewal and the restoration of reciprocal relationship is signalled by a snake, by the fact that "Old Snake's daughter moved back home" to the pool in the *Gardens* where Indigo, Sister Salt and her child finally settle (479).[4] H.D has an analogous respect for snakes and links them directly to Freud and his ability to tap into the "fourth dimension." She compares Freud to the Greek Asklepios, who incurred the wrath of the gods for raising the dead, and stresses how the symbol of the serpent is entwined with the cross of the "Hippocratic University." Perhaps ironically on one level, given the suffering that follows Edward Palmer's compulsion to collect ancient artefacts in *Gardens*, a shared love of antiquity was a primary and very meaningful bond between Freud and H.D. She had a longing to delight him by adding a Cretan serpent-goddess to the host of little statues and images that littered his consulting rooms (H.D. 64; 101; 175). Overall, however, *Gardens* could be said to owe much more to the work of Freud's disciple Carl Gustav Jung, the Swiss psychologist and life-long student of Gnosticism, than it does to Freud.[5]

"Post-Freudianism" is only part of the fascinating historical web that binds *Gardens* together. Arguably, the novel should be seen first and foremost as a Gnostic treatise, as an heretical subversion of received Christianity. Silko has confessed that she wrote *Gardens* partly because of the bestselling book *The Gnostic Gospels* written by her fellow MacArthur Fellow and now Princeton Professor of Religion, Elaine Pagels. Pagels' book was based on her work translating a library of ancient manuscripts found in 1945 at Nag Hammadi in

Upper Egypt. Her book contradicted the image of early Christian church as a unified movement, and suggested that political considerations of the time were determinant in how Christian orthodoxy developed and furthermore, that women were once prominent but were subsequently excluded from governing positions in the Church's emerging hierarchy.

In picking up and developing themes from Pagels' book, Silko has linked Native American spirituality with a set of powerful and increasingly fashionable ideas. Gnosticism originally flourished from sometime prior to the Christian era and began to decline after the second century, but currently it could be said to be undergoing a revival, both amongst serious scholars (Daniel Boyarin, John Dominic Crossan, Geza Vermes, Harold Bloom) and in popular culture (Gnostic themes are discernible in Grant Morrison's comic series *The Invisibles*, in the work of Philip K. Dick, Philip Pullman, Dan Brown and in films such as *The Matrix*, *The Truman Show*, *Groundhog Day*, *Vanilla Sky* and *Pleasantville*). As with most spiritual approaches, Gnosticism contains multiple traditions and is complex and difficult to define, but key aspects include a mythopoetic and transcendent nature, an emphasis upon knowing the self as means of knowing God, the idea that matter is a deterioration of the divine spirit and the idea that God is a duality, specifically a unity of the masculine and the feminine. In general Gnosticism has taught that the earth was ruled over by a lesser "god," the Demiurge, after Plato (Greek demiurgos — "one who shapes") and that certain humans contain a divine spark or *pneuma* that knowledge (*gnosis*) can allow to return to the source, or nothingness, from which it and all things originally came. Other leading Gnostic ideas include that of a supreme female principle (Sophia), that of magic vowels supposed to have been uttered by the Saviour and his disciples, that of a Cosmic Serpent who heroically freed Eve from the rule of Hyle or Matter through passing on *gnosis*, docetism or the belief that Jesus did not have a physical body, emphasis upon light and darkness, and belief in the power of ritual. In terms of its relationship to other spiritual traditions Gnosticism is syncretistic and inclusive. It may have been influenced by Buddhism; it has correspondences with the origins of Jewish mystical teaching and for some scholars, it is fundamentally pagan in origin. It has been criticised as being elitist (*gnosis* or "knowledge" being available only to those who know), as being heretical in that it regards figures such as Jesus simply as helpers towards individual spiritual advancement and transformation rather than as sacrificial saviours and accurately, of being a threat to ecclesiastical authority.

Gnosticism has allowed Silko another framework within which to present the history of the Ghost Dance. She realised, as she put it, "that there are lots of different Jesus Christs, and the Jesus of the Messiah of the Ghost Dance and some of the other sightings of the Holy Family in the Americas were just as valid and powerful as other sightings and versions of Jesus" (Arnold 164). Therefore *Gardens* presents a counternarrative to more usual understandings of the Ghost Dance phenomenon, one where the Ghost Dance messiah is juxtaposed to other experiences of Jesus across the globe. Very often in mainstream histories the Ghost Dance phenomenon is presented, as William T. Hagan puts it in *American Indians*, as an example of "warriors grasping at straws" and as "a completely disillusioning experience for the Indians involved" (142). In *Gardens*, rather than being presented as the millennialist pipe-dream of a depleted and desperate set of peoples or as the poorly-digested adoption by Indians of an wholly alien faith, the Ghost Dance is portrayed as a lived example of superior native spirituality, a spirituality whose impulse is to include rather than exclude, to expand interrelationship, broaden community and to foster positive reciprocal connections between land, plants, animals and peoples, regardless of heritage. In Silko's reading, experience of a messiah is not something exclusive to or owned by one group, instead it is a spiritual experience many peoples across the world have in common. Silko shows the Ghost Dance to be evidence of the power of Native American spirituality to include and absorb and she is aware that this process has a long history. As she has said with reference to early European colonisers, "It was so funny. They weren't here long, and they had to see their Jesus, their Mary, their Joseph, their saints, go native, just like that. And they couldn't stop it" (Silko qtd. in Arnold 187).

To the extent that the novel's unadorned prose encourages its readers to experience the sense of loss of the Indian peoples who danced the Ghost Dance and to feel the spiritual power of reconnection with those lost ancestors, *Gardens* successfully reinvokes the Ghost Dance ritual itself. The Dancers are, after all, dancing in spite of their experience of sustained attack upon their respective communities, in spite of the trauma Grandma Fleet describes when she points out to Indigo, "To go on living when your body is pierced by pain, to go on breathing when every breath reminds you of your loved ones—to go on living is more painful than death" (53). Most importantly, in *Gardens* it is the spiritual rather than the political significance of the Ghost Dance that is emphasised. By comparison, most historians have characterised it, and the analogous movements that came before and after it (such as those associated with the Delaware prophet in the Ohio-Great-Lakes region in the eighteenth century, or with Handsome Lake or with Tenskwatawa, also known as "the Shawnee Prophet" in the Old Northwest in the early nineteenth century), as "revitalization movements" aimed at the re-establishment of native control over

Indian cultures and lands. *Gardens* repositions the Ghost Dance so that its
spiritual foundations take primacy, in line in fact, with the focus of some of the
more recent historical analyses of such movements.[6]

Whilst the Ghost Dance is important within Silko's novel, gardens and their
history is what takes centre stage. *Gardens* re-connects landscape to storytelling,
creating an awareness in its readers of common ground and of what limits it.
Silko began writing *Gardens* as an enjoyable, apolitical "reward" for the reader,
but quickly realised that this approach was unsustainable since, as she puts it
"you just can't write an apolitical novel about gardens!" (Silko qtd. in Arnold
181). Like so many of Silko's characters, plants are travellers and migrants.
Their history provides another lens through which to view colonialism given
that the collection and use by empire of plants is so intimately connected with
the domination of peoples across the globe. The reader learns of the risibly
pathetic attempts of decaying aristocrats to use garden land as a canvas upon
which to broadcast how fashionable and rich they were and winces at the
inappropriateness of shipping wholly grown trees into alien landscapes. This
connects very meaningfully with some of the most recent approaches to the
historical study of empire. Books such as Maya Jasanoff's *Edge of Empire:
Conquest and Collecting on the Eastern Frontiers of the British Empire, 1750–1850* have
shown that the mania of imperial collectors was a metaphor for how empire was
actually formed. Rather than planned expansion, empire developed in the same
piecemeal and haphazard pattern that collectors collected. Like Silko, Jasanoff
emphasises how the empire's collectors of indigenous artefacts and plants,
because they themselves came from shallow-rooted origins, sought to "re-
fashion" themselves in their adopted countries through display. The non-native
gardens Silko's novel invokes, such as the Italian Renaissance villa garden and
the nineteenth century English bourgeois private garden, are in themselves
examples of new garden traditions developed at times of dramatic social and
political transformation for the cultures involved.[7] But unlike Edward in
Gardens, many of the agents sent to smuggle plants and seeds by the British
Royal Botanic Gardens at Kew were successful. For example, in the 1850s
cinchona seeds, capable of combating malaria, were removed from the Andes;
in 1876 latex-producing *Hevea brasiliensis* was removed from the Amazon,
facilitating the subsequent rise of rubber plantations in Ceylon, Malaya and
Sumatra and in 1893; the sisal plant, used for twine, was transferred from
Florida to German East Africa. Like Edward, the real plant smugglers of the
nineteenth century considered their work to be both good business and, given
that it was in the name of science, an unalloyed blessing for mankind. However,
as *Gardens* and the work of historians such as Lucile H. Brockway has pointed

out, such piracy had complex repercussions and was, essentially, theft at the expense of colonised nations.

In making gardens the pivot for her narrative, Silko has interposed an Indian viewpoint upon a long conversation among historians about nature, its refashioning as garden in America and American identity. Cultural historians like Perry Miller and Henry Nash Smith have described how Americans conceived of their unique national character in terms of their domestication of the wild and "virgin" lands of the New World. In *The Machine in the Garden* Leo Marx showed that it was only when Euro-American methods of cultivation had transfigured much of the continent into a productive garden that Americans were able to romanticise their republic as a place that was spiritually sustaining. And of course, as writers like Annette Kolodny have shown, this discourse of subordination was intimately bound up in the minds of American male writers with an eroticised and gendered approach to landscape.[8] Crucially, Silko's novel helps destroy the notion that colonising powers brought some compensation to the peoples and landscapes they dominated by creating "gardens in the desert." She demonstrates the superiority, rather than inferiority or absence, of indigenous methods and approaches to cultivation as well as their long-term sustainability and sacred nature. In terms of narrative and in terms of spiritual thought, *Gardens* displaces the Euro-American from the garden and makes primary the reciprocal and progressive approach to cultivation practiced by Indigo. Hartwig Isernhagen has suggested that such a correction of the historical record within native writing was inevitable. He writes, "In order to set the record straight and as a move of self-empowering, it was to be expected that a native writer would come and (re)claim the garden as cultural icon and emblem for indigenous writing, thus also reclaiming horticulture for the indigenous repertoire of self-representation and modifying the dominance of the desert in it" (176–77).

However hideous the conspicuous consumption Indigo sees as she experiences new gardens, this does not prevent her from admiring their beauty and interacting with them positively. In stark comparison to the activities of generations of sons of the English aristocracy, who since the eighteenth century undertook "Grand Tours" throughout Europe so as to inspect and collect treasures of classical antiquity for display in their landscaped parks, Indigo collects only the seeds and cuttings that are freely given to her and which she can ultimately use to sustain herself, her community and her home landscape. Significantly, *Gardens* closes with news of Indigo's successful adaptation of gladiolus spuds to the dune gardens and we learn how the flowers help foster good feeling between Indigo's community and that of another set of staunch

Christian Indians. Once again, a flower is used in the novel to celebrate the sacred and to foster inclusive community, perhaps as flowers once did before Christianity depleted flower knowledge and flower gardening during the pious Middle Ages (*Gardens* 477; 478).[9] Indigo's experience directs the reader towards a fuller understanding of how positive hybridity is, the kind of hybridity that can only benefit a spiritually dominant Indian worldview. Thus Sister Salt's mixed-blood baby speaks from within her womb using the language of the Sand Lizard people, because, quite simply, "the Sand Lizard mother's body changed everything to Sand Lizard inside her" (*Gardens* 204). This is the opposite kind of hybridity to the forced migration of plants practiced pathetically by the character Susan James with her "English landscape garden" on the East Coast. Her transfer of two sixty-foot copper beech trees appals Indigo and her reaction to the event is described in the language of atrocity:

> Indigo was shocked at the sight; wrapped in canvas and big chains on the flat wagon was a great tree lying helpless, its leaves shocked limp, followed by its companion; the stain of damp earth like dark blood seeped through the canvas. As the procession inched past, Indigo heard low creaks and groans—not sounds of the wagons but from the trees.   (185)

Edward ties many of the above themes together by exemplifying the foolish misguidedness that Silko connects with strident capitalism. He is the most vulnerable of all the book's characters and in the end his spiritual failings, indeed the sickness of his materialism and his belief in science, lead to his death. Like previous Silko characters representative of a Euro-American desire for capitalistic exploitation, he is spiritually impotent. This is connected to the fact that he is obsessed with making fresh starts, that is with denying history, like the characters Max the mafia assassin and Leah his wife in *Almanac of the Dead*. Edward's failure to gain power encourages the reader to examine what it is that he seeks, even at grave risk to his own physical and spiritual equilibrium. His consistent desire is to dominate, objectify and possess. Echoing the Gnosticism of Pagels' book, Edward's theft of fruit trees in a Corsican orchard rewrites the Biblical Garden of Eden story, making a man the wrong-doer rather than a serpent and a woman. By comparison, at the very moment when Edward is doing most wrong, Hattie is focusing upon gaining knowledge from direct and authentic experience of the divine, upon experiencing a moment of Gnostic revelation.[10]

Thus *Gardens* successfully encourages us to re-evaluate a series of established approaches to the past, even though at points that re-evaluation can be deeply unsettling. Aside from the factual historical anomalies Brewster Fitz has referred to, there is for example, the question of the alacrity with which Sister Salt approaches prostitution. Silko tells us that, ignoring the churchgoers "who pursed their lips anuslike to spit insults at her," Sister Salt "took her choice of the men willing to pay a dime for fun in the tall grass along the river" largely because, "The old-time Sand Lizard people believed sex with strangers was advantageous because it created a happy atmosphere to benefit commerce and exchange with strangers" (*Gardens* 220). Since Silko invented the Sand Lizard people, the idea of a happy Sand Lizard prostitute is, of course, possible, but it does fly in the face of much scholarship devoted to unseating historical myths that stretch back to Columbus suggesting that Indian women enjoy sexual exploitation and that such exploitation is somehow culturally sanctioned within Indian communities (Fitz 262).[11]

A large, complex theme in *Gardens* is the way it subverts conventional history through its focus upon connections between "old European" and Native American Indian worldviews. In using "old Europe," Silko is invoking a term introduced by Marija Gimbutas, in *The Goddesses and Gods of Old Europe: 6500–3500 B.C.* Controversially, Gimbutas made central use of folklore in her work, inventing a new interdisciplinary field, archaeomythology. She found evidence of peaceful and matrilinear pre-Indo-European "Old European" cultures that once worshipped a range of goddesses and gods and further argued that the Vinca-Tordis script (excavated post 1875 in Vinca near Belgrade and elsewhere) was an Old European language. Indigo's journey in *Gardens* connects "old European" and Indian lifeways. In fact, in an ironic reversal of the ethnographies of the period, the novel exposes its readers to a spiritual ethnography conducted by Indigo as traveller, as she spiritually "reads" a series of gardens and their communities. Indigo meets Hattie's Aunt Bronwyn, a follower of Gustav Theodor Fechner (1801–87), who venerates "dancing" stones and sacred groves that house of the spirits of the dead.[12] Bronwyn has a Welsh name connoting purity and lives in a house and very cosmopolitan garden near Bath. Here Indigo first encounters gladioli and detects a strong similarity in spirit with the old gardens of the Sand Lizard people. Aunt Bronwyn struggles to protect the ancient from the modern so as to salvage an old, pre-Christian spiritual understanding from loss. As the novel progresses, glimpses and varieties of this abiding knowledge are portrayed across Europe from the beginning of time up until the present.

It is with Aunt Bronwyn that Silko introduces some of the most radical re-historicising *Gardens* contains. Bronwyn explains to Indigo how the English displacement of the Scottish was fundamentally a spiritual crime, one that caused "the fairies" to wage war against Scottish sheep. She suggests that the

Irish famine of 1846 "came because the Protestants and the English knocked down the old stones" (254). "The wars of Europe," we learn "were the terrible consequences of centuries of crimes against the old stones and sacred groves of hazel and oak" (254). All this, along with talk of sightings of dancers around fires on hilltops in the mist and news that "in the fog and mist; the people saw his Mother, sometimes with a child they called the Son of God" (264), is accepted by the young Sand Lizard girl, whose eyes were "round with delight as she nodded vigorously" (264). In Bronwyn's version of the European past, the Irish play a special role. In particular, she is familiar with Derry, or, to give it its official name, Londonderry, in the North of Ireland and is vehement about its significance. She asks:

> Did Hattie know (did anyone know) how much innocent blood spilled in Derry over the years of the occupation or how much more blood might yet spill? Ireland's suffering began with the betrayal of fairies. Those who cut down the sacred groves doomed themselves and all their descendents![13]   (263–64)

Clearly, this kind of history is simplistic, since it telescopes complex waves of conquest into one relationship, that of universalised colonisers versus stones, oak groves, fairies and presumably, the indigenous Irish, but that is not to say that the spiritual and ecological change such a history speaks to should be ignored or dismissed.[14] It productively encourages us to do something unusual, that is, to consider the past over very long timescales and it has interesting interrelationships with more orthodox histories. In Derry's case, it links a past most people even in Ireland have forgotten with a present that seems wholly irresolvable. Derry's name in Irish, "Doire" does indeed translate to "oak grove" and those oak groves were used for ships, building and the plantations of non-indigenous English and Scottish settlers with intensive colonisation beginning in 1585. There is also evidence that Derry is one of the longest continuously inhabited places in Ireland, that once its giant oaks were sacred and that oak groves like Derry's were used as places of ceremony and ritual. Derry has also been the site of recurrent destruction from 783, when the Danes burnt its abbey, to the end of the seventeenth century. Today Derry continues to suffer from the serious civil conflict and sustained terrorist activity that dates from the civil rights clashes of October 1968. Undoubtedly, as *Gardens* suggests, specific ecological, social, cultural and political correspondences exist between Derry's history and that of various Native American Indian communities across time.[15]

However, Silko's conflation of a stance that is against "the Protestants and the English" with the language of mists, fairies and the ancient druids has a complex pedigree within Ireland. It connects strongly to the idealisation of the primitive that accompanied all the "Celtic Revivals" in Ireland of the late eighteenth and nineteenth centuries. Ironically, in terms of Silko's pro-indigenous re-historicising, the chief agents of such primitivism in nineteenth century Ireland were in fact the Anglo-Irish gentry. They projected ancient Irish folkways as neutral territory on which they could connect with their Catholic compatriots. In fact, as Sinéad Garrigan Mattar has recently pointed out, by the mid-nineteenth century, as a class the very survival of these Unionists, "seemed to depend upon the motivating strength of romantic primitivism" (14). This was a primitivism, an idealization of a an "authentic" Irish identity predating English colonial influence, that many scholars of the Irish past hold had as much to do with contemporary science and with constructions of the Orient, as it did with any ancient Celtic tradition in Ireland.[16] Arguably, by invoking such a romantic and primitivist version of the Irish in *Gardens*, Silko has reinscribed a set of stereotypes about the Irish that are as deeply problematic and as wedded to colonialism as those which are routinely applied to Native Americans.

Irish nationalists at the time certainly reacted strongly against the romantic primitivism of key (Protestant) literary figures such as William Butler Yeats, Lady Gregory and John Millington Synge, seeing it as a colonial slander against the good (Christian) name of the Irish nation. Frank Hugh O'Donnell said of Yeats' play *The Countess Cathleen*, that it depicted the old Irish as nothing more than "an impious and renegade people, crouched in degraded awe before demons, and goblins, and sprites, and sowlths, and thivishes—just like a sordid tribe of black devil-worshippers and fetish-worshippers on the Congo or the Niger" (qtd. in Mattar 97). Similarly, the "Irish Ireland" movement also strongly protested the "Celtic sham" as patronising, Arnoldian, and Unionist. There was deep-seated resistance to the emphasis upon the utopian spiritual and symbolic Irish at the expense of the material and actual Irish caught up in modernity. As Sinéad Garrigan Mattar puts it, "The peasant whose dream Yeats emulated lived in a pre-industrial time-warp, where the circumstances of a primitive spiritual life were more real, and more desirable, than 'reality'. The peasant of the West whom he denied had fought in the Land Wars and was religiously orthodox; his children were intent on leaving the fireside, discontent with the benefits of a fairy 'swoon', to seek material comfort elsewhere" (98). In essence, the primitivism of fairies and of a posited Celtic twilight depoliticised the Irish at a time when the political power of the Irish peasant was becoming threatening. It seems likely that Silko intended her emphasis upon fairies, twilight, oak, spirit and stone in *Gardens* at least in part as a form of nationalist solidarity with another indigenous and colonised culture, but, as so often with things Irish, the truth in terms of the operations of history, power, representation and stereotype, is not so simple.

These complexities do not mean that *Gardens* is unsuccessful in historical terms. To the extent that history can be seen as the struggle for pre-eminence between competing stories, it is another powerful and highly nuanced salvo from Silko against dominant historical narratives. Indigo's story, like that of Sister Salt, her child, their friends and Hattie is a victory, a victory of the power of lived experience over history presented simply as teleological report. Silko presents a story of successful resistance to negative Euro-American values in the past so that her readers may better imagine such resistance today and in the future. Fundamentally, she encourages us to lengthen and broaden our historical thinking so that we include native perspectives and realise the great age of those perspectives relative to dominant understandings. In marrying the nineteenth century novel form to these complex ideas she powerfully inserts an Indian reading into our literary consciousness of the past. As in her previous work, *Storyteller*, *Gardens* begins with Indian lives and perspectives under threat but ends with Indian visions and values pre-eminent. In *Gardens*, Indian ways gradually absorb and transcend non-Indian ways, strengthened by Indian interconnection between the living and the dead, between people and the natural world. This inevitable assimilation is a long drawn out process, a long war rather than an individual battle, but it is one where Silko is confident that time is on the Indian side. As she puts it, "I believe in subversion rather than straight-out confrontation. I believe in the sands of time" (qtd. in Coltelli 147).

NOTES

1. Silko's intention here contrasts sharply with Fitz's reading in *Silko: Writing Storyteller and Medicine Woman*, where he describes *Gardens* as "maudlin" and "figuratively soaked in tears shed by characters."

2. In Arnold's interview Silko was careful to point out that she is not against the free market or the concept of private property. She defined capitalism as "the middle-men, the banks, the government, that kind of economic system that favors the giant and crushes the little person." In its place she advocated a form of bioregionalism that abandons "all kinds of national boundaries" (180; 185–86; 193).

3. Silko discusses H.D.'s "wonderful" book in Barnes 82.

4. For more on Silko's personal relationship with snakes, see Gonzalez in Arnold 97–107.

5. Jung worked with G. R. S. Mead to explain the Gnostic faith from a psychological standpoint. Jung linked the emergence of the Demiurge (in Gnostic doctrine following Valentinus and John) out of the original, unified monadic source of the spiritual universe by stages to the emergence of the ego from the unconscious. However, whilst Gnostics seek a return to the ultimate source, or Godhead,

Jung did not agree that this should be the ultimate goal of the individual since this was analogous to a dangerous total identification of the self with the unconscious. See Segal, Jung and Jaffe.

6. See for example Dowd and Martin. Although Indian schools are presented negatively in *Gardens*, they were one of key means by which news of the Ghost Dance spread and several historians have stressed the positive spirit of community they fostered. See for example Lowawaima.

7. For more on this issue see Hunt 19–32.

8. See Miller, Smith, Marx and Kolodny. For discussion of why so many of the key books of this era on "discovery" of the American landscape exclusively consider the east-to-west movements of white men, and for discussion of the importance of desert gardens to WWII Japanese subject to coerced relocation, see Limerick.

9. See also Goody.

10. This is not to say that the historical record provides no evidence of female figures whose work was analogous to Edward's. Most often such women are described positively as "pioneering" scientists striking out against the gender limitations of the late nineteenth and early twentieth centuries. See for example Shindler.

11. Fitz states that it is unlikely that around 1900, a Catholic would have been admitted to Vassar or that a thesis committee would have been established at Harvard for an auditor (Fitz 262). U.S. Indian women's history is an extremely robust field. For a useful overview see Bell 307–21. See also Butler.

12. Fechner was an early experimental psychologist who carried out work on the perception of colours and who believed mind and matter were simply different ways of perceiving the same reality. See Wozniak. *Gardens* is an acutely visual novel and Indigo, like Night Swan, Ts'eh and Betbie's grandmother in *Ceremony*, is consistently associated with the colour blue.

13. The issue of the city's proper name is so violently contested that those who favour peace and who wish to avoid perpetuating blame, often refer to it as Derry/Londonderry or, for short, "Stroke City."

14. I have not dealt in detail here with the singular approach to the Great Famine expressed in *Gardens*. However, at a minimum, it should be noted that David W. Miller's work has shown that the impoverished Protestant underclass were as vulnerable to the crisis of 1845–52 as the Catholic labourers in the South and West of Ireland. To gain a broader understanding of the famine, see ÓGráda and McLean.

15. For more on "Stroke City," see O'Brien and Nolan. Ironically, "St Columba's Greeting to Ireland" speaks of Derry as "my little oak grove of Erin and concludes "As you view it afar from Derry belovèd / O the peace of it, the peace and delight!"—in Graves 17. See also Porter.

16. See for example Lennon.

WORKS CITED

Arnold, Ellen L. "Listening to the Spirits: An Interview with Leslie Marmon Silko." *Conversations with Leslie Marmon Silko*. Ed. Ellen L. Arnold. Jackson: UP of Mississippi, 2000.

Barnes, Kim. "A Leslie Marmon Silko interview." *Conversations with Leslie Marmon Silko*. Ed. Ellen L. Arnold. Jackson: UP of Mississippi, 2000. 69–84.

Bell, Betty. "Gender in Native America." *A Companion to American Indian History*. Ed. Philip J. Deloria and Neal Salisbury. Oxford: Blackwell, 2002.

Blaeser, Kimberley M. *Native American Perspectives on Literature and History*. Ed. Alan Velie. Norman: U of Oklahoma P, 1994.

Bloom, Harold. *Omens of Millenium: The Gnosis of Angels, Dreams and Resurrection*. New York: Riverhead, 1996.

Boyarin, Daniel. *Borderlines: the Partition of Judaeo-Christianity*. Philadelphia: U of Pennsylvania P, 2004.

Brockway, Lucile H. *Science and Colonial Expansion: The Role of the British Royal Botanic Gardens*. New York: Academic P, 1979.

Butler, Anne M. *Daughters of Joy, Sisters of Mercy: Prostitutes in the American West, 1865–90*. Champaign: U of Illinois P, 1985.

Coltelli, Laura. *Winged Words: American Indian Writers Speak*. Lincoln: U of Nebraska P, 1990.

Crossan, John D. *The Birth of Christianity: Discovering What Happened in the Years Immediately After the Execution of Jesus*. San Francisco: Harper Collins, 1999.

Dowd, Gregory E. "Thinking and Believing: Nativism and Unity in the Ages of Pontiac and Tecumseh." *American Indian Quarterly* 16 (1992): 309–35.

Fitz, Brewster E. *Silko: Writing Storyteller and Medicine Woman*. Norman: U of Oklahoma P, 2004.

Garrigan Mattar, Sinead. *Primitivism, Science, and The Irish Revival*. Oxford: Oxford UP, 2004.

Gonzalez, Ray. "The past is right here and now: an interview with Leslie Marmon Silko." *Conversations with Leslie Marmon Silko*. Ed. Ellen L. Arnold. Jackson: UP of Mississippi, 2000. 97–107.

Gimbutas, Marija. *The Goddesses and Gods of Old Europe: 6500–3500 B.C.: Myth, Legends & Cult Images*. London: Thames & Hudson, 1974.

Goody, Jack. *The Culture of Flowers*. Cambridge: Cambridge UP, 1993.

Graves, Alfred P. *A Celtic Psaltery*. New York: F.A. Stokes, 1917.

Hagan, William T. *American Indians*. Chicago: U of Chicago P, 1993.

H.D. *Tribute to Freud: Writing on the Wall: Advent*. Fwd. Norman H. Pearson. Manchester: Carcanet, 1985.

Hunt, John D. "The garden as cultural object." *Denatured Visions: Landscape and Culture in the Twentieth Century*. Ed. Stuart Wrede and William H. Adams. New York: The Museum of Modern Art. 19–32.

Isernhagen, Hartwig. "Of Desert and Gardens: The Southwest in Literature and Art, 'Native' and 'White'. The Example of Leslie Silko and Georgia O'Keefe." *Literature and the Visual Arts in 20th-Century America*. Ed. Michele Bottalico. Bari: Palomar Eupalinos, 2002.

Jasanoff, Maya. *Edge of Empire: Conquest and Collecting on the Eastern Frontiers of the British Empire, 1750–1850*. New York: Knopf, 2005.

Jung, Carl G. and Aniela Jaffe. *Memories, Dreams, Reflections*. London: Collins, 1962.

Kolodney, Annette. *The Lay of the Land: Metaphor as Experience and History in American Life and Letters*. Chapel Hill: U of North Carolina P, 1975.

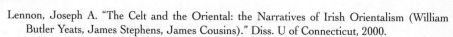

Lennon, Joseph A. "The Celt and the Oriental: the Narratives of Irish Orientalism (William Butler Yeats, James Stephens, James Cousins)." Diss. U of Connecticut, 2000.

Limerick, Patricia N. "Disorientation and Reorientation: The American Landscape Discovered from the West." *Journal of American History* 79.3 (1992): 1021–49.

Lowawaima, K. Tsianina. *They Called It Prairie Light: The Story of Chilocco Indian School.* Lincoln: U of Nebraska P, 1994.

Martin, Joel W. *Sacred Revolt: The Muskogees' Struggle for a New World.* Boston: Beacon, 1991.

Marx, Leo. *The Machine in the Garden: Technology and the Pastoral Ideal in America.* New York: Oxford UP, 1964.

Mattar, Sinead G. *Primitivism, Science, and The Irish Revival.* Oxford: Oxford UP, 2004.

McLean, Stuart. *The Event and Its Terrors: Ireland, Famine, Modernity.* Stanford: Stanford UP, 2004.

Miller, David W. "Irish Presbyterians and the Great Famine." *Luxury & Austerity.* Ed. Jacqueline Hill and Colm Lennon. Historical Studies. 21. Dublin: U Coll. Dublin P, 1999.

Miller, Perry. *Errand into the Wilderness.* Cambridge: Belknap P of Harvard UP, 1987.

Nash Smith, Henry. *Virgin Land.* Cambridge: Harvard UP, 2005.

O'Brien, Gerard, and William Nolan. *Derry & Londonderry.* Dublin: Geography Publications, 1999.

ÓGráda, Cormac. *Black '47 and Beyond: The Great Irish Famine in History, Economy and Money.* Princeton: Princeton UP, 1999.

Pagels, Elaine. *The Gnostic Gospels.* New York: Vintage, 1979.

Porter, Joy. "The North American Indians and the Irish." *Irish Studies Review* 11.3 (2003): 263–71.

Segal, Robert A., ed. *The Gnostic Jung: Including Seven Sermons to the Dead by C. G. Jung.* Princeton: Princeton UP, 1992.

Shindler, Karolyn. *Discovering Dorothea: The Life of the Pioneering Fossil-Hunter Dorothea Bate.* London: Harper Collins, 2005.

Silko, Leslie Marmon. *Almanac of the Dead.* New York: Penguin, 1991.

———. *Ceremony.* New York: Penguin books, 1986.

———. *Gardens in the Dunes.* New York: Simon & Schuster, 1999.

———. *Storyteller.* New York: Arcade, 1981.

Vermes, Geza. *The Authentic Gospel of Jesus.* London: Penguin, 2004.

Wozniak, Robert H. Introduction. "Elemente der Psychophysik." 1860. By Gustav Theodor Fechner in Robert H. Wozniak *Classics in Psychology, 1855–1914: Historical Essays.* Bristol: Thoemmes, 1999.

"WE'VE GOT TO GET OURSELVES BACK TO THE GARDEN:" INDIGENOUS VIEWS OF THE LIFE-DEATH CYCLE AS RESISTANCE IN LESLIE SILKO'S *GARDENS IN THE DUNES*

Kimberly Roppolo

> I give you back to the soldiers
> who burned down my home, beheaded my children,
> raped and sodomized my brothers and sisters.
> I give you back to those who stole the
> food from our plates when we were starving.
> I release you, fear, because you hold
> these scenes in front of me and I was born
> with eyes that can never close.   (Harjo 73)

Though the mainstream American populace was largely shocked when pictures of sexual degradation of Iraqi captives were made public, American Indian[1] and African American peoples are all too painfully aware through our personal and familial histories that rape and sodomy, that intentional miscegenation and degradation, are part and parcel of colonization. Colonization is a process, like the rapes and sodomies that accompany it, of emasculating a people to open them up, along with their land, as "virgin" territory for the taking. Colonization is a rape of a people and a land, a miscegenation designed to transfer "ownership" that creates its own justifications. It

1. Kills as many males of indigenous group as possible or demoralizes and emasculates them through the use of war technology and "rules" of warfare antithetical to indigenous concepts, including, but not limited to, forced sodomy and other tortures;
2. Utilizes rape and sexual servitude of women to miscegenate and terrorize;
3. Separates children from the group;
4. Forces assimilation of children and attempts to remake their identities;
5. Forces re-ordering of individual societies with the paradigms of the colonizer, including separation from the Land/Mother.

Helen Fein in "Genocide and Gender: The Uses of Women in Group Destiny" traces the use of such practices in contemporary and historical war, finding that "perpetrators of genocide must either annul reproduction within the group [being colonized] or appropriate the progeny in order to destroy the group in the long run" (43). Roger Smith in "Genocide and the Politics of Rape" outlines "'the pervasiveness of rape in war, its political uses, and the psychology and politics of rape as policy: it functions as a ritual of degradation, to instill terror and demoralize the victim group, to destroy the continuity of their reproduction, and as symbolic revenge and reward to the participants" (qtd. in Fein 43). Ruth Seifert in "War and Rape: A Preliminary Analysis" offers additional insight. She claims that "'rape is part of the 'rules' of war. . . . an ideal of masculinity associated with aggression . . . aimed at destroying the opponent's culture, 'the rape of the women in a community can be regarded as the symbolic rape of the body of the community'" (qtd. in Fein 43). Kathy Peiss, in *Major Problems in the History of American Sexuality*, argues that "sexual relationships between Europeans and Native Americans were shaped by the dynamics of power between their societies. Rape and other forms of sexual abuse were most frequent where European men sought to control and exploit Native Americans' bodies and land . . . . [S]ome historians argue that sexual violence was a key instrument of European conquest" (26–27).[2]

Though this happened throughout the Americas, the testimony of Junipero Serra, provides specific examples in regard to Spanish conduct in the invasion and missionization of California, the same region, though not the same locale, as the novel, in the earliest phases of colonization. Serra writes that the soldiers, in pursuit, would "'lasso Indian women—who then became prey for their unbridled lust,'" that they murdered Indian men in order to take their women, that "'even the children who came to the mission were not safe from their baseness'" (qtd. in Castañeda 47–48). Other Spanish chroniclers from Bartolomé de las Casas (32; 33; 36; 73; 74; 77; 80; 82) to Father Luis Jayme (36–38) note similar instances throughout the area attacked by the Spanish during the entire period of Spanish control, as do colonial chroniclers of other European ethnicities throughout other parts of the hemisphere, such as William Byrd (qtd. in Purdue 44). Rape and sexual degradation are not merely part of Indigenous memory and reality, they are part of the colonial record.

Certainly, this is the kind of mindset of sexual violence symbolized and actualized in the depredations of the Sand Creek Massacre, where Cheyenne infants were "shot at their mothers' breasts" (US Congress 82–83), where "bodies were mutilated in the most horrible manner, men, women, and children—privates cut out . . . one man [said] he had cut a woman's private parts out, and had them for exhibition on a stick . . . numerous instances in which men had cut out the private parts of females, and stretched them over saddle-bows, and wore them over their hats" (88–89). Though on the opposite end of the spectrum in terms of colonial sexual invasion, it is also the kind of mindset that gave rise to the practice of relationships 'à la façon du pays,' or, 'in the custom of the country' (112) between European men and First Nations women in Canadian colonization referred to by Carol J. Williams in *Framing the West: Race, Gender, and the Photographic Frontier in the Pacific Northwest*. Many of these Indigenous women were later abandoned as European wives became available, and they and their children were subject to great discrimination: their children as racially-mixed indesirables and they as 'promiscuous' and 'inferior' (114–15). In fact, the legacy of these sorts of stereotypes of Indigenous women, on the colonial record throughout the Americas to justify European's own rape, sodomy, and pillage, is manifest in the Church and State funded rape of Native children that took place in the boarding schools. To this day, the effects of sexual abuse in residential schools resound in the US and in Canada. Moreover, Native women and children are still subject to the various forms of abuse that grow out of colonial rape; in Canada, over five hundred First Nations women are reported missing, many of whom are feared fallen victim to sexually-violent predators.

This paper will show how Silko's characters, in particular Sister Salt, subvert and overcome the sexual violence of colonization in *Gardens in the Dunes*. As in many tribal stories, Silko's gardens in the novel are analogous to the cycle of life and death depicted in the human characters in the book. Using Native American Church as an intertribal context as well as tribally specific references, the idea of the Sacred Feminine within a non-binary dualist ontology will be explored to clarify the text's philosophical basis; in her "heresy," Silko uses a non-binary dualist paradigm based on intertribally-common philosophical ideals, rather than a linear paradigm, to show that life continues, both for the People and for the planet, in the face of imperialism. In this novel, for the indigenous woman who embraces the larger cycle, who maintains an indigenous worldview, sex, reproduction, birth, and death can be acts of resistance. As in earlier works, Silko depicts hybridity as strength, rather than accepting it as miscegenation. In embracing life, we as Native women take the effects of colonization into us like children into our wombs and transform them into gifts for our peoples, into survival of that very colonization itself. We are the centers of change.

Colonization, because it cannot be justified morally, is justified legally; it is grounded in a pseudo-neo-Judaic legalistic worldview. William Bradford's positing of the pilgrims as Hebrews and Indians as Cannanites in *Of Plymouth Plantation* and the use of Church/State law to justify the genocidal actions of the Spanish are perfect examples of this. Resistance entails attempts to prevent the depredations of colonization, including insistence upon continuation of indigenous definitions of relationships and identities, insistence upon continuing our worldviews.

Law vs. Nature's Ways

Based on objectification	Based on "love"
Absolutes	Paradoxical
Heterosexual and masculine-privileged	Gender-balanced and ever-shifting
Linear	Holistic
Draws separations	Finds connections
Encoded in His-story, teleological	Fights back with Heresy (Her-Say), This-story—ongoing and cyclical

Non-binary dualism can be studied in the ceremonial paths of any single tribe around the world, whether the Maori or the Blackfeet, or by the using non-linear, holistic, synthesis developed through those disciplines (as opposed to analytic, "scientific" thought of Western-born academia) and looking at intertribal commonality, which I think at this time is extremely important for us to do. In fact, the single most important reason in my mind for intertribal explorations of philosophical commonality is that they are key in restoring balance in this overwhelmingly masculine era that is prophesied and necessary in some of the cyclical ceremonial counts, such as the Mayan calendar. In this view of time, as opposed to Western notions of time, we are in an overtly masculine era prior to a return to the feminine. Characteristics of this era, well-depicted in Silko's *Almanac of the Dead* and to some extent in *Ceremony*, grow out of dualistic views of reality. This dualistic, dominant culture worldview is a refusal of the slipping signifier, of the non-binary, the non-linear, non-teleological, holistic worldviews of Indigenous reality. Indigenous realities accept multiple, eternally changing and growing explanations of Truth just as they are witness to multiple, eternally changing and growing manifestations of Life in Creation. The dominant dualistic worldview creates an attachment to certain signifier sets, privileging, along with masculinity, heterosexuality, Christianity, capitalism, and materialism. It worships its own ideas as "correct," as "the only path," as "morally right," as "logical," and as "science."

Separation of the masculine and feminine causes lack of respect and a corresponding abuse, appropriation, destruction of what is objectified in an extreme masculine appropriation of the concrete, a separation of the intangible and tangible into "not real" and "real." The materialism and capitalism made possible by this reinforce the "thingification" of the Sacred Created aspects of "Creation"—seeing these as individual, concrete, non-spirited units rather than interrelated (All my Relatives) and spirited.[3] The separation of sexuality and the sacred, generative powers of humanity, the feminine and masculine procreative powers, posits sexuality as dangerous and "bad," female sexuality particularly so as Christianity uses and used its biblical precedents to cast it as such. In contrast, in many Native languages (such as Blackfeet and Cheyenne), sexual desire is described as being "hungry for a man/woman," sex being as natural and necessary to life as eating.

Because of the importance of sexuality to life and the role women play in reproduction and survival, the Feminine is honored and Sacred in Native cultures. The feminine image is symbolized and seen everywhere around us. The sacred doorway of the vulva is manifested in emergence places, the Grand Canyon, in springs, and in the entrances to ceremonial spaces or to traditional Native homes. Entering sweat lodges, kivas, and tipis is a re-entry into the womb of Mother Earth. Desire focuses on the point of entry and upon entry itself, as what is beyond is the ultimate Eternal Feminine, the Sacred, the thing beyond the veil of the Temple; this is the space of conception, the joining of the masculine and the feminine in pre-birth being, rebirth, and transformations of all kinds. The principles taught in Native American Church serve as a good example for illustrating this.[4]

Like Ghost Dance, Native American Church is inter and extra tribal. It, too, is a blend of Native and Christian ideas—a hybrid, but paradoxically, while non-tribally specific, Indian. Many origin stories exist, but all involve a woman, sometimes with, sometimes bereft of, her offspring, attempting to survive in the desert where her child was lost from the group and return to her tribe. The knowledge of the healing and saving powers of Peyote was given to the woman, near the point of death, by the Plant itself, considered to be the Heart of Jesus. The woman brought Peyote ways back to her people; the ceremony was at first a women's ceremony. After a time passed, the women, who had held their ceremonies outside, turned the ceremony over to the men. The men moved the ceremony inside the tipi to bring in the Feminine Aspect the women had brought by the nature of who they are as Mothers of their Peoples. Today, both women and men participate in the ceremony, but we are taught that the tipi poles are our Mother's ribs, the smokehole, her mouth, that we are inside of our Mother. By simple extension, though this is not directly discussed, one can see that the doorway is the opening of the womb. This is reinforced in the morning, when a woman, the "Water Maiden," acts as the Mother of All, prays for all of creation and the people who attended the "meeting," and brings in "morning water . . . the water of life." At this point, "the circle is completed," her Sacred Femininity pairing across the fire from her with the masculinity of the Road Man, seated in the honor seat. Some Road Men, for this reason, feel that only their wives should fill this ceremonial role and will not allow their wives to act as Water Maidens in meetings run by other Road Men. Let me stress that while no sexual contact is involved whatsoever, the power of the spiritual/symbolic communion is such that it causes jealousy.

The Water Maiden sitting in front of the doorway inside the tipi, all of the supplicants with living mothers rise to their knees as the Morning Water Song is sung, honoring their mothers. Those who do not rise are mourning the loss of their own. The nurturing aspect of the Feminine and the connection of both the tipi and the woman with Mother Earth is then highlighted as she brings in the produce of Mother Earth's body, actualized in corn, fruit, and meat. In this ceremony, the whole space of the tipi is the Womb of the Eternal Feminine, the origin of our physical being in the joining of the desire of Creator and the Womb of Mother Earth. It is paralleled in what Western thought tries to separate from the idea of reproduction, the sexual and sacred desire of our biological fathers for the "vision" of the vulva of our biological mothers—the recognition of "who she is," in Marilou Awiakta's terms, an aspect of the Sacred Feminine (249). This is also mirrored in the willingness of our mothers to both sacrifice themselves to that masculine desire and be receptive physically to our conceptions and to sacrifice themselves for our gestations, birth-transformations, and nurturance throughout life. Out of respect, participants are taught to follow the "right way" to move through the sacred space of the tipi. On the physical level, this translates as appropriate movement clockwise, facing the fire, and not turning oneself in a circle or crossing between someone praying, singing, or eating medicine and the fire. This path is also manifested in symbols such as the Peyote Moon, explained as the "Road of Life," carrying the lessons beyond the Sacred space of the tipi into the Sacred space of individual life paths themselves. The respect we are taught for the tipi should extend into our lives as we encounter individual females as Mothers or potential Mothers.

Like in a Georgia O'Keefe painting, the Feminine as a Sacred and Natural focus of desire, permeates the Indigenous world, *is* the Indigenous world. The Vuvlic Doorway is the most compelling and centripetal image for all humankind as it is our point of entry and re-entry into the Sacred Feminine, our own Origin and possibility of change and growth, of continuing life. It is the point where Sacred Silence/Sacred Awe exists. Ceremonial space is of necessity representative of the Eternal Feminine because this is the place of mystery, of "fecund darkness" and transformation, the place of miracles; it is the space where the cardinal balances and the powers of thought and word in speaking, prayer, ritual, and song are utilized to create the New in the way that new life is gestated in the womb through the bringing together of masculine desire and seeking and feminine sacrifice and nurturing. It is analogous to the receptiveness of the (feminine) Earth for (masculine) rain; it is the bringing together of spirit and flesh, the intangible and the tangible, as all created things are both equal parts of spirit and flesh, heart and mind. We, the seekers, must approach and enter the Eternal Feminine with respect, in a good way, in order to precipitate transformation.

The concrete level on which heterosexual reproduction and sexuality operates and their Sacred significance in Native Cultures is perhaps the easiest way to understand this, but because in Indigenous worldviews, things are, to use Leroy Littlebear's words, in "constant flux," the manifestation of these masculine and feminine principles in same-sex desire and sexuality in these worldviews must also be explained. The intertribal teachings of Native American Church parallel those once given (and still given in some tribes) in traditional coming of age ceremonies for both females and males. Returning to this notion of doing things "in a good way," young women were traditionally taught to achieve this, taught "who they were," not only throughout the Life Path as we all do our understandings of the Sacred, but also through the Transforming to Woman ceremonies of the tribes, so that they could both respect and *expect* respect for their own Sacred Sexuality in both its reproductive (physical conception and transformative aspects) and spiritually-transformative aspects. The traditional ways of Transforming into Man taught respect for woman through taking on the feminine aspect of self-sacrifice in fasting and/or other physical sacrifice and the feminine aspect of nurturing through the act of "gifting" the instructor, the path leader who himself sacrifices some of his medicine and knowledge to the supplicant for the life of the People. Heterosexual men learned to fully recognize and respect the Feminine and its Powers both in others and the self through Ceremony. When the Transforming into Man Ceremony preceded physical sexuality on the Life Path of individual Indigenous Men, they were able to approach their physical sexuality in a "good way" more easily. This was further developed as well throughout a man's lifetime if he chose the warrior path. Women being more necessary to the survival of a people then men, males had to be willing to sacrifice themselves as protectors or in traditional warfare and raiding ways. This worldview is in sharp contrast to that of the colonizers, who saw Native women as property for the taking, and in sharp contrast to the "sex sells" world of today. Sex, in mainstream culture, has become devoid of, robbed of its meaning entirely to the point of culture boredom with sex and the rise of a selfish, ego-centric, childish impulse for the new, the novel, the "kinky" to maintain desire rather than the seeking of a Sacred Path based on mutual respect for each other as representations/aspects of Creator Spirit. Within the non-binary dualist paradigm of gender, self-sacrifice (not merely sexual or reproductive, but also ceremonial) is considered feminine, while desire (not merely sexual desire, but also the quest in its many forms, including the quest of ceremony) is considered masculine. Masculinity is also associated with the spirit (the intangible) as is the feminine with the flesh (the concrete); however, unlike in Judeo-Christian tradition, neither of these is maligned as "evil;" both are necessary in a culture. The joining of the two, whether in sex or in ceremony, is "always sacred;" this is illustrated by the Pipe (chanupa) way in Lakota tradition. The joining of cardinal balances is the causality behind the Liminal Space of transformation.[5] Through ceremony, we give birth to ourselves, as well as give rebirth and transformation to This World and all of Creation. Through our sexuality, when we see it as Sacred, we can come to understand this—there is a give and take between feminine nurturance and sacrifice and masculine strength and desire in sexual acts as in life, one in which the flux is constant and in which either party can give any of the above to the other.

Keeping in mind these ideas regarding sexuality and ceremony, in the non-binary dualism of Native worldviews, the "opposite" or cardinal balance of Death is not Life, but Birth. Death, like Birth, is simply an ultimate Ceremony, an unmitigated transformation. Like the Masculine and Feminine, death and birth are the extremes, the cardinal principles of the Sacred Life Path, manipulated for transformation in the ceremonial paths themselves through the sacrifice of those things that ensure our life force remains strong—water, food, sex—and the inclusion at times of intentional physical self-wounding. In Death, like in Ceremony, we re-enter the womb and transform. On one hand, physically we return to the Transformative and Life-Giving Womb Mother Earth to be remanifested as humus, as plant, as animal. On the other, our spiritual selves are reborn into (the) Other World(s), put on new paths.

Although signifiers in Native cultures are not fixed, but allow for much slippage, plants are commonly associated with the Feminine, aspects of Creation in which all of the above mentioned Feminine principles are also manifest. As women are associated with plants both in our reproductive capacity and through our traditional gathering of and tending of them for food, we, with our wombs, our breasts, and our plants, along with our cultural knowledge and ways, are the centers of survival and continuance for our Peoples. This is why so many Native cultures were traditionally matricentric. Though men can bring food by hunting, even the animals they seek are dependent upon Mother Earth's produce to survive. Moreover, men were taught that the animal, like woman, chooses the hunter, not the other way around, and that the animal must be properly respected and thanked. The idea of feminine self-sacrifice is echoed in the traditional life ways. The Corn Mothers of the Southwest are analogous in many ways to Selu of Cherokee tradition, who sacrifices her life for the people and gives us continually the produce of her body for our survival: corn, squash, and beans. These plants, in many traditions, are called the Three Sisters. *Gardens* shows the Three Sisters, Corn, Beans, and Squash, are all over Turtle Island (157) and suggests there are analogues worldwide: female centered, fertility centered cultures of Earth Mother and her body's produce, plants. And just as hybrid corn, when allowed to reseed itself for a few generations, returns ultimately to "Indian" corn, anything that we allow to become a part of ourselves ultimately becomes Indian. This is why in many Indigenous traditions, descent is counted matrilineally.

The same principles that underlie the story of Selu and that of the Corn Mothers elsewhere underlie the Sand Lizard metanarrative. Sand Lizard, "a relative of Grandfather Snake," had been invited to live there by him, live there and "cultivate her seeds." The ancestors of the people found her there in her garden where she gave them instructions for life based on the principles of plants in nature. They are to be generous with others: remember the ancestors with the first fruits in order to receive the rain they bring in their part of the cycle; remember their animal relatives the second fruits; remember the insect relatives with the third fruit; leave select plants to reseed, as "human beings are undependable" (17). The Garden, Mother Earth, is an Eden, a Refuge, a Womb—the place to which we are always, in William Bevis' terms, "homing." For the starving people (17) who "home" to here again and again, it is a place filled with the power of Survival, and it is this power that makes the story behind it the basis for the principles of life for those whose worldviews start here. The old gardens are full of plants, all pregnant with life—from the squash, gourds, and the pumpkins to the "sunflowers . . . heavy with seeds" (18). Mama, despite the fact she is raped by the Presbyterian missionary, returns home to give birth to Sister Salt where the plants give birth, in the garden were she herself was born (18–19). It is important to note here that Salt, despite her mixed ancestry, her "lighter hair and skin" (204), *is* Sand Lizard. This fictional culture, like many indigenous cultures, is matrilineal and matrilocal; the children are of the mother's people and place. The unnaturalness of the rape parallels the slaughter of the government given sheep and cattle (19), a thing out of balance, unlike hunting in Native paradigms, as mentioned above, but Mama overcomes this by maintaining her ways and beliefs. The idea that she prevails by maintaining her tribal ways is also supported by the ceremonial fashion in which Mama returns four years later to give birth to Indigo, also Sand Lizard, despite her uncertain paternity (19). Seeing herself connected to the cycle of nature means Mama keeps doing what is natural: bearing the future Sand Lizard generations and bearing Sand Lizard culture to transmit to them. We see she has succeeded as for Sister Salt, the "baby's head peek[ing] out from between her mother's legs" is both a natural and sacred thing (20); the fruit of our bodies *is* the fruit of Mother Earth. Survival and continuance are, after all, our primary business as Native women.

Grandma Fleet is the head of this matrilineal family, the elder who passes knowledge down to the rest. In always seeking survival, Grandma Fleet is a "recycler"—she looks for what can be "made new" and for the seeds that will renew themselves in a dump (16; 24). "Home" is a "lean to made of old crates and tin" (16). They themselves are a quilt, just like the sewn one by Mama from a "singed blanket and . . . ragged towels" with a "sharpened wire and string Grandma Fleet retrieved from the dump" (22). Protection is maternal and based on survival, with Grandma Fleet pretending to be "crippled" and sitting hen-like on the girls who are under the quilt/nest to protect them from the Indian policemen and whites who want to place them within the patriarchial world of residential school (23). This philosophy of recycling, of sustainable use of Mother Earth's resources, extends to the self, as the self is integrally part of nature and the larger cycle. When Indigo fears the future, Grandma tells her, "Anything could happen to us, dear . . . . Don't worry. Some hungry animal will eat what's left of you and off you'll go again, alive as ever, part of the creature who ate you" (53). Becoming part of the physical cycle again immediately, as she divides and her spirit goes on to bring rain, is Grandma's goal in building her "burrow below the apricot seedlings" (52). Epitomizing the idea of sacrifice in women's reproductive capacity, she teaches the girls that, having been close to death several times, particularly in the birth of her first child, "dying is easy—it's living that is painful . . . to go on living when your body is pierced by pain, to go on breathing when every breath reminds you of your lost loved ones—to go on living is far more painful than death" (53). In short, she teaches the girls as she is dying, as she is preparing to separate and become apricot and rain bringing spirit, that as women, they are part of the cycle of sacrifice, survival, and continuance, that the "rules" of life taught by the Sand Lizard's Garden will serve them well. And Salt's remembrance of Grandma with food, her unqualified love for her living and dead, shows she has spiritually, mentally, and emotionally become the woman her physical body is about to become. Indigo, still a child, accepts the worldview transmitted by Grandma mentally, but is spiritually, emotionally, and physically still too immature to handle this; she accepts that Mama is likely now "crawling around as a worm or running as a coyote," but with tears on her face (53). And when Grandma falls asleep for the final time, Indigo at first refuses to accept this, only joining Salt in the parting feast because of hunger. She then digs herself a womb beside Grandma's grave, where she longs for her mother's return (54–55).

The use of Ghost Dance in the novel further reinforces the paradigm of intertribal non-binary dualism and the view of the death/rebirth/life cycle through Sister Salt's eyes later in the novel as a member of an imagined Native culture, one based, however, upon real intertribally-common philosophical tenets. Ghost Dance, based on renewal and rebirth is spiritual and metaphysical subversion of colonialism—and the US government fears this (16). Like Native American Church, Ghost Dance is a blend of Christian and indigenous ways. However, the Messiah the Indians await is not the white Jesus. Despite the fact that both mainstream Christianity and Ghost Dance are built on resurrection, the resurrection of Ghost Dance is indigenous. "Jesus promised Wovoka that if the Paiutes and all the other Indians and danced this dance, then the used-up land would be made whole again and the elk and the herds of buffalo killed off would return . . . the winds would dry up all the white people and all the Indians who followed the white man's ways, and they would blow away with the dust" (25). This "Jesus wore a white coat with bright red stripes; he wore moccasins on his feet. His face was dark and handsome, his eyes black and shining. He had no beard or whiskers, but thick eyebrows" (25). This religion allows for the unmediated contact with the ancestors and the non-binary dualistic, matri-cyclical deities of the Mother, the Christ, his wife, and their offspring in the spirit world, moreover, while awaiting resurrection and renewal or rebirth of the Earth herself. This Christ is Queztacoatl, the Morning Star that returns each day to guide the people as they survive hunger and fatigue (33; 392).

Love, the connecting language of creation, both living and dead, acts as a lingua-franca for the dancers who, Mormon or Indian, are "all the children of Mother Earth" (34) as they instruct each other for preparation in this intertribal gathering and communicate with the Divine and with the ancestors. The dancers must enter the liminal zone of ceremony, where all cardinal balances converge, where death and life exist in equal measure. Crows, like owls, mark of crossings between worlds, and the Paiute woman shares that "the flocks of crows were a sign that Wovoka and the Messiah were coming" (26). Later in the novel, we will see that this can happen in various places on Mother Earth; the blackbirds in New England are a sign that the ability to "cross over" is everywhere (161). The dance circle is made of red earth, and red paint marks the doorways of the homes. Red earth, or paint, is sacred; it "belongs to the spirits" (27), because it is the lifeblood of Mother Earth. Here, the meaning is a perfect representation of non-binary dualism in cardinal balances—it is both "the color of old blood" (26), representing death, and blood that accompanies birth, marking both vulvic doorways of the homes and of the dance circle. The dancers wear white shawls and white paint, the color of death, to enter that realm despite their living bodies. The change is not merely symbolic. In the liminal zone of the dance, neither Mama nor Grandma can "recognize" the girls. Death and life are fluid, not discrete. Like Mother Earth, we are all in a cycle, not in permanent states of being. And death is necessary to renewal. In the midst of the destruction of colonization, the "invaders made the Earth get old and want to die" (28). This desire for death is not suicidal or apocalyptic. The lyrics to the song, "The black rock is broken and from it pours clear fresh water" (28) are indicative that the apparent sterility of death, like the apparent sterility of rock, is merely temporary, and that life will return.

Salt participates in the dances and gains spiritual knowledge there that Indigo will have to wait for. The spirits teach Salt "how beautiful we are, how beautiful we will become" (30), the beauty in both the life-giving way of woman and in death, which she no longer fears. Prior to young womanhood, knowledge of both death and of life-giving is not appropriate for Indigo, as Grandma indicates (31). When Sister Salt has her first menses, as the matrilineal family had predicted, the girls "celebrated [her] womanhood" with a modest feast. Her welcome into the cycle of generations has been preceded by years of daily teaching of feminine knowledge by Grandma and Mama, but Salt knows she will be the only "one to teach Indigo everything" (58), a task she is separated from as she is separated from Indigo. For now, this pan-Indian way of Ghost Dance has continued to acculturate Salt in the midst of the dissolution of her own cohesive culture; "Sand Lizard people weren't afraid of horned owls the way some people were," or by extension, within the symbolism of many Native cultures, of death, and Ghost Dance has reinforced the principle right before Salt comes of age in the absence of her matrilineal elders (61). And with the soldiers' prophesied disruption of the ritual (34), Salt has been prepared to guide Indigo as the girls themselves experience a kind of death, a death of the life they have known before with Mama and Grandma, in which they dig into Mother Earth's womb for warmth and protection (35) and must ritually re-feed over a four day period on the mild food of cattail roots (36).

Salt, as the older sister, is the one who must first take the role of woman taught to her by Mama and Grandma. A Survivor looks for nourishment for her and her children where she can, as life must continue, and it is her role as an aspect of the Sacred Feminine to carry it on. With Mama and Grandma away, Salt becomes Mother to Indigo: "When there was nothing else to eat, there was amaranth; every morning and every night Sister Salt boiled up amaranth greens just like Grandma Fleet taught her" and later, she makes seed tortillas when the greens are gone (16). This philosophy also manifests in he natural Sand Lizard view of sexuality that Salt has. Salt's Chemehuevi friends, Maytha and Vedna, see her as "like the old-time people their mother talked about—before the missionaries came. In those days, the Chemehuevis really knew how to enjoy one another; only Sand Lizards knew how to enjoy sex more . . . . Sand Lizards practiced sex the way they all used to" (208). However, with genocide, no Sand Lizard men are available as sexual partners for Salt. Luckily, for the Sand Lizards, "Sex with strangers was valued for alliances and friendships that might be made," and she has an open, natural attitude toward what she jokingly refers to as "the Sand Lizards' wild sexual practices" (204). And alliance and friendships are exactly what Salt needs to survive at Parker and remain in control of her own Sacred Sexuality. Salt and the other Indian women are in constant danger; "they all knew stories about women and even little girls attacked by whites or black men or Mexicans who worked for them," and a Cocopa girl had been "beaten and bloodied" after one such attack (209). She finds both a lover and a protector with Big Candy, the African American camp cook, who himself has Creek ancestry, "Baton Rouge" here likely referring to Red Stick Creeks, the portion of the tribe that most strongly resisted colonization. Candy is patient with her sexually, "content just to hug her close and kiss her and touch her breasts without intercourse" for weeks (211). When Salt and the Chemehuevi sisters are jailed for three months for pilfering soap from the school laundry to run their own side business, Candy pays Salt's fines and takes her to live with him in his tent (213). Salt feels safe enough here to enjoy a more natural attitude about her body, slitting her skirt and cutting off her sleeves to ease the heat and even going nude when she was alone (214). However, assumptions arise about Indian female sexuality; Candy moves Salt into her own place amid rumors that Candy is starting a "whorehouse" (214). Candy does, however, bail out Maytha and Vedna to join her, giving her the female companionship and extra protection other women would bring (216).

Candy understands that this is time of survival for Indian women; he often gave out leftovers from the camp to "hungry Indian women and children" on the streets of Needles (216). And he equally understands that he does not control or own Salt's sexuality. Salt engages in prostitution by choice, considering the money capitalism now necessitates they have a nice byproduct of the natural practice of sex as viewed in her tribal ways:

> The only time she wasn't homesick was when she was flirting with handsome strangers or lying with one of them on the sandy riverbank in the shade. The old-time Sand Lizard people believed sex with strangers was advantageous because it created a happy atmosphere to benefit commerce and exchange with strangers. Grandma Fleet said it was simply good manners. Any babies born from these unions were named 'friend,' 'peace,' and 'unity': they loved these babies just as fiercely as they loved all their Sand Lizard babies.
> Sister Salt took her choice of the men willing to pay a dime for fun in the tall grass along the river. Maytha and Vedna said Chemehuevi-Laguna women like them knew how to enjoy life, but this Sand Lizard woman was lusty! Candy did not mind—he was making good money and busy himself. Her body belonged to her—it was none of his business. (220)

He also seems to engage in sex with a Mojave woman outside of his relationship with Salt, showing a similar attitude toward sexuality (219). Salt realizes he has other women and thinks his "kindness to women [is] his best quality," especially not minding when he sleeps with her friends (220).

When Salt becomes pregnant, she is unsure whether the baby is Charlie's, a married Mexican man she had been involved with briefly, or Candy's. No matter, the baby is "Sand Lizard," and with her Sand Lizard beliefs, Salt feels the child will resemble both Charlie and Candy since "both men had sex with her regularly. But now that Charlie stayed away, the baby would become more and more like Big Candy until it was his child. That was what sex during pregnancy did" (222). Salt's view of her child's identity reflects the principles explained in the first section of this article: "Sand Lizard mothers gave birth to Sand Lizard babies no matter which man they lay with; the Sand Lizard mother's body changed everything to Sand Lizard inside her. Little Sand Lizards all had different markings, and some were lighter or darker, but they were all Sand Lizards" (204). The Sand Lizard baby, like the ancestors who speak to the living in dreams, talks to Salt and lets her know in her language that it wants to go home, to return to the old gardens (335). Pregnancy makes Salt miss Indigo as her remaining maternal family and miss home as well (340). It also makes her crave "Sand Lizard food," as that is what the baby wants to eat. When Salt goes out to gather the produce of the Earth in the form of the best local substitutes, the melons, themselves pregnant with life in a way reminiscent of the old gardens, she goes into early labor (341–42). Salt gives birth alone, the way in many tribal traditions:

> . . . she bit through the cord that connected them. He was a tiny shrunken old man . . . . She tore her skirt and gently wrapped him . . . . She was still bleeding, and the cramping did not stop. She thought, My Sand Lizard grandfather has come to take me home . . . [S]he curled around the little black grandfather . . . . She did not lose consciousness, but she was so weak she felt the pull of the earth bring her to the ground, and she thought, So this is how we return to Mother Earth. She was happy to return because she missed Grandma Fleet so much.   (343)

Death and Birth, cardinal balances, are part of the same cycle for Salt; both should bring joy. Salt, the little grandfather, and Grandma Fleet, all maternal family, are equally connected in this cycle. This connection is emphasized when the "rain cloud ancestors" come to "greet" the baby, knowing that "if not properly welcomed, a baby that tiny might give up this world and leave" (348). Each new Sand Lizard needs to be shown that they are still connected with their extended Sand Lizard maternal family on this side as well as in the Spirit World, that Birth and Death are part of one cycle. As Delena, the Mexican woman who reads Salt's cards and who herself has an agenda of Indigenous revolution says of the Death card, La Muerte: "Death's here, death's there—that's nothing unusual. That's the way life is; it means some sort of change" (370).

As danger increases around them, it is the baby who reminds Salt that she must leave (358–59). "Bright eyes" (401), as Salt comes to call him, is like the bright morning star; he is a resurrection of life for his people, Salt's grandfather returned (468), the missing masculine element of matrilineal family, and they must return to the safety of home. "He wanted to return to the old gardens. Money wasn't necessary there—all the food the two of them would need could be gathered there. His little auntie, Indigo, would return there—she wouldn't forget the way home" (400). He, Indigo, and the gardens are the constants in Salt's world, not Candy, who by now is behaving unnaturally (367) and cares more about money than the love of either Salt or his child (387). For Salt to achieve balance, she must reconnect with Indigo and return home. Hattie, having undergone great change herself throughout the course of the novel, reconnecting with the ancient goddess traditions from her own European ancestral past, learning from Aunt Bronwyn and Laura as well as Indigo, brings Indigo to Salt at Road's End.[6] Returning to Ghost Dance at Needles with Salt and the Chemehuevi sisters, Indigo communicates with Grandma and Mama in her dreams and matures in her understanding: "She felt so much love she wept; she knew then where Mama was and always would be" (470), as does Salt (478). The connecting language of love, which knows no boundary between life and death, gives the girls the strength to reach the gardens. Despite the slaughtering of the big snake and the chopping down of Grandma Fleet's apricot trees, life has returned in the form of a new snake and fresh shoots that grow out of the old trunk (478–79) as well as the new generation of Sand Lizards. "Old Snake's beautiful daughter," the mother of the people, now manifest in Sister Salt, "moved back home" (479).

NOTES

1. As I have stated in other forums, I will use the terms American Indian, Native American, First Nations, and Indigenous interchangeably throughout my work as none of these terms are correct, and I refuse to privilege any of them, though some term must be used in order to address the ideas we as Indigenous peoples often share in common.

2. Rape was uncommon in traditional Indigenous American cultures. In fact, among the Plateau tribes, there is evidence that the rare rapists were turned over women who "physical molested and publicly humiliated" them (Ackerman 87).

3. I choose the word "spirited" here over "anthropomorphized" or "magical realism" dismissals of Indigenous worldviews to show how profoundly different these ontologies are.

4. All Native American Church information is from my own experience and from the teachings of Eugene Blackbear, Sr., whom I have taken as a grandfather in Cheyenne tradition.

5. Here, it is important to distinguish that the "feminine" does not always mean female, and the "masculine" does not always mean male. The power of sexuality is, after all, more than even the miraculous power of producing life itself, because certainly, this power, the cardinal balances of masculine and feminine joined, manifest themselves in ways that *do not* produce actual new human lives. The paths of lesbianism and homosexuality reproduce on the spiritual level rather than the physical one, and, in many tribes, were considered sacred because of their very ability to do so in the intangible. The Contrary, the Wintke, path is one of these ways, and the ceremonial manifestations of that path are a recognition of this. The ability of a female able to gender masculinely in her sexuality is another, also Sacred, but commonly seen in tribal intellectual/philosophical/spiritual inheritances as different from the way of the Contrary. This is why the Lakota signs that a fasting supplicant is to become a Contrary have a separate application for female supplicants, one that *is not* lesbianism as one might expect in a Western worldview as the counter-part of the Contrary's Sacred Male Homosexuality, but rather the fullest possible Feminine and Female manifestation of the Sacred self-sacrificing impulse of Wintke way. Despite the physical sex of the participants, the principles of Sacred Sexuality do not change. The physical sexes of individual humans is less relevant than the masculine and feminine procreative and generative *roles* that are taken in human sexual acts and that *reflect* the manipulation of these balances within ourselves and throughout creation in the act of ceremony.

6. Hattie, whose white privilege has not protected her from being objectified and ignored by Edward and later raped, undergoes a rebirth in coming so close to death. Her finding of true religion,

of 'religere', relinking with her ancestors, is what leads her to join the Chemehuevi sisters, Salt, and Indigo at the second Ghost Dance of the novel (464). Indigenous principles of connectedness with Mother Earth, of the Sacred Feminine and Masculine, are for all who seek the ways of the ancestors. Ultimately, Hattie, too, returns home to England seeking balance (476).

WORKS CITED

Ackerman, Lillian A. "Gender Status in the Plateau." *Women and Power in Native North America*. Ed. Laura F. Klein and Lillian A. Ackerman. Norman: U of Oklahoma P, 1995. 75–100.

Awiakta, Marilou. *Selu: Seeking the Corn-Mother's Wisdom*. Golden: Fulcrum, 1993.

Bevis, William. "Native American Novels: Homing In." *Critical Perspectives on Native American Fiction*. Ed. Richard Fleck. Washington: Three Continents, 1993. 15–45.

Castañeda, Anonia J. "Sexual Violence in the Spanish Conquest of California." Peiss 47–56.

De Las Casas, Bartolomé. *The Devastation of the Indies*. Baltimore: Johns Hopkins UP, 1992.

Fein, Helen. "Genocide and Gender: The Uses of Women and Group Destiny." *Journal of Genocide Research* 1.1 (1999): 43–63.

Harjo, Joy. *"I Give You Back." She Had Some Horses*. New York: Thunder's Mouth, 1997. 73–74.

Jayme, Father Luis. "Father Luis Jayme Attacks the Sexual Abuse of Indian Women, 1772." Peiss 36–38.

Littlebear, Leroy. Personal interview. 28 Feb 2005.

Peiss, Kathy, ed. *Major Problems in the History of American Sexuality*. Boston: Houghton Mifflin, 2002.

Purdue, Theda. "Columus Meets Pocahontas in the American South." Peiss 39–56.

Silko, Leslie Marmon. *Gardens in the Dunes*. New York: Simon and Schuster, 1999.

United States. Cong. Joint Special Committee to Inquire into the Condition of the Indian Tribes. *Condition of the Indian Tribes. Report of the Joint Special Committee, Appointed Under Joint Resolution of March 3, 1865*. Microfiche. Washington: GPO, 1867.

Williams, Carol J. *Framing the West: Race, Gender, and the Photographic Frontier in the Pacific Northwest*. New York: Oxford UP, 2003.

GHOST DANCING THROUGH HISTORY IN SILKO'S *GARDENS IN THE DUNES* AND *ALMANAC OF THE DEAD*

David L. Moore

The question [is] whether the spirits of the ancestors in some way failed our people when the prophets called them to the Ghost Dance.   (*Almanac* 722)

The farther east they traveled, the closer they came to the place the Messiah and his family and followers traveled when they left the mountains beyond Paiute country.   (*Gardens* 320–21)

The Spirits of the Night and the Spirits of the Day would take care of the people.   (*Almanac* 523)

GHOSTS IN THE GARDEN

This article is conceived as a sequel to my earlier piece, "Silko's Blood Sacrifice: The Circulating Witness in *Almanac of the Dead*." There I argued for an understanding of *Almanac* as an elaborate performance of the Arrowboy myth that stands as a central dynamic of Leslie Silko's former novel *Ceremony*. *Almanac* was perplexing to many readers for its vast and dark vision, yet a focus on Arrowboy as witness sets that epic vision in Silko's mythic context. As readers recognize how Silko draws them into Arrowboy's and her own act of witnessing, the novel comes more into focus. Yet its challenge of facing the brutalities of history remains daunting. *Gardens* is perplexing to many readers for opposite reasons, for its seeming lightness and gentleness. Due largely to her choice of a juvenile narrator's predominant point of view, among various colonial voices returning to their roots, some readers have felt that *Gardens* was not a radical enough response to her *Almanac*. Not as a defense or apology, this paper tries to critique thematic links in *Gardens* with Silko's oeuvre that reflect this delicate orchid of a vision.

Perhaps because of a spirit of experimentation, or because of the different spirits of different days and eras, certainly because of her discursive gifts, each of Silko's books is unique and strikingly distinct, even divergent, from her others in tone, style, and structure. Yet a rhythm is evident. After the global witchery of *Ceremony* and *Storyteller* in the oceanic surge of *Almanac of the Dead*, Silko swam back upstream to quieter headwaters in her photographic essay, *Sacred Water*, and then let those waters flow into *Gardens in the Dunes*. While all of her works share a fundamental affirmation of Native survivance and a critique of colonialism, each takes a different approach. If *Almanac* is epic, *Gardens* is lyric. If the one is historical, the other is psychological. *Almanac* examines vast social and historical forces; *Gardens* explores individual lives in that history. The cacophony of global mixtures in *Almanac* finds some incomplete harmony in *Gardens*—because both are mythic, like all of Silko's work, and in her mythopoetics their opposite qualities interpenetrate. Thus the parlor novel that is *Gardens* takes place in the vast edifice that is *Almanac*. *Garden*'s orchids grow out of *Almanac*'s blood-soaked soil.

The roots are specific. Just as *Almanac* had roots in *Ceremony* via affirmations about Arrowboy, *Gardens* has roots in *Almanac* via affirmations about the Ghost Dance. Indeed, *Gardens* challenges readers to think in cross-cultural ways that *Almanac* prophesied. The spirit of Native continuity that the Barefoot Hopi affirms in *Almanac* is enacted precisely, carefully, and cross-culturally in *Gardens*: "Calabazas took the words of the Hopi to heart. He believed the change was in motion and was a process that had never stopped; it would all continue with or without him" (739). Near the end of *Almanac*, Wilson Weasel Tail raises the key challenge for the characters of *Gardens*: "The question as to whether the spirits of the ancestors in some way failed our people when the prophets called them to the Ghost Dance" (722). And Weasel Tail's comeback also measures the frame of *Gardens*: "the Ghost Dance was to reunite living people with the spirits of beloved ancestors lost in the five-hundred years war" (722). *Gardens* follows that effort at reuniting with beloved spirits by enacting the Ghost Dance across continents.

It is worth mentioning that the use of the term "ghost" instead of "spirit" in "Ghost Dance" has a long cross-cultural history of mistranslation from languages of Native spirituality into the discourse of colonial Christian prejudice against and even fear of Native spirituality. Thus many places sacred to Native cultures across the Americas are translated into American English with diabolical monikers. Look on any state road map. Near Ithaca, New York in Haudenausee country, as in Pend d'Oreilles country on the Flathead Reservation in Montana, modern travelers may stand in awe before the beauty of "Lucifer Falls." Devil's Lake in North Dakota certainly had other sacred meanings to the Chippewa and others who preceded the white map makers there as well. Topographical examples of Christian projection of evil onto Native translations are countless. In this vein, the Ghost Dance was indeed a source of apprehension to the frontier settlers and military, while the dancers themselves swooned in devotional communion with the spirits of their ancestors.

Ancestry itself is patently cross-cultural across time, or timeless and placeless in any present, as well as buried in the land. A number of other contemporary Native writers, including Linda Hogan, Sherman Alexie, and Gerald Vizenor, employ the imagery of ghost dancing to reaffirm not only the suffering of the ancestors on the ground and in the air we breathe, but also Native survivance in the present and future. Silko's novel begins with intimate imagining inside the Ghost Dance, moving from the skin of the dancers to the larger mythic landscape:

> The painting and the wrapping in white robes took a long time, but the people were happy and excited. . . . The white clay on Indigo's hair and face felt odd when she moved her mouth or eyes; her hair felt stiff. . . . They moved together and began to join hands in a circle around the fire. The voices of the dancers rose softly at first from low undertones, but gradually the singing seemed to rise out of the earth to surround them. . . . They were moving from right to left because that was the path followed by the sun. Wovoka wanted them to dance because dancing moves the dead. Only by dancing could they hope to bring the Messiah, the Christ, who would bring with him all their beloved family members and friends who had moved on to the spirit world after the hunger and the sadness got to be too much for them. The invaders made the Earth get old and want to die. (28)

The energy of a young dancer's experience of the Ghost Dance flows out into a mythic history of the Earth. By such patterns, *Gardens* manages to contribute to contemporary affirmation of Native survivance while carrying it in unexpected directions: to the tribal cultures of pre-Christian Europe and Africa, following their parallels with Native American mythic landscapes. The novel travels in those global directions specifically through the chosen trope of the Ghost Dance. Silko is ghost dancing through history to keep the spirit alive.

In addition to Weasel Tail's explicit reflection on the question of ghost dancing's potency, *Almanac* offers a number of expressions of the persistent ghost dance spirit as it will carry on in *Gardens*. For instance, the revolutionary leader, El Feo, muses, "Politics didn't add up. In the end only the Earth remained, and they'd all return to her as dust. . . . El Feo himself did not worry. History was unstoppable. The days, years, and centuries were spirit beings who traveled the universe, returning endlessly. The Spirits of the Night and the Spirits of the Day would take care of the people" (523). Similarly, Tacho affirms the mythic strategy: "The battle would be won or lost in the realm of dreams" (475). In a dramatic complication, the revolutionary Angelita voices the same vision, although skeptically: "All money went for food; the people were protected by the spirits and needed no weapons. The changes might require another hundred years, until the Europeans had been outnumbered and the people retook the land peacefully. All that might be okay for Wacah and El Feo, but Angelita had plans of her own" (710). And Calabazas prophesizes in direct resonance with Wovoka's discourse that established the Ghost Dance of the 1880s and beyond: "He had reminded the people of the prophecies different tribes had. In each version one fact was clear: the world that the whites brought with them would not last. It would be swept away in a giant gust of wind. All they had to do was to wait. It would be only a matter of time" (235).

These ghost dancing affirmations in *Almanac* function as expository explorations that then map the narrative structure of *Gardens*, where spirits direct the action. Sister Salt, for instance, consults her Gypsy cards as she is fleeing across the California desert: "Still, she could feel the golden threads of the radiance from across time that turned the cards and spoke the truth about her pursuer, like it or not" (391). Similarly, young Indigo, at Christ Church in England with Hattie and her eccentric Aunt Bronwyn, recognizes "the eyes of the original Mother, the Mother of God, the Mother of Jesus" in the ancient stones surrounding the church (267). The characters of the novel are steadily dancing with ghosts. Indeed, Indigo's involuntary travels across Europe are animated by her love of the Ghost Dance Messiah, as she follows in his peripatetic footsteps. The energy of that attraction is the motivation driving the novel itself, as in this exclamation following her perception of the eyes of the Mother of God in England:

> Indigo felt a rush of excitement and raced over the fragrant damp turf to the center of the great circle, where she sang out the words of the song from long ago: "The black rock, the black rock—the rock is broken and from it pours clear, fresh water, clear, fresh water!" Yes! The Messiah and his family stopped by this place on their journey to the east; Indigo felt certain of this.   (267)

The youthful enthusiasm of Indigo, insisting on this spiritual experience, effectively challenges Silko's readers to consider such a mythic substrate of history in just the innocence and simplicity that it suggests beneath the complications of the colonial archive. After the grotesque complexities of *Almanac*, Silko offers through Indigo's eyes in *Gardens* the beauty of simplicity. Telescoped dramatically in Indigo and Sister Salt, *Gardens* reaffirms the life of Ghost Dance spirits across generations of assimilation and oppression. The sisters' separate journeys across the globe follow their return, and echo a general Native American return, to the spirit of the Ghost Dance Messiah. Indigo weeps and prays early in her travels, here at Hattie's parents' house on Long Island en route to Europe: "'I'm trying to get back home,' she whispered to Mama and Sister Salt, and hoped when they dreamed they'd see her in this room and hear her message" (178). Ghost dance spirits travel in all directions. Later onboard their cross-Atlantic ship, Indigo addresses Ocean as Earth's sister, and again tries to commune with her Sister Salt: "Please help me, Ocean! Send your rainy wind to my sister with this message: I took the long way home, but I'm on my way. Please don't worry" (226).

Through a child's eyes, a fundamental optimism animates *Gardens*. In *Ceremony*, where "there are no boundaries, only transitions though all distances and time" (258) under the ancient shadow of witchery, myths link to history by the evil realities of colonialism itself as witchery's bloody feast. *Almanac* delves deeper into that same shadow. In *Gardens*, however, where "spirit is everything," where the Ghost Dance Messiah travels on a global journey, where Indigo prays to her long-lost sister, "Please don't worry," the shadows of witchery are flushed with light. A mythic power of life prevails over death. Toward the book's conclusion, as Indigo and Sister Salt watch the oppressive white town of Needles burn after interrupting their unconsummated Ghost Dance, "At first they didn't mention what night this was to have been or that somewhere in the mountains the Messiah and the ancestors still waited and loved them" (475). Even after being prohibited from their crucial fourth night of dancing to welcome back the Messiah, they know the loving strength of radical patience. By the end of the narrative, the well-traveled and reunited sisters move back to the old gardens in the dunes where, "something terrible struck there, but whatever or whoever, it was gone now. . . . Old Snake's beautiful daughter moved back home" to the hidden spring (479).

In addition to setting tone and framing structure, Silko's choice of a juvenile narrator also addresses a fundamental philosophical and religious question embedded in colonial history: the suffering of the innocent. If spirits do indeed direct history (if there is a God . . .), why do children suffer? Whether or not the question is properly constructed, I don't think that Silko pretends to answer, though she allows a paradox to finesse it in *Gardens*. The point of focus in *Gardens* is not the history or fact of suffering, but the story or imagination of deliverance, as in *Almanac*'s question, "Why had Yoeme called the story 'Day of Deliverance'?" when she survived "The Great Influenza of 1918" (580). As a keeper of the Almanac, her survival meant that the dreaming and the waiting and the watching could continue. If tribal sovereignty honors the suffering of the ancestors, ghost dancing is as much invoking those ancestors in their suffering as imagining a future. The paradox is that the past as present is that future for the ghost dancers. "In the Americas the white man never referred to the past but only to the future. The white man didn't seem to understand he had no future here because he had no past, no spirits of ancestors here" (*Almanac* 313). Silko offers *Gardens* to her white audiences to suggest a spiritual past in pre-Christian Europe, and thus a future in America. Indigo is full of delight, even in her sorrow. Is her delight the delusional fantasy of ignorance or the creative faith of genius? Silko's story, disguising such questions in the voice of a child, leaves that for her readers to decide.

REINVENTING THE HYBRID

A further religious question implicit in the imagery, language, and plot of the novel is the question of syncretism, religious mixing, or in the lamentable theoretical qua horticultural discourse some might prefer as more appropriate to *Gardens*, hybridization. Indigo identifies the Mother of Jesus with the family of the Ghost Dance Messiah. Christ Church in England is the site of the Mother's eyes in ancient pre-Christian rocks. A miraculous schoolhouse wall in Corsica becomes another visionary screen for this modern mixture of mythologies. European corms and bulbs are replanted in a spring-fed hideaway of an American desert. *Gardens* is a novel of botanical and cultural syncretism. For a measure of theoretical precision, it is worth examining the question of hybridization in the context of *Gardens* to clarify what Silko is and is not doing with her mingling of plants, peoples, and myths.

In looking at this question of hybridization, I am compelled to respond to a particular line in the recent call for papers of the 39th Annual Western Literature Association Conference, which offered this tack: "Analyze hybridity as a *necessary* component of western identities—in places, populations, and cultures" (emphasis added). Obedience to this call may get me in trouble, but I am not sure why or how hybridity must be necessary, if more useful mappings make visible the triangulations and quadrangulations, the larger systems, or the reappropriative disseminations and dialogics of power. Frankly, I don't like even the sound of the term "hybridity" in cultural or literary studies, nor its further nominalization "hybridization," nor its verbal "hybridizing." Not only does it miss the embrace of *Gardens'* simple, domestic fierce love of "glorious new plant life," it misses fundamental issues. The polysyllabics of hybridization bleep on the theoretical radar with all the wrongheadedness of reductive dualisms, thence of correspondingly reductive dialectics. I prefer analytical lenses that open up more complex fields of liability, impact, and activation.

The term "hybrid," which the OED says was virtually unused until the nineteenth century, comes from Latin roots that connect it first with "offspring of a tame sow and wild boar," then leaps by some logic of scientific racism to the following formulation: "hence, of human parents of different races, half-breed." Gerald Vizenor, noted Anishinabeg writer and postmodernist, embraces use of the affectionate term "mongrel" in his fiction, a metaphor which at least retains the imagery of a mammalian subjectivity. Unfortunately, modern usage of "hybridity" suggests a grafted woody plant stem, lovely enough, but suddenly hierarchical. One half of the shaft is cut to receive the wedge of the other. One half roots, the other flowers and fruits. One half supports, the other flourishes. One sits below, mostly, in the moist dark, the other rises above, wafting in the air and light. They work together in tandem, one dominant, the other subordinate, yet which is which? The story of dominance goes back and forth.

All the gendered dynamics of a dominating model of colonialism drive the image of a hybrid, as in Edward's attempted mercantile theft of Corsican citron cuttings for profit, or, one may say, graft:

> He was still a bit out of breath himself from the exertion of carrying the tripod and the camera case, heavy now with dozens of twig cuttings carefully rolled in oil cloth to sustain them until they returned to the hotel. There he would hollow out little receptacles in the potatoes to provide the moisture and nutrients that would sustain the cuttings on their long journey to California. . . . Edward was in rare high spirits and talked excitedly about the joint venture with Dr. Gates—shares in the citron stock in exchange for shares in the meteor iron mine. (322)

His care for the plants is focused not on their animistic presence but on his own exploitative profit. His eventual failure is predicated on his insensitivity to the mythic dimension that even he is enacting. Edward, by his genteel but brutal greed, is associated with signs of "the destroyers" in *Ceremony*, *Storyteller*, and *Almanac of the Dead*, and with "the aliens" and "the invaders" in *Gardens*: "The Sand Lizard people heard rumors about the aliens for years before they finally appeared. The reports were alarming, and the people had difficulty believing the bloodshed and cruelty attributed to the strangers. But the reports were true. At harvest, the aliens demanded and took everything" (17). Not only is Edward willing to drain even his wife's finances for his contraband, he loses no love in the loss. "He had no regrets—he was accustomed to the single state" (403). Indeed, he lived and died as the alien expected by the Sand Lizard people.

In direct contrast with Edward's attempt at illegal hybridization, the passage above of Edward's smuggling attempt is interwoven with Hattie's and Indigo's spiritual epiphany over the Corsican vision of the Blessed Mother, which celebrates a syncretic mix of Christian and Native mythologies. Edward, in his colonial blindness, cannot read their devotional delight: "He thought Hattie and the child were rather subdued but he chalked that up to fatigue" (322). Instead, they have just seen a confirmation of global guidance, of a sustaining spirit in the Ghost Dance that beats beneath economy and history, as in Indigo's voice:

> The rocky dry hills and their people were poor; their lives were a struggle here; that was why the Blessed Mother showed herself here; the people here needed her. Although she didn't see the Messiah or the rest of the family or her mother with the dancers, Indigo was much heartened; all who are lost will be found, a voice inside her said; the voice came from the Messiah, Indigo was certain.   (322)

In the spiritual light of Indigo's Ghost Dance visions—in contrast with the dark, profiteering vision of Edward's ultimately self-destructive projects—she is able to bring exotic plant life home to California.

These distinct mythopoetics spread far beyond the hierarchies of hybridization. Indigo conceives of an archetypal originary prior to the dialectics of colonial history. I have written elsewhere about the limits of dualistic analytical tools (see bibliography). Let me just say here that a focus on "hybridity" can reify problems of agency, in contrast with the opportunities for agency in the free play of wider connections. Hybridity's roots in scientistic discourse reduce the subjects of hybridity to a state of entrapping polarities, not only encapsulating them in historical and biological dialectics that erase narratives of choice, but metaphorically shoveling them into a kind of cultural compost. "Hybridity" does this reductive work by eclipsing multiple alternatives outside the colonial system. Leslie Silko's work is about imagining just such alternatives, and *Gardens*, which opens and closes with interrupted Ghost Dances, tries to narrate how and where those alternatives may reside and survive.

As a farewell to the term, Lenape scholar, Jack Forbes, explored hybridity in *Black Africans and Native Americans*:

> "Hybrid" formerly referred to almost any type of mixture including that between "wild" and "tame" or between "citizen" and "stranger." Mestizo commenced its history as an equivalent of "hybrid" and originally was applicable to animals as well as humans, and to mixture that was religious, ethnic or cultural as well as "racial." ... But in the nineteenth century, and especially after the US Civil War, greater and

greater emphasis was placed upon wholly biological or "racial" categorization and differentiation in North America. (268–69)

According to Forbes' genealogy, the term has marinated in the bitter soup of scientific racism. Bruce Simon, in "Hybridity in the Americas: Reading Condé, Mukherjee, and Hawthorne," points out that "Forbes's carefully historicized research implies that the current emphasis on cultural hybridization, rather than insufficiently breaking with racial science, might instead be something of a return to an older usage" (415–16). Similarly, Robert Young, in *Colonial Desire: Hybridity in Theory, Culture, and Race*, also links hybridity to nineteenth century racial science, pointing out the more recent echoes: "In the nineteenth century it was used to refer to a physiological phenomenon; in the twentieth century it has become reactivated to describe a cultural one" (qtd. in Simon 415).

Thus, discourses of hybridity are implicated problematically in colonial and postcolonial projects—whether your definition of "postcolonial" means since the colonists arrived or since they left. In contrast to Silko's recasting of history as a quest for beloved spirits, a focus on hybridization replays history in the terms of settler culture. Colonial implications function not only contextually but in the logical syntax of the very structure of a hybrid. For all the mixing and blending seemingly implied in hybridization, it has a reverse effect of separation and alienation precisely because of its dualistic limits, where hierarchies build on binaries. Social attention to either this or that blood sets up discrimination based on slight differences of mixture. Terms for human hybrids carry such social discriminations, as in "half-breed," "mixed-blood," "quadroon," "octoroon," or any other form of the generally pejorative "mulatto." The post-Allotment history of Native American "competency" trials based on blood-quantum, or equally the contemporary issues of tribal membership based largely on blood-quantum, are weighted with these colonialist separations of the hybrid. Such language of marginalization becomes the self-reflexive center of domination. As Homi Bhabha suggests in "Signs Taken for Wonders," the colonial project itself is exactly hybridization: "the effect of colonial power is . . . the production of hybridization . . . the business of colonialism is the production of hybrid subjectivities" (112). That is, the racial differences generated by hybridization are those that colonialism sets up to maintain its hierarchies. Slave owners used their female slaves sexually to produce more slaves for the cotton trade. Fur trappers used their Indian wives to produce laborers and translators for the fur trade. Hybridization is the project of power to dominate. Thus when the disenfranchised tell stories that affirm their own difference as prior to or indifferent to colonial centers of power, they try to elude hybridization, its discriminations, and projected dynamics of colonization itself. They write stories different from the common use of hybridization as exploitation.

So why am I even deflecting the term? Only this once, precisely because of the opportunity to register its colonialist, hence racist, connotations by contrasting Silko's resistant discursive strategies, and to show how she reinvents the meaning of hybrids in *Gardens*. Silko's radical "ghost dance" mythopoetics specifically contrast with hybridization's linear colonial narrative strictures. Her novels take the radical step of claiming what could be called pre-colonial hybridity. She invokes alliances and spiritual sources that not only precede the colonial era, but that pre-empt history itself. Perhaps a term such as Gerald Vizenor's "paracolonial" (12) might suit, meaning beside or parallel with colonial history, except that Vizenor's term actually emphasizes "colonial" as the determining force, in "the simulations and cruelties of paracolonial history," i.e., history written as the voice of colonialism. Silko's narratives suggest that there is an entirely different yet forceful story that constitutes our experience apart from that history. The almanac in *Almanac of the Dead* and the quest in *Gardens* focus on that different story, that "Day of Deliverance," to clarify the suffering of the innocent. By way of the intercontinental ghost dancers of *Gardens*, Silko makes visible an alternative chronology.

If it is not standard hybridization, what is it? Silko's characteristic use of cyclic time suggests an alternative, and a brief look at Mikhail Bakhtin's notion of chronotopes is useful here to account further for the significance of Silko's tactic. The term "chronotope" mixes Greek roots for time and space: ". . . chronotopes are images that integrate the temporal processes and spatial selections of a literary text" (Keunen 420). There are micro and macro levels of chronotopes. On the micro level of a story, a chronotope might be a microwave oven in a suburban house versus an open fire at the center of a tipi. While both images convey space, they also convey time, one setting us in the twentieth or twenty-first century, the other in some previous time-space (unless we are in a twenty-first century tipi—the ambiguity is immediate). On the macro-level, a chronotope, "should be considered a text's fundamental image of the world," according to Bart Keunen. His commentary on Bakhtin offers clarity on the narrative effects of Silko's global and mythical chronotope of ghost dancing through history.

> The dialogue between [micro] chronotopes, created in the text by its producer, causes the reader to experience one particular type of image as dominant and to select it as the 'overarching chronotope'. The overarching chronotope plays an important

part in the process of interpretation, because the nature of its spatial indications (an idyllic setting, a commercial-industrial environment, a desolate landscape, the simultaneous chaos of a city) and its specific vision of temporal processes (the cycles of nature, the historical development of society, the subjective moment, the discontinuous temporal experience of a dream or of intoxication) set the boundaries within which fictional events can take place. As a result, the kind of agent and action created in a narrative is always related to the world model it presents.   (421–22)

The "kind of agent and action created in a narrative" remains a primary concern of Native writers searching for channels of agency through colonial history, and Silko works with these general elements specifically to present an alternative "world model" that makes global room for Native culture through mythic connections.

Manipulation of chronotopes thus specifies how subjectivity masquerades as objectivity in a text. Social assumptions of history and human interaction need not rise to the surface, yet they drive the narrative. The myths we live by subjectively or even unconsciously play out in the objective world of a story. If "the overarching chronotope plays an important part in the process of interpretation," it does so by funneling subjective expectations of "spatial indications" and "temporal processes." In these terms, Silko produces an overarching chronotope that overturns colonial interpretations of history and nation. Both *Almanac*'s and *Gardens*' chronotopes summon images of global mythology, global travel, human interaction and confrontation in biological and cultural spheres, and, especially in *Gardens*, global botanical migration, to affirm an alternative history and subjective agency apart from colonial subjection.

For Silko and many other Native writers, the opposite of colonial subjection is tribal sovereignty or indigenous nationhood. The context of tribal sovereignty returns us to the significance of her ghost dance through history. Analyzing the trajectory of colonial history, Homi Bhabha links the chronotope in visual imagery to nation-construction, suggesting that a national identity is the triumph of one competing image:

> The recurrent metaphor of landscape as the inscape of national identity emphasizes the quality of light, the question of social visibility, the power of the eye to naturalize the rhetoric of national affiliation and its forms of collective expression. There is, however, always the distracting presence of another temporality that disturbs the contemporaneity of the national present . . . National time becomes concrete and visible in the chronotype [sic]of the local, particular, graphic, from beginning to end.   (143)

A prevalent chronotope is the image of a nation, a people on the land, "the inscape of national identity." These terms are useful to make visible how

America's "national timespace," its repetitive present, strives to surmount the ghostly presence of Native America as its always already "vanishing Indian."

Yet Native writers recognize, as do Bhabha, Keunen and Bakhtin in their view of contested chronotopes, the fragility of that consistent, repetitive national effort to erase or surmount the presence of Native America in its midst. As Chief Justice John Marshall's early Supreme Court decisions established Indian policy in the 1820s and 30s, he admitted in court decisions that America's own dispossession of Indians was and is uncivilized and unaccountable by any legal standard. Yet Marshall makes that dispossession the foundation of American law on and of the land, thus the foundation of American civilization. A necessary past of conquest is constructed in the American imaginary that relegates "Indians" to a chronotope of the beginning, not the end, never the contemporaneous, never the present or future of America. Thus simply to revive the "Ghost Dance" is not only to subvert the American national narrative, but to insert the uncanny, the even terrifying nightmare of America's own unplumbed conscience into the ongoing story of American domination. Writing the Indian back into history is to interrupt America dreaming of itself. Silko's *Gardens*, like her other works, subverts American identity by reinserting the Indian as that "distracting presence of another temporality that disturbs the contemporaneity of the national present" (Bhabha 143).

That subversion is seductive, and thus Silko in *Gardens* portrays Hattie's gradual liberation from Edward's dominating, puritanical, impotent rigidity: *"there are no sins of the flesh, spirit is everything!"* (452). Because domination forces hybridization into the erotics of subordination, colonial domination has co-opted and hierarchized hybridization itself. In contrast, natural hybridity is simply a ubiquitous pattern of cross-pollination, so Silko reappropriates that originary hybridity in a cornucopia of botanical images to affirm global mythic, cultural connections.

Thus if the term "hybridity" tends to reinscribe power relations across colonial exchange in the hand of the colonizer through a dialectic of authority and difference, the trick remains to see where the colonized may summon some prior, subsequent, or inherent power. Silko's invocation of ghost dance spirits is significant especially in its ability to elude this colonial dialectic of dominating hybridization along a linear timeline of progressive history. *Almanac of the Dead* and *Gardens in the Dunes* examine and contrast two types of hybridization and two types of globalization, as we shall see further: a colonialist capitalist type in Edward versus (for lack of a non-temporal word) a precolonial mythological type in Indigo, each with very different narrative structures of colonial domination versus indigenous survivance. "How strange," Indigo ponders the orchids transplanted to California, "to think these small plants traveled so far with so many hazards, yet still thrived while Edward died" (449). Silko is envisioning alternative global narratives, one capitalist and hybrid, the other communal and diverse. She depicts an inhumane globalization of capital with currency in spilled human blood versus a humane globalization of mythology with currency in the circulation of living things, plants, animals, humans. *Almanac* establishes the mythological history of the former, *Gardens* the latter.

GHOST DANCING TO KEEP THE SPIRITS ALIVE

Especially because Silko's stories elude the reductive binaries of hybridization, it is important to highlight her evocation of ancient European mythologies. If each of her fictions reorients time through alternative chronotopes, each text approaches this overall strategy with a different tactic. The precolonial witchery of *Ceremony* carries over into *Storyteller*. *Almanac of the Dead* invokes the cyclic chronotopes of Mayan cosmology. In the wedded mythologies of Africa, Old Europe, and Native America of *Gardens*, Silko trumps the mercantile narrative of authority and difference, of center and margin that would merely hybridize the European and Native on a dualistic colonial field. Her chronotopes expand globally beyond the western hemisphere and beyond history, as in *Almanac* where Montezuma and Cortez are connected as "blood worshippers" (570) or in the powerful Black Indian of Tampico in *Gardens*, daughter of African and Mayan spirits (429). Transcontinental mythic schemes and collaborations precede colonial conflicts, subordinating those colonial relations to prior mythic ones.

This mythopoetic alternative to colonial domination may be subject to criticism as merely discursive or rhetorical. One response in Silko's work, already prior to the critique in her non-linear time, is that these mythologies are in the land, and that the land has "time" on its side beyond human constructions or even depredations. As Calabazas declares early in *Almanac*, verbalizing a past in the present tense,

> We don't believe in boundaries. Borders. Nothing like that. We are here thousands of years before the first whites. We are here before maps or quit claims. We know where we belong on this earth. We have always moved freely. North-south. East-west. We pay no attention to what isn't real.

> Imaginary lines. Imaginary minutes and hours. . . . We have always had the advantage because this country is ours—it's our backyard . . .   (216–18)

He asserts an inverted reality, a reality of Native culture on the land prior to "imaginary" laws and claims of the gringos. "We pay no attention to what isn't real." Silko's mythopoetics make the claim to an inverse reality. Still, this essential current in Silko works through an ethos of life on the land, on indigeneity, and leads to an increasing rhetorical engagement with the material specifics of the land, carried furthest so far in *Gardens*. Elaborate depictions of plants (orchids, citron) and animals (Indigo's parrot "Rainbow," her pet monkey "Linnaeus") occupy central narrative positions in this text precisely for the reason that the earth carries the spirits of survival, and languages of the earth invoke those spirits.

The net is thrown as widely as possible, for surviving spirits in *Gardens* link Native American to Celtic, Coptic, and other myths. By means of the elusive travels of the Ghost Dance Messiah across Europe to the Holy Land, his itinerary, like apocryphal stories of the wanderings of Jesus, traces the global path of myth itself. "The Paiutes said Jesus traveled east across the ocean from time to time, but was careful not to show himself because of the danger from police and soldiers. If the Messiah and his followers crossed the ocean, it might be some time before they returned here" (57). "Oh the Messiah and his family traveled the earth—they might be seen anywhere" (471). The Messiah's movements ahead of the other characters' travels across Europe (and back to the southern California desert) further map those mythic links and create a mythological originary that is precolonial and pluralistic in its invocation of ancient traditions.

When Hattie, Edward, and Indigo are visiting Hattie's Aunt Bronwyn in Britain, the narrative welds numerous links between what the texts call "the Old Europeans" and Indigo's Native traditions. Invoking a precolonial network of Celtic myth, Aunt Bronwyn expatiates on the censorship the ancient Christian administrators imposed on Old European spirit traditions:

> For centuries the clergy made war on the ways of the old ones! . . . The Council of Tours decreed excommunication for those who persisted in worshiping trees; the Council of Nantes instructed bishops and their servants to dig up and hide the stones in remote woody places upon which vows were still made. . . . Ireland's suffering began with the betrayal of fairies. Those who cut down the sacred groves doomed themselves and all their descendants!   (263–64)

If the homesick Indian child, Indigo, listens to this with her eyes "round with delight as she nodded vigorously," she takes strength from mythic connections across the same ocean where history has forced her to wander. Aunt Bronwyn's description of European sightings of the Divine Mother and the Son of God indicate to Indigo's delight that "yes, the Messiah and his dancers were safe" in their travels for refuge (264).

This dream of reassurance comes even in the context of the Wounded Knee Massacre of 1890—the crushing historical moment generally regarded as the death of the Ghost Dance. Hattie has just related how "six or seven years before" she "followed the reports in the *New York Times*. It all ended rather badly; settlers feared Indian uprisings, and in South Dakota the army killed more than a hundred dancers" (264). As Hattie laments and Aunt Bronwyn turns solemn at this account, Indigo remains sanguine. ". . . she told them not to worry: the soldiers would not find the Messiah and his family or the dancers because they fled far away to the east. By winter it would be safe, and the Messiah would return with the first snow" (264). This moment in *Gardens* encapsulates the entire project of the novel: one of the most infamous episodes in colonial history transforms into a stage for mythic survivance.

The gendered muscles of colonial domination are accented also in contrast to this global embrace of the Sacred Mother, as Hattie is herself a victim of academic sexism. Her male professors had rejected her Master's thesis on "the equal status accorded the feminine principle in Gnostic Christian tradition" (101) and the "female spiritual principle in the early church" (102). Yet she is vindicated by others' research before the end of the novel. She thus is alerted to alternatives. Edward, her husband, stands in for the parasitical colonial male. Indigo, though a child, stands in for a Native voice.

To underline these contrasts, the spirits of the American Ghost Dance seek refuge with ancient European ones, just as Celtic spirits are shown in the novel at an archeological dig to have joined in the past with Roman gods, who now join again with the ancestors dancing in spirit with the Ghost Dancers.

> As Hattie took a step down, the major announced she was now standing on the earliest Roman occupation level, from the time the sacred hot springs were first contained in a pool of cement and limestone; the construction of a Roman temple dedicated to Sulis Minerva followed. Its name was somewhat of a mystery, Major Davis explained, because Sulis was a Celtic deity of the sun and Minerva was the Roman goddess of the moon . . .   (257)

The major is mystified because he cannot conceive of syncretism. The ancient history of merging gods and goddesses validates the novel's contemporary affirmations of Ghost Dance acculturations, where Wovoka's movement itself is expressed as syncretic, merging Native and Christian revelatory traditions.

Documented history of Jack Wilson, the Northern Paiute who became Wovoka, suggests syncretic aspects of the chronicled Ghost Dance through

material connections as well. Mark T. Hoyer in his study of the writer Mary
Austin and her experiences with Nevada and California tribal cultures,
describes Wilson in the 1880s as a ranch worker whose conversations with
Nevada Presbyterians instilled in him the Biblical discourse of the Messiah.

> Like most Paiutes in the area, Wovoka himself was employed by a white rancher,
> David Wilson. The Wilsons, from whom Wovoka, according to custom, drew his
> Christian name, were devout Presbyterians. According to Ed Dyer, a white store
> owner and friend of Jack's who later functioned as the prophet's unofficial
> secretary, it was during the regular "Bible readings, evening prayers, grace before
> meat, and similar family devotions" that Wovoka developed his lively interest in
> Christian stories and teachings.   (3–4)

Hoyer goes on to make the case that the principal aim of Great Basin religious
traditions—gaining power or *puha*—would have made Wovoka "particularly
attracted to those biblical figures with the most *puha*,"

> . . . not only Old Testament prophets such as Moses, because he led his people to the
> Promised Land, and Elijah, because his power included controlling the weather and
> raising the dead (feats that would later be attributed to Wovoka, too), but also Jesus,
> because of his miraculous powers over the elements and over death.   (4)

Wovoka's eventual vision incorporated such imagery, as well as traditional
Paiute aspects. Thus the discourse of the Ghost Dance itself may have drawn
syncretically from the symbolism of both Biblical and Paiute traditions. His
father had been a follower of "wodziwob, or 'Fish Lake Joe,' a Paiute spiritual
leader whose prophecies spurred an earlier Ghost Dance movement" (4) in the
1870s when Wovoka was a boy. The dance Wovoka was taught in his vision
was "a variation of the traditional Paiute Round Dance" (1).

    That vision occurred on New Year's Day 1889, during a total eclipse of the
sun, when, "Wovoka, known to whites as Jack Wilson, fell into a trance in the
Pine Nut Mountains of western Nevada, where he had been cutting wood. On
reviving, he reported that he had died and gone to heaven, where he had talked
to God and seen 'all the dead people,' Indian and white alike . . ." (1). One may
characterize a vision of Indians and whites together in heaven as syncretic in
itself, and Hoyer emphasizes Wovoka's peaceful message embracing both: "To
secure Wilson's authority, God granted him power over the elements,
specifically in the form of five songs for controlling the weather. He then
instructed Wilson to command the Indians to cease all lying, stealing, and
fighting, and to work peaceably with whites . . ." (1) Silko's mythopoetics
maintains these historical parallels in *Gardens*:

> Mama made friends with a Paiute woman who talked about Wovoka. Wovoka lived
> an ordinary life until one day he died and saw Jesus in heaven. Jesus was sad and
> angry at what had been done to the Earth and to all the animals and people. Jesus
> promised Wovoka that if the Paiutes all the other Indians danced this dance, then
> the used-up land would be made whole again and the elk and the herds of buffalo
> killed off would return. The dance was a peaceful dance, and the Paiutes wished no
> harm to white people; but Jesus was very angry with white people. As the people
> dance, great storm clouds would gather over the entire world . . .   (25)

Silko tries to account for both the peaceful message and the brutal reactions
against the early Ghost Dance, contrasting the feminine, embracing circle of
the dance with the intrusions of the whites, "what had been done to the earth."

Yet for historical accuracy, it is important to emphasize how the
syncretically peaceful foundations of the Ghost Dance may have been changed
by its further proliferations, as Hoyer explains:

> Although Wovoka's message enjoined Indians to get along with whites, the content
> of his revelation changed in several ways as it traveled, due in part to the vagaries
> of translating between different languages; in part to the fact that Wovoka could not
> write and so never recorded the prophecy in a fixed form; and in part to the
> divergent needs of the various peoples the prophecy reached. Thus, both the
> prophecy's meaning and particular tribes' reaction to it varied according to specific
> cultural contexts.   (1–2)

For all the diversity within the movement, Hoyer attributes the warlike images
of the Ghost Dance primarily to the American newspaper industry, that needed
a "war dance" to sell their newspapers, instead of "[d]ancing, peaceful Indians
awaiting their divine redemption" (2). Evidently another peaceful movement
for cultural survival was traumatized into warfare. The indication is that
material events overwhelmed mythological momentum.

In the Beginning is the Myth

However, as in each of Silko's books, *Gardens* posits the reverse: myths move
the world. There remains a causal relationship between mythological and
historical events. In what one might say is a Hegelian dialectic, similar to
Hegel's phenomenology of spirit directing history, Silko affirms a pre-Marxist
relationship between mythic cause and historical effect, with myth as thesis and
history as antithesis. (This mythic primacy over historical and economic events

is why La Escapia's and others' Marxism, which would set Hegel on his head by giving primacy to economic rather than spiritual factors, in *Almanac* fails to gain the momentum of the spiritual revolution.) For example, after Aunt Bronwyn in *Gardens* has described what seemed to be an innocuous collection of doddering English elders meeting as the "Antiquity Rescue Committee," she suggests that the repercussions are, faithfully, historic:

> As they walked back through the garden toward the house, her aunt said something that surprised Hattie. The old people had warned her even would-be rescuers of the old stones must use great caution because it was dangerous to tamper with the standing stones or to cut down the sacred groves. The stones and the groves house "the good folk," the spirits of the dead. Never interfere with the fairies! . . . The terrible famine in Ireland in 1846 came because the Protestants and the English knocked down the old stones. The wars of Europe were the terrible consequences of centuries of crimes against the old stones and the sacred groves of hazel and oak. Still, the destruction of the stone circles and groves did not stop; now the reckoning day was not far off — twenty years or less.   (254–55)

The narrative, taking place in the 1890s, is forecasting World War I in a direct causal relation with "crimes against the old stones."

Silko's mythopoetics thus function not only by her creating or invoking the myths that her characters perform, but also by the myths themselves creating the life of the world. If the Greek root, poew, ΠΟΕΩ, as in "poetry," means "to make," then mythopoetics generally indicates myth-making, the making of myth by the author. Silko's mythopoetics means also the making of the author and her world *by* myth, i.e., not only myth-creating, but also myths creating things, myths creating realities. Myth is not only the object, but also the subject of her mythopoetics. As she makes myth, so myth makes the world in her cosmology. In the beginning was the myth.

Indeed, myth in Silko is the organization of creative energy itself, a morphogenetic field of meaning. To convey this organizing force, Silko invokes modern physics to envision a sense of energy, as spirit living on in matter. For example, Lecha muses in *Almanac* on spiritual energy in the context of world history:

> Old Yoeme had always said the earth would go on, the earth would outlast anything man did to it including the atomic bomb. . . . The energy or 'electricity' of a being's spirit was not extinguished by death; it was set free from the flesh. Dust to dust or as a meal for pack rats, the energy of the spirit was never lost. Out of the dust grew the plants; the plants were consumed and became muscle and bone; and all the time, the energy had only been changing form, nothing had been lost or destroyed.   (718–19)

This view of energy that can be neither created nor destroyed is not always benign, especially in *Almanac*: "Knives, guns, even automobiles, possessed 'energies' that craved blood from time to time" (512). Behind the options of benign or brutal appetites, the field on which those opposites dance remains the wider mythic structure.

Those changing cravings of eternal energy are shaped then by myth, and Ghost Dance prophecies are one of those mythopoetic forces, again: "He had reminded the people of the prophecies different tribes had. In each version one fact was clear: the world that the whites brought with them would not last" (235). As Calabazas remembers in *Almanac*, "It would be only a matter of time," precisely because the myth had already shaped the eventual rebalancing of the world's energies. And Sister Salt muses on the fundamental mythic construction in *Gardens*: "What confused Sister Salt was why the Messiah didn't stop the killers. The Messiah told the people here not to take up weapons but to dance until the great storm winds of heaven scoured the earth of killers. She did not like to admit she was beginning to have some doubts about the Messiah's promises . . ." (356). That mythic dictum not only soothes a Native sense of despair. By pre-empting and directly contradicting historical frustrations, it retells the story of victimhood in ways that can envision surviving desperate changes. If energy is never lost as spirit plays through matter, if "spirit is everything," even in the white man, then Native America will survive.

Thus mythic bonds between Old Europe and Native America continue to appear as the troupe travels farther through the continent to Italy and Corsica. There the causal potency of myth grows clearer through their outward travels and eventual, difficult discoveries. Edward's devious agenda for smuggling Corsican citron cuttings stages Hattie's and Indigo's visionary journey precisely as the larger errant history of colonialism reveals global mythic connections. Despite material domination and exploitation, mythic interconnection and reciprocity prevail. Aunt Bronwyn's friend, *professoressa* Laura, tends a garden in Lucca that is full of ancient fertility symbolism resonating with Indigo's indigenous American experience. "To the Old Europeans, black was the color of fertility and birth, the color of the Great Mother . . ." (298). In the garden of tall black gladiolus, they see pre-Christian sculptures, a "small terra-cotta was a snake-headed figure with human arms and breasts that held a baby snake, but her legs were two snakes!" (298). This imagery recalls for Indigo the great rattlesnake, a central figure, by the desert pool at her home.

Indigo rejoined the others on the terrace below, where they stood before a stone pedestal with a seated figure of carved sandstone that gazed at them with the round eyes of a snake. The snake-headed mother had human arms and in them she cradled her snake baby to human breasts; but instead of legs, she had two snakes for limbs. Indigo took a deep breath and the others looked at her. Well, what did she think? Indigo didn't know what to say. Grandma Fleet used to talk to the big snake that lived at the spring above the old gardens; she always asked after the snake's grandchildren and relatives and sent her best regards. . . . As they made their way to the niche on the terrace below, Laura described the remnants of snake devotion still found in rural villages of the Black and Adriatic Seas . . .   (299–300)

Welding a qualitative relationship, the familiar imagery of Old Europe in the garden continues, drawing her home to Native America:

The figure was a seated bear mother tenderly cradling her cub in her arms; Indigo could feel how much the bear mother loved her cub just from the curve of the clay. She stayed by the bear mother even after Hattie and Edward followed Laura to the next niche; Indigo felt embraced by the bear mother, loved and held by her even as she stood there. The bear mother's affection made her smile for Mama and Grandma Fleet—they'd held Sister Salt and her just like that, even after they were big girls . . .   (298–99)

The sentimental memories invoked by these ancient images characterize some of Indigo's childlike voice and point of view.

Offsetting and toughening that innocence, Silko's lens on mythic globalism is also focused ironically through the colonialist's eye, as Edward's jaundiced view rebalances the significance of the prose. His puritanical responses to stone sculptures of fertility gods in the Italian garden contrast with Indigo's and the women's delight, dramatizing their thematic engagement in the underlying mythic kinship:

There were no other objectionable objects as Edward had feared but it was just as well Indigo missed the serpent figures. The child was from a culture of snake worshipers and there was no sense in confusing her with the impression the old Europeans were no better than red Indians or black Africans who prayed to snakes.   (304)

Edward's bigotry highlights by his blindness the equality of these various cultures, not by way of cultural relativity, but by way of an archaic unity underlying cultural diversity. If the white male colonist remains alienated from all of this, and if his eventual defeat and demise are the consequence of his blindness, the white woman, Hattie, reconnecting with her Celtic roots emerges as a kind of heroine. For instance, moved to tears by the maternal figure cradling her baby in stone, Hattie recognizes Edward's modern illusions: "Edward would not understand; he'd think she was ill again. How dare Edward call these Old European sculptures boring or ugly?" (300). The characterization of this unhappy couple plays on the feminist movement against colonial patriarchy, while highlighting the global mythic possibilities.

Those uncanny possibilities trumpet the radical multiculturalism of the novel. Myth outpaces pluralist history in these pages, precisely to make myth the prime mover. Nowhere is this claim for myth made more strongly than in the strange travels across Europe by the Ghost Dance Messiah, voyaging east to the Holy Land to get away from persecution in California.

> Hattie was about to caution Indigo about exaggeration and falsehood when Aunt Bronwyn asked Indigo if she had seen the Messiah. Indigo nodded eagerly; they were all so beautiful. Aunt Bronwyn smiled and nodded. Here on the remote islands people sometimes heard the sounds of voices and drums in the night; through the fog or rain mist at night people sometimes saw the silhouettes of dancers around fires on the hilltops. Indigo's eyes were round with delight as she nodded vigorously . . . Hattie was at a loss for words. Her mother . . . never mentioned Aunt Bronwyn's enthusiasm for Celtic mythology. Why, her aunt had left the church altogether! (264–65)

As the loose-knit American family travels from England to Italy, they seem to be following the Ghost Dance Messiah himself. On the island of Corsica, gazing at a newly famous miraculous image of "the Blessed Mother herself" on the whitewashed stone wall of a schoolhouse,

> Indigo gripped Hattie's hand tightly as she felt the excitement all over her body. The farther east they traveled, the closer they came to the place the Messiah and his family and followers traveled when they left the mountains beyond Paiute country. (321)

The causal connections of myth between Old Europe and Native America, accentuated by the Ghost Dance Messiah's being at home on either continent, are triangulated by connections between indigenous Africa and America. By this mythic map, the precolonial tapestry thus is woven tighter and more broadly than any particular colonial enterprise. The western and southern hemispheres join in mythic conspiracy to pre-empt the colonial project. On a Caribbean voyage to gather orchids early in the novel, Edward, as the book's representative of EuroAmerican male dominance and crass mercantilism, is blown off-course to the Mexican port town of Tampico. Using science as an excuse, he continually seeks material profit from spiritual materials, such as meteors, orchids, and cultural artifacts. He was "pleased for the opportunity to have a look around the public market in Tampico. He had made it his practice to collect samples of local and regional agriculture. The natives might possess unknown medicinal plants with commercial potential or a new variety of citrus or a new source for rubber. He was also eager to purchase archeological artifacts and curiosities . . ." (88). Toward the novel's anticolonial thrust, in an attempt to buy a collection of meteorite ore, he is unnerved by "a huge blue face" that appears in the window of a shop. "The old woman's long tangled hair and her ample chest and arms all had been painted a bright blue that emphasized the woman's Maya features. . ." (89). Her blue paint reflects the name of the main Native character in the novel, Indigo, and echoes blue symbolism in other Silko novels of ocean, river, and cloud waters that give life to the southwestern desert lands and cultures. It turns out that Edward has faced "the Black Indian of Tampico" (90) who, the sailors say, raises storms on the Bay of Campeche. "They said she was a daughter of the African spirits and the Maya spirits as well" (91). This cross-cultural, cross-continental invocation packs the double potency of precolonial mythologies, a kind of antediluvian solidarity.

Back aboard a tossing ship, Edward, "said nothing about his encounter with her lest they accuse him of bringing down the storm" (91). Nearly four hundred pages later, after Edward's various mercantile schemes have collapsed, exposed as multifarious forms of international and personal thievery, his hallucinations on his death bed take him back to "the hostile blue-faced woman" and he dreams he rests his dying head "in the big Negress's lap" (429). Yet his subconscious ravings prove his unregenerated condition.

> What bothered him most was his memory of the piles of meteor irons he left behind in Tampico; he always intended to return to the town market to acquire those meteor irons from the hostile blue-faced woman. Oh the burn of regret lest someone knowledgeable see the neat pyramid stacks of the irons and buy them before he did! He drifted off. . .   (429)

The spirit powers of Africa and Mexico have manipulated the death of this colonialist like the doom of those who cut down sacred groves or disturb the dancing stones. The effect of this spiritual solidarity of the colonized is, again, to establish a chronotope that is global and universal, though connected to local myths of land and water.

Midway through the novel, another important story emerges of the early connections between Native Americans and Africans, here among scenes of a construction camp for a dam in the desert land along the Southern California and Arizona border. Alluding to the historical Red Stick faction of the

Muskogee (Creeks) of Alabama, who later waged war with Andrew Jackson in 1813–14, Silko's narrative recounts the stories that an emancipated slave,

> . . . heard as a girl about the Red Stick people who adopted the escaped African slaves. Even before the Indians ever saw an African, the old Red Stick dreamers described them and said they had powerful medicine that the people here could use. So they welcomed the fugitives when they appeared, and it wasn't long before the Red Sticks were given some of this medicine, which allowed their warriors to move through the swamps as silently and swiftly as smoke. Heavy casualties were inflicted on the French soldiers by only a handful of warriors, and later they routed the British. (219)

This reclaimed history is chronotopic background for Big Candy, a mixed-blood character whose good nature is hardened by his own entrepreneurial capitalist ambitions. As he dies in the desert after trailing after his stolen money, like Frank Norris' McTeague, his demise is anything but naturalistic as he too is the pitiful object of spirits joining actively from Africa and Indian America:

> The last he remembered was the animated voices in a heated discussion louder than the drumming he heard; they talked about him. The Africans and the Indians—all his ancestors argued whether they should bring him home or let him stay longer. He didn't remember his ancestors or care about their feelings; yes, he was a good boy and loved his mama, but once a grown man he wasn't worth a damn except for moneymaking. (445–46)

Again, these are the ancestors invoked by the Ghost Dancers, whose purpose is "to reunite living people with the spirits of beloved ancestors lost in the five-hundred years war." Those who turn away from the ancestors, even good-hearted gamblers and capitalists like Candy, are doomed in this mythological universe.

It is a universe without racial boundaries. Even marginalized whites are gathered into this mythic system in the form of a non-Indian Mormon ghost dancer who is integrated into the dancers' camp.

> The old Mormons believed they were related to the Indians, and the U.S. government feared the old Mormons and Indians might band together against the government. The old Mormons who answered the call of Wovoka were hated most of all. How dare these Mormons take an Indian to be the Messiah. Federal officials feared the dancers were a secret army in disguise, ready to attack Needles. (46–47)

If Indians as the Lost Tribes of Israel are connected to Christians and Mormons, what is the effect of such a global mythology? It confounds the colonial frontiers. It sets the officials on edge, scurrying into wasteful defensive postures in the Mojave Desert and the Colorado Basin, while believers in the mythic connections celebrate. "Small groups of Mormons came because the Mormons had been waiting for the Messiah's return; they became very excited after they heard Wovoka preach" (31). It pre-empts the colonial enterprise itself by establishing connections for transcendent and subversive resistance among colonized peoples.

"Sex with strangers was advantageous"

This vast global mythology is then matched materially in the novel with botanical globalization. The lyricism of *Ceremony*'s psychic and cultural landscape and the epic sweep of *Almanac*'s political and mythic landscape are focused in *Gardens* on botanical pleasures of assorted gardens or arcane orchids on rainforest cliffs. What saves such a seemingly limiting stylistic and rhetorical decision is Silko's trope of gardens and orchid commodification as indicative of human/nature relations. The various characters in the novel, depending on their colonial identities, relate differently to gardens, gladiolus bulbs, orchids, cuttings of citron branches, or seeds in either commodified and exploitative or animated and nurturing ways. Edward exploits and extorts, while Indigo has already learned from her mother how to gather and nurture plant spirits. Hattie gradually learns from Indigo and the ancient spirits of Europe. Thus there is resonance in the language that links the imagery of *Gardens* to Silko's ongoing themes of cross-cultural identity, communication, miscommunication, and capitalist-colonialist commodification.

For instance, in Italy when the *professoressa* bestows Indigo with seeds to take home, Edward's racism dismisses the Indian child's capabilities.

> He found himself a bit irritated at the *professoressa*'s attention to the child, especially her generous gifts of packets of seeds and corms from her hybrids, although he could see that she made an identical bundle for him and Hattie. It seemed a bit ludicrous for Laura to pretend the Indian child would ever plant the corms or seeds, much less perform the pollination process for hybrids, even if she did take notes on all the necessary steps. Of course Laura could not be expected to know anything about American Indians. (305)

Edward's ignorance and arrogance only highlight Indigo's indigenous agency. These power are affirmed, characteristically, "in the realm of dreams." Indigo's dream that night will eventually come true, and more: "back home at the old gardens; but where the sunflowers and corn plants and squash once grew, tall gladiolus bloomed in all colors . . ." (306).

In the juvenile voice of Indigo, many of the book's mythic and historical reaffirmations are made through the medium of botanical mobility or transplantability. Silko's catalogues and invocation of botanical images follows a certain invocative, spirit-infused register of song and word in oral storytelling and ritual where the names invoke the plant spirits. Yet here those spirits are international. At the *professoressa's* table in Tuscany, Indigo delights in Native American foods translated into Italian cuisine:

> Then came a warm bowl of stewed sweet red peppers with yellow squash. Indigo's eyes widened at the sight of food she knew, and as she tasted the peppers she thought of them grown so far from their original home; seeds must be among the greatest travelers of all! (293)

Dissemination of Native American agricultural developments to Europe and the migration of Native or Asian plants to colonial centers functions as a trope throughout the novel for anticolonial possibilities. These cross-continental patterns of influence erode the force of Eurocentric narratives.

> . . . Aunt Bronwyn . . . explained the roses, the lilies, the hollyhocks, and the pear trees did not originate in England but in the Near East and Asia. "Your people," she said," the American Indians, gave the world so many vegetables, fruits, and flowers—corn, tomatoes, potatoes, chilies, peanuts, coffee, chocolate, pineapple, bananas, and of course, tobacco. (246)

Indigo's childlike though informed response is sudden embarrassment that her own Sand Lizard people of the desert were "barely were able to grow corn, and they had no tomatoes, peanuts, or bananas" (246). Her tribally specific perspective, however, does not erase the global narrative of botanical integration that Aunt Bronwyn, and apparently Silko, offer here.

Indeed, another moment in the novel affirms the parallel value of racial integration in Indigo's Sand Lizard culture, in one of several references to widening the gene pool:

> The old-time Sand Lizard people believed sex with strangers was advantageous because it created a happy atmosphere to benefit commerce and exchange with strangers. Grandma Fleet said it was simply good manners. Any babies born from these unions were named "friend," "peace," and "unity;" they loved these babies just as fiercely as they loved all their Sand Lizard babies. (220)

This affront to mainstream "good manners" reflects the novel's ultimate reversal
of hierarchies, upsetting not only Edward, but his Great Chain of Being as well:

> Aunt Bronwyn agreed; if a garden wasn't loved it could not properly grow! She was
> an avid follower of the theories of Gustav Fechner, who believed plants have souls
> and human beings exist only to be consumed by plants and be transformed into
> glorious new plant life. Hattie had to smile; so human beings existed only to become
> fertilizer for plants! Edward and her father would have a good laugh at that! (242)

The male dominators in Silko's text are incapable of recognizing the power of
a spiritual quality that animates growing things.

At the first Ghost Dance camp early on in the novel, we get the plain
language of this elusive, animistic quality:

> When Sister Salt excitedly told Mama and Grandma what she had heard [that the
> Messiah spoke in a language that all the people from different tribes and even
> whites could understand], a Paiute man standing nearby smiled and nodded his
> head. In the presence of the messiah and the Holy Mother, there was only one
> language spoken—the language of love—which all people understand, he said,
> because we are all the children of Mother Earth.   (34)

One language animates the mythic reality. In *Gardens* that language of love,
which we find in *Almanac* is spirit energy moving in matter, returns us to
Hattie's feminist critique of Church history and the nurturing, maternal spirit
that she discovered in the Gnostic texts.

Her peculiar academic background, perhaps, makes her susceptible to an
epiphany that she experiences, of a "luminous glow" in Aunt Bronwyn's
English garden and several time later in her travels. This "soft yellow glow"
(470) that we see through Hattie's eyes is another symbol of the novel's mythic
affirmations. Hattie sees it around the sighting of the Virgin Mother on the wall
in Corsica, and at the anti-climactic Ghost Dance near the end of the story. Just
as other female characters "could feel the golden threads of the radiance from
across time that turned the [Gypsy] cards and spoke the truth . . ." (391), at the
novel's final Ghost Dance camp, Hattie reconnects this luminous glow with the
Native ancestors:

> . . . As she approached the blanket over the lean-to entrance, the light outside
> became brighter and more luminous—she recognized it at once and felt a thrill
> sweep over her. How soothing the light was, how joyously serene she felt . . .
> The girls were surprised to find Hattie up when they returned to the lean-to after
> midnight. She told them how she woke feeling so much better and then noticed the

beautiful glow outside the lean-to, so much like the strange light she saw before. The light she [Hattie] saw was the morning star, who came to comfort her, Sister explained. How could she have seen the same light in the garden in England and in a dream on board the ship? Oh the Messiah and his family traveled the earth—they might be seen anywhere. (471)

What does it mean then to invoke mythic and spiritual connections that not only offset but pre-empt history? Is it naïve? Is it a desperate expression of colonial denial?

Certainly, Silko does not reject material history—indeed she faces it in harsh detail—but she insists on mythic history as present in the conflicts on the land. Silko is persistent in imagining various nonmaterial perspectives on human events. Nor is she didactic as she speaks through her characters' epiphanies. Reading *Gardens*, we are not asked to set aside the history and economics of *Almanac*, but we are asked to recognize in the Ghost Dance her "mythification of lived experience" (100) to use Paul Zumthor's phrase for the impulse of oral poetry traditions, as a primary aesthetic and ethic of her text. Where her literary explorations affirm the animistic universe of an oral tradition, her "mythification" portrays life as mythic, and myths as alive. Here in a full circle, the written word affirms animistic perceptions of the oral world.

In Albuquerque, before the novel's finale, Hattie, newly liberated white feminist and supporter of the Ghost Dancers, muses on this primary, global, mythical dimension, where the written word, even a shelved Master's thesis, possesses the animistic power of speech in the oral tradition.

My Mother, my Spirit—words from the old Gnostic gospels sprang into her mind. *She who is before all things, Grace, Mother of Mythic Eternal Silence*—after months in the oblivion of its shallow grave, her thesis spoke to her. *Incorruptible Wisdom, Sophia, the material world and the flesh are only temporary—there are no sins of the flesh, spirit is everything!* (452)

WORKS CITED

Bhabha, Homi K. "Signs Taken for Wonders: Questions of Ambivalence and Authority under a Tree Outside Delhi, May 1817." *Critical Inquiry* 12.1 (Autumn 1985): 144–65.

——. *The Location of Culture.* New York: Routledge, 1994.

Forbes, Jack. *Black Africans and Native Americans: Color, Race and Caste in the Evolution of Red-Black Peoples.* Cambridge: Basil Blackwell, 1988.

Hoyer, Mark T. "Prophets of a New West: Wovoka and Mary Austin." *Dancing Ghosts: Native American and Christian Syncretism in Mary Austin's Work.* Western Literature Ser. Reno: Nevada UP, 1998.

Keunen, Bart. "The Plurality of Chronotopes in the Modernist City Novel: The Case of Manhattan Transfer." *English Studies: A Journal of English Language and Literature* 82.5 (Oct. 2001): 420–36.

Moore, David L. "Decolonializing Criticism: Reading Dialectics and Dialogics in Native American Literatures." *Studies in American Indian Literatures* 6.4 (Winter 1994): 7–33.

———. "Return of the Buffalo: Cultural Representation as Cultural Property." *Native American Representations: European and North American Perspectives.* Ed. Gretchen Bataille. Lincoln: Nebraska UP, 2001. 52–79.

———. "Silko's Blood Sacrifice: The Circulating Witness in *Almanac of the Dead.*" *Leslie Marmon Silko: A Collection of Critical Essays.* Ed. James Thorson and Louise Barnett. Albuquerque: New Mexico UP, 1999. 149–83.

Silko, Leslie Marmon. *Almanac of the Dead.* New York: Penguin, 1991.

———. *Gardens in the Dunes.* New York: Simon and Schuster, 1999.

———. *Storyteller.* New York: Arcade, 1981.

Simon, Bruce. "Hybridity in the Americas: Reading Condé, Mukherjee, and Hawthorne." *Postcolonial Theory and the United States.* Ed. Amritjit Singh and Peter Schmidt. Jackson: Mississippi UP, 2000. 412–43.

Vizenor, Gerald. "The Ruins of Representation: Shadow Survivance and the Literature of Dominance." *American Indian Quarterly* 17.1 (Winter 1993): 7–30.

Young, Robert. *Colonial Desire: Hybridity in Theory, Culture, and Race.* New York: Routledge, 1995.

Zumthor, Paul. *Oral Poetry: An Introduction.* Trans. Kathryn Murphy-Judy. Minneapolis: Minnesota UP, 1990.

OLD COMPARISONS, NEW SYNCRETISMS AND *GARDENS IN THE DUNES*

David Murray

As the focus of critical discussions of Native American writing has moved from crises of identity, authenticity and origins to the creative possibilities within hybridity and transnationalism, so the treatment of Leslie Silko's works has reflected these changes, not least because her later works have also foregrounded these ideas. *Almanac of the Dead* and *Gardens in the Dunes* have both offered ambitious explorations of the newer themes, while maintaining a clear continuity with the concerns and locales of her earlier work. But while it is certainly possible to see *Gardens* as continuing the strongly hybrid and transnational orientation of *Almanac of the Dead*, the shift back to the end of the nineteenth century in the later novel also suggests another older intellectual context, that of comparative religion and mythology, and it is this context which I want to explore here. My argument will be that the similarities between these earlier comparative impulses and Silko's own approach in this novel suggest some problems not addressed in the more celebratory characterisations of the postnationalist and hybrid qualities of the novel.

One of the most striking things about Silko has always been the fruitful tension between her rootedness in a specific cultural and religious provenance (Laguna and more broadly the Indian Southwest) and the ambition and range of her novels, which develop connections and comparisons well beyond that local base. Her work has always been widely appreciated for its ability to cross boundaries and to speak at a global or even universal level, whether in the extension of the Pueblo idea of witchery and healing to the level of world politics, and what has been called radioactive colonialism in *Ceremony*, or the linking of Indian prophesies with contemporary transnational movements of trade and capital in *Almanac of the Dead*. In *Gardens* we find a similar blending of local narrative into a larger international framework of colonialism, but also the combining of very disparate religious phenomena. Silko links these religious experiences and movements to debates over comparative religion at the time when the novel is set, but her material also inevitably—and I think problematically—suggests similar comparative and universalising claims made within New Age writings. In this essay I want to explore some of the implications of Silko's comparativist and synthesising impulses in *Gardens* in this double context of the beginning and the end of the twentieth century.

Both *Gardens in the Dunes* and *Almanac of the Dead* address similar issues, and use overlapping sets of imagery. While they both end with the image of a returning snake, representing the traditional beliefs of a very specific and localised group, they also both employ a much larger range of reference, and entertain comparativist claims. In *Almanac of the Dead* this has clear political ramifications. The later sections of the novel describe the coming together in Tucson of a range of different indigenous revolutionary groups, within the protective disguise of a New Age 'International Holistic Healers Convention'. The figure of the African American Clinton is significant in the novel because of his attempts to fuse Indian and African American concerns. He worships African deities, particularly Ogoun, but he also has Cherokee ancestry and feels that "great American and great African tribal cultures had come together to create a powerful consciousness within all people" (Silko, *Almanac* 416).

The hope held out here, and implicitly in the novel as a whole, however conditionally, is of a unification of spiritual traditions which will sweep away the corruptions of international capitalism, in a movement comparable to—but more practically effective than—the Ghost Dance of the late nineteenth century. In *Gardens* many of the same themes are present, particularly the commonality of spiritual experience, set against the corruption of international commerce and colonial power, but in a wholly different register and historical time. The novel returns to the time of the original Ghost Dance, and records the scattering of Indian communities by following the lives of the Sand Lizard family of Indigo and her mother and sister. The parallel and gradually coalescing spiritual experiences of the white woman Hattie and the young girl Indigo in their encounter with pre-Christian European religions are contrasted with a heartless and reductively rationalist masculine world of science and commerce. Though the spiritual experiences themselves are presented as transcending time, Silko is careful to situate the action historically at the intersections of various developing forms of Western scientific enquiry (comparative religion and botany) with indigenous belief systems which were themselves undergoing profound change as a result of larger economic and political forces associated with colonialism and the workings of international capital. As a way into Silko's concerns I want to look more closely at one of these contexts, that of comparative religion.

The fields of comparative religion, represented from the middle of the nineteenth century by Max Müller, and comparative mythology which developed later in the century, and culminated eventually in the work of G. S. Frazer, seemed to offer a comprehensive scientific account which linked all the disparate phenomena of religion and belief. At the time these approaches held powerful disciplinary sway, but have since been extensively critiqued, not so much for the details of their explanations but for their fundamental assumptions. Recent critical accounts of the comparativist method in general have viewed it as a totalizing gesture, which organises similarities and differences within an overall framework or overview available only to the outsider/scientist. To the degree that this overview relies on knowledge gained by colonial structures of power, it replicates that political situation of inequality. The claims implicit within many comparativist enterprises for universal or underlying values can then be seen as suspect in the same ways that the larger Enlightenment claims for universality are suspect—namely that they may incorporate ethnocentric Western values which are assumed to be universal. According to this critique the comparativist impulse, rather than decentring the West always comes back to reconfirming a centre, or an overall intellectual structure established by that centre.[1]

It can be argued, though, that this is too monolithic a picture of Western scientific enquiry, and does not allow, for instance, for the less disciplined and more inclusive approach found in folklore studies of the time. Many folklorists took what was in some ways a more positive view of primitive religion and magic, and it is here that we can see the idea of a Western rationalist centre unravelling, as the widespread beliefs, which had been dismissed as lingering superstitions to be swept aside by science, were taken seriously, and shown to share common ground with primitive religions. The folklorist Andrew Lang, for instance, challenged the comfortable distinctions made by Müller and others between religion and magic, and science and folk belief, which he saw as reflecting and supporting a whole implicit hierarchy which reflected assumptions of Western progress and superior rationality. Admittedly the folkloric approach often shaded off into an indulgent enjoyment of faery and whimsy, as with Lang, or Charles Leland, and it did retain a racist condescension even while enjoying the frissant of a common belief in the supernatural. It does, nevertheless, reflect a centrifugal impulse which is present in the collecting and comparing of materials from a wide range of cultures—a potential to relativise or de-centre the assumptions of the collector, which the stress on a unifying model and on a scientific method held in check. In this way it may offer interesting material for comparison with later New Age thinking, as I will show later.

The description and systematic comparison of disparate religions was parallel to the discovery and taxonomy of exotic specimens found in far-flung places by botanists and others, an activity represented in the novel by Hattie's husband

Edward. The name of his parrot, Linnaeus is a reference to this, but Edward's own dubious activities reflect the way that such collecting is linked to structures of imperial power and economic exploitation. Whereas Indigo relates to Nature with a childlike directness, reveling in the physical sensations of color and smell, and loving some animals like people, Edward is a scientist and collector, concerned with the propagation and hybridization of plants for commercial exploitation. Through his unsuccessful ventures Silko gives a historical dimension to the concept of hybridity, showing how plant collecting and taxonomy were related to commerce and to European control of the resources of the rest of the world. In the novel mining and plant collecting are fuelled by the same exploitative motives, since Edward's illegal activities in Brazil and Corsica all involve the collection of specimens for commercial exploitation. In the same way that comparativism's relativising and centrifugal properties are nullified by the scientific method, so the rich disseminative and creative possibilities of hybridity are controlled and exploited in what we see here as simply a commercial exploitation of nature. Significantly, Edward is terrified by the racial dimensions of hybridity, which is reflected in the threatening presence of a woman who is part Mayan and part African and appears almost as a magical figure.

The recent postmodern critique of comparative approaches to religion outlined above, which stresses the imbrication of scientific knowledge and classification with power, also chimes in some significant ways with indigenist and nationalist discourses, which defend the uniqueness and untranslatability of the local, and suspect the scientific approach of establishing objective grounds for comparison and taxonomy, as part of a larger tactic of control. To assume that everything is commensurable means establishing grounds for that commensurability and the suspicion is that these grounds are determined by those with power to make their view prevail. An important difference, though, between indigenist and poststructural approaches occurs over the claims for validity of any local or particular religion. Poststructuralists and indigenists may seem to be arguing the same thing in defending the local, and suspecting the grand narratives of Western science and progress, and they may combine in defending the right to believe in the power of a stone snake in the American Southwest, for instance, and similar rights to local and indigenous beliefs across the world. They would diverge, though, when that belief is claimed to have a more general validity—for instance, when a local prophesy claims to have a truth which is more than relative and local, and applies to the whole world, whether this is Jesus of Nazareth or the prophet of the Ghost Dance. While a fully postmodern scepticism would reject the scientistic underpinning of comparitivism it would also reject any idea that one local religion was absolutely valid because of recourse to a centre or source, or any appeal to a general shared spiritual truth of the sort claimed by New Age syncretisms. It is in this context that the combination in Silko of the local and indigenous with a wider comparitivist and even universalising sweep raises such interesting issues.

Ami Regier sees Silko's connections with other religions as an aspect of her advocacy of hybridity and syncretism,[2] which represent the way forward for Indigo and her fellow survivors of colonialist expansion. She focuses on Silko's use of the Ghost Dance, which is presented as something adaptable to many purposes, by different tribes and also by the Mormons who appear in the novel. Regier links this with the transnational sweep of the novel and James Clifford's concept of 'travelling cultures' and it is true that this is a constant and important theme in Silko. Regier argues that in highlighting the pre-Christian elements in Christianity Silko is also showing that even the supposed centre is 'always already' as the deconstructionists would put it, deeply hybrid—an idea reinforced by the early images of animal and human hybrid forms that Hattie and others find.

Regier's enthusiasm for the instability and creativity to be found in the hybrid and transnational space created in the novel extends to its revolutionary potential, but it is here, I think, that the precise nature of Regier's claims needs to be pinned down. As she points out, the end of the novel presents a Ghost Dance (though Silko's characters always refer to it as the coming of the Messiah) the culmination of which, on the fourth day, is prevented by the arrival of the police and soldiers. At this point a half-crazed Hattie, believing in the coming of the Messiah, burns down part of the nearby town of Needles, and Regier sees the fire as a 'metonym' of the millenarian change promised in the Ghost Dance. Silko has clearly brought the events into conjunction for this purpose, but here, as in *Almanac*, in specifying the actual relation of ceremony to political or practical consequences Silko is perhaps more cautious than Regier's account might suggest. Regier's essay in fact makes close links between Silko's own writing and the effects claimed for a Ghost Dance when she argues that "written narrative may function as a ghost of the Ghost Dance carrying out the oral tradition's revolutionary work in latter-day performative forms that are magically real enough to be powerful" (135). But what does this last phrase really mean? We could read it as saying that the book is powerfully persuasive as writing, and that therefore, *like* the ceremony, it may have effects on people and change the world through their actions, but I am not sure that Regier is not implying a lot more with the word 'magic'.

It may seem pedantic to focus on what I see as a slippage between different sorts of claims here, but I think it points to a larger issue. This is the simultaneous situating of Silko within a poststructuralist framework of hybridity and transnationalism and a traditional Indian one of rooted and local spiritual truths. The former context would suggest (certainly if the hybridity was seen through Bhabha's influential formulations) an absence of any absolute claims for a rooted or essential position of truth, while the second would not. Traditional and indigenous peoples may reasonably suspect any celebration of diasporic and transnational identity if it is going to be used to challenge their unique and local rights and values, as writers like Elizabeth Cook Lynn have argued. It is for this reason that Silko's position may be more ambiguous than Regier suggests, but this is linked to another issue. What sort of common ground would these hybrid formations have which would bring them together in revolution or unified belief? This brings us back to the issue of comparativism, and it worth looking at just what sort of religious experiences we find in the novel.

The fusions and commonalities of religious experience in the novel operate at several levels. One is through the linking of similar visions and traditions across continents and centuries. In focusing closely on the experiences and reactions of the child Indigo, Silko is able in these parts of the novel to endow the world with a strangeness and newness. This viewpoint is shown to be close to Hattie's growing spiritual awareness, and in fact the novel is held together by what we might call feminine and sentimental sensibilities, which are clearly contrasted with the coarse and reductive attitudes and actions of men, notably Hattie's scientist husband Edward.[3] We are presented with a union of sensibility which crosses boundaries, a peaceable kingdom of animals (parrot and monkey) and children and women, related through gardens and redemptive visions. One corollary effect of this cross-cultural blending is that we have little sense of the Indian characters coming from any specific culture. We first encounter them swept up in the Messiah religion, and they are then cut off from their own particular people, who Silko has invented and named the Sand Lizard people. In an interview she revealed that she wanted her characters to come from 'one of those remnant, destroyed, extinct groups' (Arnold 164). This does mean that any positive hope of identity and continuity in the novel is going to involve not the regaining of a tribal whole but a forging of new identities and unities. In this sense we could say that, though the characters are Indian, the world-view or spiritual orientation is generalised within the novel.

Through the travels of Indigo with her white guardians we are introduced not to a modern scientific or industrial Europe but to one of pre-Christian survivals and syncretisms, surviving in old gardens, buildings and beliefs. Here the figure of Hattie becomes central, in that she has visions and sensations that allow her (and the reader) to connect up her ideas with various Roman and Celtic relics.

Her visions are often linked to stones and light; a strange light she experiences in her aunt's garden in Somerset; a recurrent dream of a stone; and an experience of light in Corsica, when she and Indigo join Christian believers who have been attracted to a schoolhouse wall where an image of Mary is said to have appeared. She sees a glow, which "grew brighter with a subtle iridescence that steadily intensified into a radiance of pure color that left her breathless, almost dizzy" (Silko, *Gardens* 321). She half-doubts her experience ('was it an odd reflection off metal or glass? . . . . but here she was with dozens of witnesses!') but Indigo, and the local Christians see much more. Indigo has been waiting for the return of the Messiah, because she has been removed from her people, who had been practicing the Ghost Dance, and dancing for the coming of the Messiah. Looking at the wall she sees "tiny reflections glitter on the surface of the whitewashed plaster that she recognized as the flakes of snow that swirled around the dancers the last night when the Messiah appeared with his family" (321).

The underlying common ground invoked is of a spiritual presence, experienced here through visions and stone remnants of Celtic and other pre-Christian religions across Europe, which the Christian church has continually and unsuccessfully attempted to eradicate. Hattie has already experienced the repressive force of Christian and academic orthodoxy as a would-be student of Christian heresies at Harvard, and Silko's use of Gnosticism in the novel is in many ways fundamental to the book. She actually draws on some later discoveries of the Gnostic Gospels at Nag Hammadi in the 1940s to give the sense of Hattie's 'shock of recognition', but in fact her account of Hattie's developing ideas is not so anachronistic as this might suggest.[4] There was already an interest in the nineteenth century in those Gnostic materials which were then available, and by the end of the century new discoveries were much debated, both on the fringes of the academy and within it. Silko's account of what Hattie finds in the Coptic scrolls of Dr Rhinehart, and of the dispute over their authenticity is therefore plausible, as is her account of Hattie having devoured all the mythology she could find, before her time at Harvard. Her mother's fear that Hattie's views would associate her in the public mind with scandalous feminist and spiritualist movements does reflect tensions through the nineteenth century, and Silko has acknowledged Margaret Fuller as in some ways a model for Hattie (Arnold 179). Hattie's offence is not just that she uses 'unauthenticated' material (in the sense that it had not had the age and origins of the text itself authenticated). Her more fundamental offence is that the material challenged the narrow and misogynistic orthodoxy, which had developed as Christianity. The ideas she finds there are shown to fit with older woman-centered and earth-centered beliefs, including Indian ones—though these latter are only very thinly sketched in the novel.

The two Gnostic passages supposedly found by Hattie, and actually slightly adapted from Elaine Pagels, reflect two important aspects of the novel. One asserts the central role of women, with Eve, as the instructor of Adam, associated with the snake as female principle. Its description of the primary role of Eve and the serpent Satan in the creation of the world encourages Hattie to pursue the importance of the "female spiritual principle" in the early church (Silko, *Gardens* 102).[5] The serpent found here is linked up in the novel with a snake, which guards the spring near the Sand Lizard women's old gardens in the desert. This has earlier been killed, but the novel concludes with the appearance of a new snake, and the words "Old Snake's beautiful daughter moved back home" (479). Natural (and female) forces have re-established continuities, so that even if the interruption of the Ghost Dance has prevented the Messiah from returning in that particular form, the implication is that the same spirit is evident elsewhere. There are resonances here with the stone snake at the end of *Almanac of the Dead*, which is linked with the prophesy of a world-wide political and spiritual revolution to come. In the later novel the political resonances are more muted, but the religious connections between Indian prophesies, as in the Ghost Dance and pre-Christian European beliefs are more explicitly made.

The other Gnostic passage, which acts as a revelation for Hattie, stresses the idea of an individual knowledge of God, rather than it coming through Church or dogma. This is crucial in the book, in that the spiritual core of the book is the coalescence of the individual visions and spiritual experiences of the powerless characters in the book. In an interview Silko agrees with Ellen Arnold's description of Gnostic experience as 'unmediated' and comments "that's why ultimately I hope this is a gnostic novel" (186). It is precisely this lack of mediation that allows Silko to connect the different experiences in the book, but it is worth looking further, and questioning whether this very dream of something direct and pure and beyond ideology and dogma may not itself carry ideological baggage. Silko has explicitly acknowledged the importance of American Transcendentalism, and refers to the Transcendentalist Margaret Fuller, who combined spiritual independence and political/feminist radicalism, as one of the models she had in mind for Hattie. In an interview she stresses the effect of the land itself on settlers, whereby European and Eastern ideas become changed by the experience of America—a sort of spiritual Turner thesis. Americans as a whole, then, have already begun to fulfill the old prophesies described in *Almanac of the Dead*, which said that the older indigenous values and spirits would return.[6] But this would be to assume that both the new American forms and the older indigenous religions have in common something close to Gnosticism. Harold Bloom, an unlikely bedfellow for Silko, has argued that the fundamental impulse of American religion is in fact Gnostic, based on a belief in the inviolability of an original individual vision which precedes church or community.[7]

Judging from her interviews, Silko has clearly been forcefully impressed by the common grounds of belief to be found in Europe, and the novel does dramatise some of this, but I think it does also leave open the question of what links the various spiritual experiences. Does everyone experience the same unmediated vision, or does each local community need to clothe it in its own imagery or language? In which case how do we know it's the same? Brewster Fitz provides some helpful close analysis of the ways in which Silko presents religious experiences by focusing on her use of the idea of glossolalia or speaking in tongues, a form of communication which transcends any specific local language and obviates the need for translation. The crucial thing about it is not that everyone shares a meta-language, but that each person hears the message in their own language. We can see this as miraculous because it both allows and affirms difference while transcending it, rather than making everyone the same in order to affirm a single truth, as missionaries had to do. In other words it obviates the need for translation and for the reduction of experience to terms common—and general—enough to be readily translatable.

Fitz looks very closely at how the actual communication is taking place in the novel between characters speaking different languages, and gives close readings of scenes where a communion of spiritual perception and understanding seems to be taking place. In wanting to pin down just what is happening, he is, I think, probing at the heart of the larger claims of the book. He questions how characters and readers know what experience or understanding is being shared, that is, what sort of actual communication is taking place across languages, and asks a question which can also apply to the communicability and translatability of the spiritual experiences which are presented as uniting them. "[I]s the close reader who asks questions from a realistic point of view a traitor to a text that is constructed around the dream of unmediated communication and epistemological communion?" (Fitz 211). This is a crucial question to be asked also about the syncretism of New Age spirituality, in that its claims to able to use very disparate traditions seem often to depend on assuming that what is being experienced is the same and can be subsumed under a general umbrella of spirituality. Thus the invocation of spirituality itself becomes a way of not having to address questions of cultural translatability.[8] Interestingly, Ami Regier wants to read the scene where speaking in tongues seems to be taking place rather differently. She explains away Indigo's view of it as 'a child's vision of cross-cultural perception and understanding' which is to secularise the scene considerably, and remove the possibility of something miraculous taking place (Regier 144).

Silko's use of the Ghost Dance inevitably raises questions about the particular and general meaning and status of religious visions. She does not use the actual term Ghost Dance in the novel, but she describes the Sand Lizard people as one of many groups influenced by the Paiute prophet Wovoka's original vision.[9] Recent work has allowed us a fuller picture of Wovoka and the Ghost Dance than the early white panic reactions to it as a militant movement, but even at the time James Mooney for one recognized its underlying similarities with other religious movements. His account, from which Silko seems to have borrowed, and adapted some songs, is both a powerful recognition of the material reasons for dissatisfactions and longings which would find expression in a shared prophetic movement, and an insistence on the common elements in all religions.

> The systems of our highest modern civilizations have their counterparts among all the nations, and their chain of parallels stretches backward link by link until we find their origin and interpretation in the customs and rites of our own barbarian ancestors, or of our still existing aboriginal tribes.[10]   (Mooney qtd. in Stowe 128)

This is an expression of the comparativist impulse I have described earlier, as is his comment that "the doctrines of the Hindu avatar, the Hebrew Messiah, the Christian millennium, and the Hesûnanin of the Indian Ghost Dance are essentially the same, and have their origin in a hope and longing common to all humanity" (Mooney 1). Michael Elliott has argued that the narrative frame that Mooney provides runs counter to the evolutionary assumptions of unilinear progress, implying a cyclic return, which has more in common with Silko's approach. He points to an impulse to present the 'real' in the late nineteenth century, and the development of modes in which to do it, namely realism and ethnography, which are at odds with powerful counter-impulses, which want to preserve the area of the unreal. Thus, although Mooney makes the comparative connections with Christianity and is sympathetic to the impulses of the Ghost Dance he does not himself subscribe to the belief in the power of the Ghost Dance, and this is where he makes an interesting complement to Silko. In Mooney there is the ethnographic impulse to present what he sees as the unvarnished reality, which means presenting Ghost dancers accurately and voicing their grievances, but not accepting their terms of belief. Mooney is totally confident in explaining away the magical or supernatural elements. He reports background information about the occurrence of an eclipse which 'seems to explain the whole matter' and to undermine the validity of Wovoka's vision of the death of the sun. Similarly he reports the views of two Indian witnesses, the sceptical Cheyenne Tall Bull, a man "of good hard sense and disposed to be doubtful in regard to all medicine men outside of his own tribe" and the Arapaho Black Coyote, "of contemplative disposition, much given to speculation on the unseen world." After Wovoka had waved a feather over his hat, the latter had seen "the whole spirit world" where the former had seen "only an empty hat." Mooney stresses that to his knowledge "both men were honest in their statements" but the tone of the rest of Mooney's account leaves little doubt that he himself sees Wovoka as ultimately a powerful hypnotist (18; 187).

Mooney's own Irish origins have been cited as a relevant factor in his sympathy with the oppressed Indians, and his reading of the Ghost Dance as expressive of political as well as millenarian longings, and his emphasis on Plains manifestations of the movement has been seen to have led to an over-concentration on its political and secular dimensions.[11] Silko restricts herself to the Southwestern occurrences, and does not bring out the political dimensions in the way she does in *Almanac*. By presenting the Ghost Dance mainly as experienced by a child, the visionary and prophetic aspects are foregrounded, and it is these elements which Indigo recognizes in the other religions she encounters. Other characters make the comparative connections more explicitly. Sister Salt recognizes the same ideas in a description of the Valley of Bones from *Ezekiel*, which is read out in a fortune-telling exercise. "Here it was even in the Bible—everything Wovoka said was true" (Silko, *Gardens* 362). The conjunction in the scene of Tarot cards and Ezekiel, and, in the European scenes, Celtic and Arthurian Grail legends, sacred groves and circles, suggests the comparative mythology which influenced Modernist writers, most notably Eliot's *Waste Land* and its acknowledged debt to Jessie Weston, though it is also reminiscent of the contemporary mix of many of the same ingredients to be found, together with elements of Native American religion, in New Age spirituality.

Silko's relation to Modernism has been the subject of some debate. Comparisons of her work by critics with the Anglo-American canon have sometimes been seen as appropriative ways of ignoring or misreading the specifically Native American resonances of Indian texts, but in this work at least Silko seems to insist on being seen in this context as well as a Native one, in keeping with its larger themes of hybridity and syncretism.[12] The comparison with New Age spirituality seems equally unavoidable, even if the question of what distinguishes the sort of syncretic spirituality being celebrated may be an uncomfortable or even impertinent one. One clear difference may be Silko's strong political awareness of the power relations between different groups. In this novel she provides a much fuller sense of the colonialist power structures which underlie all the phenomena that she presents than is ever to be found in New Age or Modernist syncretisms. Another is provided by Regier's view of the way the conjunction of elements in Silko create hybrid and syncretic forms which are dynamic and unstable, in contrast to the assertion of underlying constants which inform the older comparative activities, or the bland New Age syntheses.

These are two strong areas of difference, but they seem to me to apply more to *Almanac of the Dead* than to *Gardens in the Dunes*, where the overlaps with New Age materials are so strong as to prompt a different question. Instead of finding ways in which Silko's syntheses are different from, and superior to New Age syntheses here, perhaps we should be asking whether Silko, intentionally or otherwise, is providing us with a more positive way of seeing at least some aspects of New Age syncretism. Just as the revolutionary political movements in *Almanac of the Dead* emerged from under the guise of a New Age holistic healing conference, perhaps Silko is finding the new spiritual renewal, the new Ghost Dance to be within the yeasty mix of New Age spirituality, rather than separate from it. Certainly the similarities of sources and themes here make it hard for this reader to see any clear distinctions between Native and New Age syncretisms and spiritual claims. If so, this really would make *Gardens* in its own way perhaps just as revolutionary a book as its predecessor, and even more uncomfortable for those wanting to maintain the purity and distinctiveness of Native spirituality.

NOTES

1. See Kimberley C. Patton and Benjamin C. Ray.

2. Recent postcolonial celebration of syncretism tends not even to acknowledge what a controversial term this has been in anthropology, because of the tendency in the past to efface the damage done to native cultures in the process, or even to equate changes with a progress towards the dominant civilisation.

3. With the word 'sentimental' here I invoke the large body of work demonstrating the strength and coherence of a distinctive way of thinking and responding within women's writing, of course, rather than the more pejorative general use of the term.

4. She uses Elaine Pagels' influential book based largely on these discoveries. See Elaine Pagels 164.

5. See Pagels 57.

6. See Arnold 180.

7. See Davis.

8. Laura E. Donaldson has given a sharp account of the use of objects from different cultures invoked by the would-be shaman Lynn Andrews. Against such blatant and indiscriminate appropriation she argues the case for the non-exchangeability of cultural property. See also Lisa Aldred, and for a less

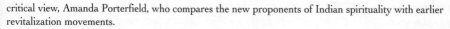

critical view, Amanda Porterfield, who compares the new proponents of Indian spirituality with earlier revitalization movements.

9. In an interview Silko mentions an actual Ghost Dance that took place in 1893 in Kingman, which she moves in her novel to Needles. See Arnold 167.

10. Stowe's account of the Ghost Dance and its songs brings out the movement's syncretism and Mooney's reactions.

11. See Michael Hittman. Ronald Niezen quotes Mooney's recognition of the importance of returned pupils from boarding schools, whose writing skills helped to spread the message (132). Their role also suggests how much more complex the movement was, at least in some of its forms, than simply an expression of regressive longing.

12. For a survey of approaches see Kenneth M. Roemer 10–37.

WORKS CITED

Aldred, Lisa. "Plastic Shamans and Astroturf Sun Dances." *American Indian Quarterly* 24.3 (2000): 329–52.

Arnold, Ellen L., ed. *Conversations with Leslie Marmon Silko.* Jackson: Mississippi UP, 2000.

Davis, Erik. *TechGnosis: Myth, Magic and Mysticism in the Age of Information.* New York: Harmony, 1998.

Donaldson, Laura A. "On Medicine Women and White Shame-ans: New Age Native Americanism and Commodity Fetishism as Pop Culture Feminism." *Signs: Journal of Women in Culture and Society* 24.3 (1999): 677.

Elliott, Michael A. *The Culture Concept: Writing and Difference in the Age of Realism.* Minneapolis and London: U of Minnesota P, 2002.

Fitz, Brewster E. *Silko: Writing Storyteller and Medicine Woman.* Norman: Oklahoma UP, 2004.

Hittman, Michael. *Wovoka and the Ghost Dance.* Lincoln and London: Nebraska UP, 1990.

Lang, Andrew. *Custom and Myth.* 1884. London: Longman, Green and Co, 1910.

Mooney, James. *The Ghost-Dance Religion and Wounded Knee.* 1896. Abr. ed. Chicago and London: Chicago UP, 1965.

Niezen, Ronald. *Spirit Wars: Native North American Religions in the Age of Nation Building.* Berkeley, Los Angeles, London: California UP, 2000.

Pagels, Elaine. *The Gnostic Gospels.* New York: Random, 1979.

Patton, Kimberley C., and Benjamin C. Ray, eds. *A Magic Still Dwells: Comparative Religion in the Postmodern Age.* Berkeley, Los Angeles and London: California UP, 2000.

Porterfield, Amanda. "American Indian Spirituality as a Countercultural Movement." *Religion in Native North America.* Ed. Christopher Vecsey. Moscow: Idaho UP, 1990.

Regier, Ami M. "Revolutionary Enunciatory Spaces: Ghost Dancing, Transatlantic Travel, and Modernist Arson in *Gardens in the Dunes.*" *Modern Fiction Studies* 51.1 (2005): 134–57.

Roemer, Kenneth M. "Silko's Arroyos as Mainstream: Processes and Implications of Canonical Identity." *Modern Fiction Studies* 45.1 (1999): 10–37.

Silko, Leslie M. *Almanac of the Dead*. New York: Penguin, 1992.

———. *Gardens in the Dunes*. New York: Simon and Schuster, 1999.

Stowe, David W. *How Sweet the Sound: Music in the Spiritual Lives of Americans*. Cambridge, Mass and London: Harvard UP, 2004.

A GYNOSTEMIC REVOLUTION: SOME THOUGHTS ABOUT ORCHIDS, *GARDENS IN THE DUNES*, AND INDIGENOUS FEMINISM AT WORK

Deborah A. Miranda

In *Gardens in the Dunes*, Leslie Marmon Silko's exploration of colonization, patriarchal ideology and gendered power, we see a vision and definition of "indigenous feminism" at work in a quiet revolution that describes feminism not by what it looks like, but how it functions in our lives. Having last left readers within the devastation of *Almanac of the Dead*, which she herself has called 'toxic,' Silko has already identified for us—with painful clarity—all the ways human beings can, and do, perpetuate the imbalance between creative and destructive energies. Now, in *Gardens*, Silko presents us with characters whose lives and actions respond to the aftermath of that imbalance: confronted with loss, destruction, violation, insanity, betrayal, greed and cruelty, protagonists like Sister Salt and Indigo do not wilt, self-destruct nor destroy others. Instead, Silko's indigenous women consistently turn to actions that honor balance and feed the creative, illustrating that a profoundly important restoration of right relationship between humans as well as between humans and the Earth is not only possible but necessary for our survival. Through the use of richly layered non-human characters such as orchids, gardens, seeds and water, Silko enables us to read this book as a distinctly indigenous feminist text, and simultaneously urges us toward an understanding of feminist practices that are particular to each culture. To that end, Silko's ambitious text also prominently focuses around Hattie, a white woman academic whose father "agreed with the theories of Mr. John Stuart Mills about the education of women and . . . was proud of his precocious child" (74), underscoring that this novel, ostensibly about Indians, is actually (like Silko's previous books) about saving the world we human beings—all of us, native or non-native, male or female—inhabit. In essence, then, if *Almanac of the Dead* exposes us to the workings of destroyers, *Gardens* is a loving, inclusive and creative instruction manual that teaches us appropriate responses to such devastation through the practice of a feminism that serves the needs of indigenous women while also providing guidance for

Western women who desire indigenous ways of knowing, yet want to resist falling into the familiar trap of appropriating Native culture.[1]

THE 'F' WORD IN INDIAN COUNTRY

Long ago, Cherokee writer Marilou Awiakta tells us, an important negotiation meeting occurred between Cherokee and whites. Expecting to see proper representation of white community leaders, the Cherokee were amazed to see only a group of white men. Attakullakulla, a Cherokee leader, asked these white men, "Where are your women?" (92). Contemporary Western feminists might read this question as a powerful feminist statement by a well-educated Cherokee man. Awiakta, however, tells us that an accurate interpretation of his question is most closely phrased, "Where is your balance?" The Cherokee women and men who made up that delegation of representatives felt that without women present in the white delegation, there could not be a sincere, balanced effort at negotiation on the part of the white community. This *sounds* like an ideal form of what we call "feminism," and yet today a problematic relationship continues between Western feminism and North American indigenous communities, a history of suspicion, wariness, and outright distrust. Paula Gunn Allen writes that "Many Indian women are uncomfortable with feminism because they perceive it (correctly) as white-dominated" (747). Diné poet Laura Tohe declares, "There is no word for feminism in my language . . . there [is] no need for feminism because of our matrilineal culture" (110). Lakota scholar Joyzelle Godfrey goes so far as to flatly state that "feminism really has no place in native cultures and native traditions" (qtd. in Cotera 62), while Lisa Udel remarks in her article, "Revision and Resistance: the Politics of Native Women's Motherwork," that politically savvy indigenous women from diverse backgrounds "articulate a reluctance to affiliate with white feminist movements of North America" (43) in large part because Indian women see white feminism as advocating "a devaluation of motherhood and refutation of women's traditional responsibilities" (45). Udel's use of the word "traditional" does not indicate a fearful or blind adherence to patriarchal rule, as Western feminists may automatically conclude; instead, "traditional" here means a cultural practice with deep tribal legacies of feminine power.

All too often, Indian women feel that Western feminism demands this kind of spiritual and painful divorce from male relatives and male energies, even those male energies within our female bodies; and in fact the early days of radical feminism and mass media's demonification of anything remotely 'feminist' probably contributed greatly to misunderstandings of a feminist project in Indian Country.[2] Founded by white, middle-class white women, Western feminism started from a narrow platform that did not address the unique situation Indian women found themselves negotiating. Indian women's resistance was (and is) based on an indigenous worldview that cannot view maleness as separate from femaleness, or vice versa. Maleness is a form of power; in fact, one half of the energy that governs the world; the other half, of course, is female energy. For an Indian woman to accept the essentializing rhetoric that *all* men were members of an anti-female patriarchy felt nothing less than dishonorable and nothing more than sacrilege, given indigenous beliefs in a complementary power structure based on continuous balancing of power rather than division or separation.[3] Without embracing and internal balancing of female/male energies, Native communities cannot maintain healthy, strong infrastructures in the face of racism, paternalism, and genocidal colonizing experiences, something Native women exploring feminism recognized on conscious and subconscious levels.

In short, inflexible categories of male/female simply did not work for a culture in which traditionally community-oriented relationships relied upon, respected, and utilized both male and female energies (often within the same person, rather than separated into two individuals) in order to maintain healthy, creative, responsible lives.[4] The duality imposed by male/female is at odds with indigenous understandings of gender and gender roles, as well: limiting a person's rights and actions by extremely narrow definitions of 'masculine' and 'feminine' makes no sense to an Indian community in which survival is always the foremost goal. For Indian women, Western feminism not only created bitter division where, traditionally, there were *differences*, but it also served to weaken a culture already under attack from all sides. I have come to believe that ideas about gender are at the heart of indigenous resistance to feminist projects: a refusal, consciously or unconsciously, to accept this separation of male energy and female energy. Each human being is composed of these two forces in infinite diversity, but to imagine these forces as separable or able to exist on their own is not just impossible, it is evil. To separate these energies is to destroy the balance of the world; literally, to destroy the planet. To set these two energies at odds with each other is to self-destruct and to perpetuate an incredible betrayal of one's responsibilities toward one's community, one's ancestors and descendents, and the earth itself.

But the reality is that as we enter the twenty-first century, Western feminism has in fact developed a less divisive discourse around both patriarchal ideology and 'male/female' binary straightjackets. In *Feminist Theory: A Comprehensive Introduction*, Rosemary Tong outlines this move, writing, "Patriarchal ideology, according to [Kate] Millet, exaggerates biological differences between men and women, making sure that men always have the dominant, or masculine, roles and women always have the subordinate, or feminine ones" (49). In other words, patriarchal ideology (notice it's not "men") doesn't just exploit existing differences between men and women, it actually invents those differences and turns them into sources of power for one group, disempowerment for the other; a patriarchal ideology forces conformity to extreme gender roles in order to better control the disempowered, and in fact makes up rigid gender roles of 'masculine' and 'feminine' which it then relentlessly polices. Resistance to a system that fragments the power of the whole is something that makes sense to Indian people, or rather, *would* make sense if that message were actually heard. Hence, Silko's desire to re-open an exchange of knowledge between indigenous communities and contemporary Western feminism, especially in her portrayals of white women such as Hattie, Aunt Bronwyn and Laura (the professoressa). A close reading of the novel's running commentary on gender and patriarchy reveals that Silko intends information to travel both ways through her novel: into Western feminist communities to communicate strengths from indigenous women, and into indigenous communities to communicate ideological developments from twenty-first century Western feminists.

CHILDHOOD IN THE GARDEN OF GRAFTING

Early in *Gardens*, the Indian child Indigo runs away from an Indian boarding school and ends up in the neglected garden of Edward and Hattie, two recently married mid-nineteenth century characters. Hattie, out searching for her wayward pet monkey, Linnaeus, sees Indigo and sets out to "lure the child from under the lilac bushes" (74). Leaving food and water on a tray on the lawn near Indigo's hiding place, Hattie marks time by walking an adjoining area of garden and planning improvements. She is on her husband's family's land, and cautious about moving too quickly or too boldly into new territory. Silko signals the underlying importance of the orchid in this novel here, where Hattie contextualizes the garden's history:

> During his mother's last illness the orchid house and gardens were neglected, but the acres of lemon and orange trees were tended by Edward to occupy himself. He did not talk about those difficult years, so Hattie did not press him, but she saw evidence of some sort of breakdown in the neglect of the orchid house.   (75)

As we discover in the course of the brief discussion about Edward's childhood, the lemon and orange orchards were his elusive father's domain; an exclusively adult, male, scientific zone where his father grafted one fruit onto another out of curiosity and pleasure rather than for economics. The orchid house, however, came under the direction of Edward's mother. Even when she and Edward's sister were away, Silko writes, "he did not feel as lonely in the greenhouse, surrounded by his mother's orchids" (93). Thus Silko situates her male character as a child who grew up in a strictly gendered—i.e., patriarchal—world, one in which men and women literally had separate and different 'houses' or spaces, and very limited roles. Edward travels between these male/female worlds as a small child, visiting both the masculine and feminine models of his small experience, symbolic of at least a tenuous connection between two fixed genders. However, when he is only seven years old, his mother announces that Edward is "old enough to stay with his father" and begins a yearly six month absence in which she and her daughter travel to Long Island (93).

This absence of the feminine and the subsequent focus on masculinity (as defined by his culture) causes seven-year-old Edward great trauma at first, and he has no choice but to find ways to cope on his own. Eventually he learns "to overcome the sadness by following his father to the greenhouse or orange groves" (93). In one short move, Edward's whole world is run by a man who "tolerated him as long as he did not speak unless spoken to" (93)—both the female (orchid) house and the lemon and orange (male) orchards now under one dispassionate, unpredictable, and basically vocation-less man. The beauty of the orchid house is eclipsed by the science of his father's workshop, "with its odors of paraffin, sulfur, and damp earth . . . [which] had been Edward's childhood haunt" (93). Grafting and the collection of orchids, here, seem metaphors by which Silko illustrates patriarchy as an irrational and impractical force which takes over *both* the feminine and masculine energies of creativity, enforcing an artificially separate space for each while allowing no female autonomy or voice at all, and a kind of nurturance that practices scientific attentions—water, temperature, soil—rather than any personal or aesthetic investment.

In fact, Edward's father is a man who is obsessed with constructing an end product not for beauty, profit, or sustenance, but as a gamble, casual messing around with the ways life is constructed, so inattentive to the complexities of life around him that he acts like a bored child in a chemistry lab, mixing and playing with materials whose labels he can't read and whose properties are unknown and unknowable. He cultivates an imitation of creativity. Via a technique known as grafting, Edward's father creates his masterpiece: "lemons, grapefruits, and tangerines all grew on the same tree," not caring for his success or failure except as it pleases his sense of risk (92). Grafting is a gardening technique that does not deal with seeds, pollination or fertilization, nor with the intricate relationship between plants, insects, birds, animals, soil, or weather but rather replaces those inter-related systems with surgical additions and subtractions of a tree's branches by human beings. It is not about a process of transformation but amputation and sutures, an artificial and isolated means of change which eliminates most elements of chance and closely controls how, when, and what the tree grows. Perhaps this infatuation with controlling chance is also reflected in the fact that Edward's father is a compulsive gambler who spends long periods of time determining his "lucky numbers," stays away from home for weeks on gambling binges (during which Edward, still a child, is presumably left in the care of servants), and who eventually dies while on one such adventure. Edward's role model for male creativity, then, centers around the artificiality of the 'grafting' metaphor—detach a limb from one place, and inveigle it to grow on a 'foreign' or new plant. Silko tells us that Edward embraces this role, grafting "The dwarf tangerine trees along the back wall of the red garden" when he is only twelve—a strangely appropriate manhood ceremony that cements his future (93). Edward's role model for female creativity, orchids, resonates with European domesticity theories about separation, containment or captivity (a greenhouse rather than a jungle), the passive presence/absence of the feminine (the flower and his mother), and his own childhood unfulfilled longing for intimate contact and comfort. In this world neither male nor female roles, Silko seems to say, are truly acts of creation, but rely on artifice, manipulation, and domination. Significantly, when (as a newly married adult) Edward desperately searches for a way out of personal and financial hardship, he turns once again to grafting as a source of salvation: he undertakes a trip abroad with Hattie and Indigo in large part to gather citron cuttings from Corsica. Not only would he "own some of the first citron cuttings ever imported to the United States," Edward explains to his sister and her husband, but he also has "the advantages of grafting the newly obtained cuttings of *Citrus medica* onto the limbs of [his father's] mature lemon and orange trees. They would have a crop of *Citrus medica* in eighteen months or less" (164). In response to pending destruction, Edward's action is not to create, but to surgically construct an artificial way out that takes shortcuts through maturation processes and manipulates, rather than works with, creation.

When we first meet Edward, he has already spent twenty years unsuccessfully attempting to bring these two gendered worlds, or energies, back together in the only ways he knows how—by becoming an orchid hunter. He travels the risky worlds of 'undiscovered' orchids in order to find, steal, ship or smuggle into the U.S. new plants for 'private investors.' He removes an orchid from its natural habitat, transports it to an artificial habitat (someone's greenhouse); in effect, he 'grafts' the orchids just as his father used to reconfigure citrus trees. Edward has combined his father's patriarchal form of creation (which requires no female/male contact, or any 'sexual' involvement) with his mother's aesthetically pleasing but 'tame' orchids which she does not grow but merely attempts to keep alive as long as possible for what she perceives as an innate beauty. In actuality, neither act of 'reproduction' is true, or at least not truly creative or generative, as orchids have such specialized reproduction processes that it was not possible for the casual collector to pollinate orchids (the method of orchid pollination is so environmentally-dependent and subtle that it wasn't until 1922 that Lewis Knudson, of Cornell University, determined how to actually accomplish reproduction of orchids in captivity). Silko reifies this lack of sexual relationship again when Edward's orchid-hunting wound prevents him from consummating his marriage to Hattie. Male and female energies have been so segregated that no communication is possible or permitted, and hence each is limited, perhaps even damaged (in fact, Edward is so inflexible that he literally "breaks," time and time again, suffering a broken and infected leg, a sliced hand, various recurring fevers and finally, his inelegant death from pneumonia). Whether Edward suffers from true impotence or merely exhaustion from his wounds, it is clear that for Edward, sexual intimacy with his wife is impossible.

Thus the attempts that Edward and Hattie make at creating a union as sexual partners and life partners consistently fail throughout the novel, in large part because Edward does not know how to create, how to access and allow the sharing of gendered powers. He will not nurture the "feminine" powers within himself, and he will not learn them from Hattie (who is simultaneously at battle with authority figures over her own intentional accessing of "male" energies in her academic and personal lives). He is trapped in his role as a patriarch whose identity denies the value of the creative. Edward is convinced that the only sure way to possess wholeness, financial success, and freedom from self-doubt is to steal, control, or manipulate it, and this conviction is manifested in the novel by Silko's excruciating chronicle of Edwards's obsession with orchids.

The theft of the orchids from their native lands stands at the heart of *Gardens*. In comparison to the indigenous gardens of the Sand Lizard people, which Silko portrays as both beautiful and producers of sustenance, the artificial, costly, 'alien' orchids are objects of trauma, greed, and danger. Something has been stolen from its place of emergence, and forcibly transported to an 'unnatural' place; something has been changed not through the slow process of transformation, but by man's theft and annihilation of orchid communities left behind.

Clearly, the breakdown that Hattie intuits when she sees the abandoned orchid house was not only Edward's own emotional pain at tending plants that belonged to a dying or dead mother, but sign of a longer, pervasive breakdown in the human relationship between man and woman. After the loss of his mother, Edward completely neglects the orchid house, which at some point further suffers damage during an earthquake. Symbolically, this is the long-delayed echo of Edward's loss of the feminine in his life, the loss that precipitates his adulthood of imbalance. Always already somewhat unbalanced by his parents' strange separation and the artificially rigid, non-communicative gender roles established as normal 'marital' practice, now Edward has lost even the partial presences of both father and mother. He flails to establish himself as an adult, as a whole human being, but he (and, Silko implies, any man raised in such a culture) is not prepared for that task. Edward is unable to be present for Hattie in any significant partnership.

WHERE IS YOUR GYNOSTEMIC BALANCE?

Silko has not created a simple metaphor here, however, in which an orchard equals masculinity and orchids equal femininity. Love and the erotic are powerfully creative forces in human lives, in what Joy Harjo calls, "The epic search for grace"—grace being another word for a self-sustaining matrix, a wholeness, the act of living as a balanced being within a balanced world—and of perpetuating that balance through one's actions and intent in the world. But both love and the erotic are at odds with the violence and domination that structures any patriarchal culture. Thus, in patriarchy love is turned into grief, and the erotic is distorted into the pornographic oppression and exploitation. These oppressors are those of any gender, any age, who seek power in a patriarchal system any way they can get it. It is clear that Silko uses the story of the nineteenth century orchid trade in part to discuss the economic and ethnocentric forces behind colonization, land theft, and the environmental and spiritual destruction of the earth. It's always about land, and in this novel, references to violation and rape are everywhere. But Silko layers her symbols still more deeply in choosing orchids as her central metaphor, implicit in how orchids are gendered and how that integration of male-female energy becomes something else that is neither male nor female but purely creative and powerful.

The word orchid derives from the word for testes—because the 'roots' of the plant often form into two small spheres. But the flower of the orchid has long been recognized and often feared because of its resemblance to female genitalia (at one time proper women in polite society couldn't legally own orchids). Alec Pridgeon, in *The Illustrated Encyclopedia of Orchids*, states that the diversity of orchids is phenomenal—but adds that

> . . . one feature above all others defines the orchid and differentiates it from virtually all other flowering plants—the fusion of the male portion of the flower (stamens) and female portion (pistils). Orchids have three stamens and three pistils, but unlike those of the lily, for example, which are separate from each other, those of the orchid are fused into a structure termed the column or gynostemium, which is located to one side of the flower. (7)

This word—gynostemium—is a fusion itself, 'gyno' being from the Greek for female and stemium from stamen, from the Greek for standing, a base, upright, the male organ of the flower. Gynostemium, then, means *female-male*, or *female phallus*. Thus in construction, in function, and in the naming of its sexual parts, the orchid is an integrated and doubly gendered plant. One is tempted to say, in fact, that the orchid family is a 'third gender' that naturally occurs in the flora of our planet. Unlike almost all other plants the single anther at the tip of the column produces pollen that is not free and powdery but held in waxy masses of two, four or six pellets called pollinia. In human terms, we would call this semen, and some orchids even eject pollinia quite forcefully onto passing insects for best distribution. However, this same column also *receives* the pollinia from other orchids, and becomes a vessel of conception much like a human womb; in other words, this very male organ simultaneously functions as the model of female gestation.

Silko uses the idea of gender, the concept of having a gendered energy, to talk about gendered power, but it's not necessarily power that's tied to one gender or the other being 'better,'—rather, it's about learning to know and appreciate the inherent abilities of each 'gender,' and the practice of living in balance with the knowledge of those powers, irregardless of rigid gendered identities. Further, through her use of orchid imagery, Silko asks us to question the strict boundaries between male and female, and accept that true balance makes use of fluid, changing, mutually-sustaining energies of both—or all—genders. I think, in many ways, Silko is working to explore creative and empowering ways for healing from and even reviving older ways of viewing gendered oppositions (patriarchy) and violent conquest (colonization).

Unfortunately, use of the root word *orchis* emphasizes the male aspects of the plant rather than the inherent gender-bending qualities which Silko has carefully implanted throughout her novel. The column rising from the center of the flower is, as I've noted already, called the gynostemium. As a reproductive structure derived from the fusion of both male and female parts into a single organ that both releases the pollen and also receives it (ideally from another individual) for fertilization, the gynostemium itself informs us that the orchid is clearly a plant in which reproduction does not privilege nor subjugate either 'gender'. I'm drawn, then, to the word "gynostemic," as a word which in fact describes the truer nature of orchid, and their work in *Gardens*.

Using the orchid both as a symbol and as a real, living example of balance, Silko points out that our focus on artificial gender roles perpetuates patriarchy, which feeds itself on colonization and destruction of human relationships with each other, and with the earth itself. Interestingly, with *Gardens*, Silko does not direct her message solely to Indian women, or even Indian people; nor does she position Hattie as a white woman who finds herself through some spiritual feeding off of indigenous lives, but as a woman who ultimately realizes her wholeness comes from embracing both the male and female energies within herself and within the world. Let me be clear: Silko is not advocating a cavalier philosophy in which who we are and where we come from is not important, or worse, that anyone can make up an "Indian name," help out a few needy Indians, and "become" instantly indigenous. Rather, she structures the narrative around perceiving, seeking, and honoring the balance of all energies within human nature and human, including and especially the sexual, creative energy present in (as?) gender.

Here, we see a direct connection between what Silko does in *Gardens*, and the indigenous erotic currently surfacing in many Indian women's writings. The blossoming and persistence of Indian women's erotics is about being Indian women who still survive and resist colonization and systemic genocide. This writing is also about being female—capable of creation, birth, renewal—within a viciously patriarchal, militaristic, violent culture. But more than simply a form of declaring some kind of 'female superiority,' an indigenous erotics works via the creative life force to re-establish a whole, *balanced* energy: to remake the ground, both physical and spiritual, that humanity has lost in an unwise and out of control worship of the destructive. In this system of balance, race and gender are significant not because of any inherent power, but because each has an important source unique to itself where it can best function.

Contrary to Western ideas about the erotic as a hedonistic, excessive, selfish indulgence in purely sensory pleasure, Silko describes the indigenous erotic in four words: "Share. Don't be greedy" (17). This is the heart of what being in the erotic means to a truly indigenous (symbiotic) people: to harvest, care for, and assure the reseeding of the world in responsible and pleasing ways. Perhaps this is because we humans are the only ones who still have this lesson to learn—how to be in balance—that perpetual act of balanc*ing*—that 'epic search for grace' that Joy Harjo articulates.[5]

Not only does the orchid balance this male/female energy, but it also lives a symbiotic relationship with its host plant. Many orchids must live with, even on, another plant—but they are not parasitic. In addition, the transfer of pollinia from one flower to another, though highly efficient, is often reliant upon one species of insect. In some ways, then, orchids are the product of not two but three parents—for the insect, while not a genetic contributor, is so important to the work of reproduction that it can be catastrophic for a plant if its pollinator disappears. In many ways, Silko's exploration of fertility and survival in *Gardens* works to explore creative and empowering ways for healing, and even reviving older ways of viewing, gendered oppositions, limiting dualities, and resulting conflicts.

This is what I see behind Silko's luscious, long descriptions of Hattie's journey to the gardens in Europe. She provides Hattie (the white woman who reminds me a great deal of other white women searching for a way out of patriarchal straitjackets and looking to indigenous cultures for clues, a la Lynn Andrews) with a completely alternative path, a viable way out of patriarchal religion that doesn't attempt to ditch European identity in exchange for "wannabe" American Indian identity, but instead incorporates and even admires a white, European indigeneity. She's showing European-Americans a possible place and belief system available to them, in hopes that they not only stop appropriating Native spirituality, but actually find something their own histories and bodies emerged from, and thus access a more powerful source in terms of creating an identity. The book's intricate descriptions of Hattie's explorations in the gardens in Europe—the goddess cultures, the fertility and sexual symbols found there—persuade me that what saves Hattie is not the Ghost Dance, nor Indigo's innocence or innate Native presence, or even the collective assistance of Indian and white women. What saves Hattie is her search for, and embracing of, a source of creativity and healing that is particular to her own culture. Early on in *Gardens*, we learn that Hattie marries Edward in the awful aftermath of a double trauma: first, her thesis on the Gnostic Gospels is rejected by her professors as "unacceptable Gnostic heresy, pure and simple" (79), and second, a sexual attack by a male student who sees Hattie's work with that material to mean she is an advocate of "free love." Yet although Hattie puts aside her thesis, she never burns it or gives up on her ideas that put women at the heart of the sacred, and it is this research that continues to call to her as she strolls through those amazing Gardens in Europe, discovering a kind of female empowerment that, unlike the patriarchal power she's used to, does not seek to dominate but merely to balance. In effect, Hattie's character allows Silko to tell non-native women, *you have your own place of emergence. Find it. Seek out your own source of origin, and then decide if this continent is where you belong, and if so, determine how best to live here.* In doing so, Silko addresses an issue that has very real connections to her perceptions of contemporary feminist experiences with "other" cultures—the issue of appropriation.

BALANCE AND THE LESSONS OF APPROPRIATION

In fact, in many ways *Gardens* can be read as a response to *The Bean Trees*, by Barbara Kingsolver, which also involves a white woman who takes on the role of caretaker of an Indian child, and for which Silko has expressed severe criticism. Silko writes pointedly about Kingsolver's plot in the preface to her own essay, "Books: Notes on Mixtec and Maya Screenfolds," saying that:

> Books were and still are weapons in the ongoing struggle for the Americas. Only a few years ago, a best-selling novelist breathed new life into old racist stereotypes with a portrayal of the Cherokee reservation people as pitiful drunks and child abusers whose children are better off with any white woman who comes along. Such sentiments soothe the collective conscience of white America. The subtext of such stereotypical portrayals is: take the children, take the land; these Indians are in no condition to have such precious possessions.   (Silko, *Yellow Woman* 155)

Silko insists that the foundation of a plot like Kingsolver's asserts and perpetuates a paternalistic relationship between whites and Indians even within a white woman's "feminist" search for identity and autonomy, and that this is, in fact, an ongoing offensive in American culture that pervades American literature. Not only does Kingsolver's white woman character, Taylor, make herself the guardian of an Indian girl, she also re-names the child "Turtle,"— never asking the child what her name might be, or even supposing that she has one. "Turtle Island," however, has long been used by Native peoples as a description of the North American continent.[6] What the naming of Turtle by Taylor allows Kingsolver to do, then, is arrange for a pathetic, beaten, fearful Indian woman to symbolically hand over the entire North American continent to a white woman who is passing through. Taylor is literally handed the opportunity to become the symbolic Indian mother. The implication—that Natives willingly, if wearily, turn over stewardship and thus ownership of North American to the 'new' race—is a stunning repetition of the original rationale for European colonization: ownership is established via use and occupation (*European* definitions of use and occupation). Throughout *The Bean Trees*, Taylor defines her role as woman, mother and colonizer by the raising and "taming" of this girl child. In effect, the book's plot revolves around the rescue of an Indian child by a white woman, and that white woman's development of an identity which appropriates large parts of itself from Indian culture. If there is any doubt about the role of the Indian child in this novel, it is cleared up when another character reminds Taylor about a tragic air crash. Taylor thinks to herself, "I did remember that airplane crash. On TV they showed the rescue helicopter dropping down a rope to save the only surviving stewardess from an icy river full of dead people. I remember just how she looked hanging on to that rope. *Like Turtle*" (emphasis added, 75). Here is the image of Turtle, and through Turtle, all Indians, that Silko so objects to: a battered and traumatized survivor, being plucked from a "dead people" and hanging for dear life onto the rope extended by her rescuer, a white woman, Taylor. Taylor, who began the novel as a plucky but inexperienced young girl, makes the transition to a strong, independent, capable woman—a feminist Bildungsroman that feeds off indigenous culture in a pattern that denigrates and exploits Indian lives and spirituality.

This paternalistic feminism is completely reversed in Silko's portrayal of the relationship between Hattie and Indigo. For example, Hattie is not "given" Indigo (Turtle is handed over to Taylor by an Indian woman in a parking lot, and Kingsolver indicates that Turtle has been physically and perhaps sexually abused by her Indian parents); instead, Indigo has already freed herself from the white man's abusive boarding school and is merely resting in Hattie's garden—after feeding herself from the plants she knows are good to eat. Additionally, Hattie does not re-name Indigo, because Indigo does not give her the chance; rather, when Indigo sees the plant for which she is named, she presents it to Hattie along with the Sand Lizard word for it, and tells Hattie, "This is the plant I am named for" (113). Self-naming is a clear indication of autonomy, and Silko sets up an unusual relationship right from the start, one in which Indigo nurtures and teaches Hattie and in fact "de" civilizes Hattie, or opens Hattie to the possibilities of her own indigeneity. And finally, at the end of *Gardens*, Indigo and her sister take Hattie in and care for her when the white woman has been beaten, raped, and left for dead—ironically, while bringing blankets and supplies for the winter to the two sisters, in an effort to help them.

Every step of the way, Silko creates a plot in which feminism for Hattie is not based on paternalism but mutual humane treatment and a profound respect for the connections a person feels to her place of emergence. A white woman does not save an Indian girl child from the degeneration of her race, as in Kingsolver's plot; instead, Silko creates an Indian girl who holds her own with white culture while drawing strength and power from her own, and who offers sustenance and tenderness to a white woman while that woman explores her own indigenous roots, particularly the goddess and feminine pre-Christian spirituality she has been punished for examining in her academic thesis. In fact, Silko emphasizes the communal effort of saving Hattie, destabilizing the paternalistic culture that tells Hattie a woman doesn't know what's good for her: Indigo, Aunt Bronwyn and Laura form a network of spiritual education and support for Hattie, and later, when Hattie is attacked by white men and left to die, "Indians found her. She remembered that . . . one of the women spoke English and told her not to be afraid, they would take her to their house and send for help" (459). This is a far cry from the *The Bean Trees* and other portrayals of white-Indian relationships and is a clear response from Silko to those plots which pitch feminism at the cost of Native culture.

Silko's response to the paternalism in Western feminism is not an assertion that "Indians are better," but instead offers this idea that we are all indigenous, made explicit in *Gardens*. However, as Silko has remarked, becoming indigenous to a place may take thousands of years—it can't be done instantaneously; because the atrophy of one people's indigenous connections can't be undone instantaneously.[7] Silko seems to argue that being indigenous is not purely a question of blood, but of responsibility to the relationships between earth and human spirituality, and that while our paths to fulfilling that relationship may be different based on our biological places of emergence, in the end it is of primary importance to us all. Much like reminding us that there is no such thing as race, that we are one race—the human race—Silko constructs this trinity of Sister Salt, Indigo and Hattie to point out that arguing about who is and who isn't indigenous is useless, because unless you're from Mars, we are *all* indigenous to this planet. This isn't as generous or as wishy-washy as it sounds: claiming indigeneity requires acceptance of responsibility, constant attention to balance and intent, in ways most non-Indians have rarely contemplated.

It's a tricky, tricky negotiation, and that's one of the reasons I think Silko spends so much time developing and following Hattie's transformation. Using the orchid both as a symbol and as a real, living example of balance, Silko points out that our focus on separated, rigidly artificial gender perpetuates patriarchy, which feeds itself on paternalism, colonization and destruction. By following Hattie's journey out of patriarchal confines, Silko structures the narrative around perceiving, seeking, and honoring the balance of all energies within human nature and human. Her characters Indigo, Sister Salt, and Hattie, all define indigenous feminism via attention to the erotic in order to retake the ground, both physical and spiritual, that humanity has lost in an unwise and out of control worship of the destructive and imposition of paternalistic relationships between peoples.

By setting male and female energies in opposition to one another patriarchal ideology destroys life and encourages antagonism, misunderstanding, and fear. When Silko asserts that patriarchal oppression is damaging to everyone, she means everyone—including, and especially, the Earth, the elements, the life found on there and the cosmology that holds the Earth together. Silko's feminism does not advocate a war between genders or races, but rather asks us to see, as in Awiakta's story about the lack of women at a negotiation, "that the balance is absent" (92). In *Gardens*, Silko gently insists on a gynostemic revolution in which indigenous feminism works to decolonize such systems as patriarchy and paternalism and encourage symbiotic interchange between equals as the actions that can help us all in our perpetual act of finding, and maintaining, balance.

NOTES

1. Here, I believe that Silko engages with a long, problematic tradition of Western European women who, while struggling toward autonomy and freedom from patriarchal oppression, turn to American Indian ideology in order to gain personal identity and enlightenment—for example, Mary Austen, or more recently (and more aggressively), Lynn Andrews. This tradition uses or exploits American Indian culture purely for the benefit of these Western European women who take strength from indigenous belief systems (particularly as they apply to women) without giving anything back. For a fine discussion of this pattern, see Donaldson 677.

2. For example, in her essay "All My Relatives Are Noble: Recovering the Feminine Ella Cara Deloria's *Waterlily*," Maria Eugenia Cotera writes that ". . . the politics of Native feminism are 'first and foremost' the politics of tribal survival, even as the nationalist agendas of sovereignty and self-determination are intimately intertwined with a woman-centered Native feminist perspective. Therefore, someone like Deloria who identifies 'first and foremost as an Indian woman' has as her most immediate goal the act of decolonization." When this decolonization is taken up via traditional female ways of knowing, culture and education (such as the many daily acts of a Lakota woman as depicted by Deloria), Cotera argues, that decolonization is a feminist act. Thus the definition of feminism is greatly different from an indigenous woman's point of view than from a Western feminist perspective, especially one that regards "woman's work" as always particularly confining and oppressive.

3. For further explication of this gender complementarity, see Hollrah.

4. Although space does not allow for discussion of the contemporary indigenous "Two-Spirit" movement here, or for older "third gender" examples from pre-contact, see Will Roscoe's *Living the Spirit* and *The Changing Ones*, as well as *Two-Spirit People: Native American Gender Identity, Sexuality, and Spirituality*, Sue-Ellen Jacobs et al., eds. for more information about the power inherent in one human being whose body contains "two-spirit" energy.

5. See Harjo's poem "Grace" in the collection *In Mad Love and War*.

6. Steve Talbot describes the origins of the term "Turtle Island" in the excellent reference book, *Native America: Portrait of the Peoples* (1994). As part of the earth-diver tradition of Creation Stories,

many tribes tell of an animal diving deep below the original waters of the world, over and over, each time bringing up a "tiny bit of mud to form the earth island" (446). In many versions of this story, Turtle offers her back to serve as the foundation of the land, thus the name "Turtle Island." The term is well-known by most who have done any reading about American Indians.

7. In an interview with Thomas Irmer, Silko says, ". . . my interest is in people that were connected to the land, indigenous all over the world including in Europe. The idea is if you were born — sure you have a place in this world. So everybody is indigenous. More specifically, I mean it to apply to populations who have been connected to a land for at least some thousands of years."

WORKS CITED

Allen, Paula Gunn. "Kochinnenako in Academe." *Feminisms*. Ed. Robyn Warhol and Diane Herndl. New Brunswick: Rutgers UP, 1997. 713; 131.

Awiakta, Marilou. *Selu: Seeking the Corn-Mother's Wisdom*. Golden: Fulcrum, 1994.

Cotera, Maria E. "All My Relatives Are Noble: Recovering the Feminine in Ella Cara Deloria's Waterlily." *American Indian Quarterly* 28.1–2 (2004): 52–72.

Donaldson, Laura. "On Medicine Women and White Shame-Ans: New Age Native Americanism and Commodity Fetishism as Pop Culture Feminism." *Signs: A Journal of Women and Culture in Society* 24 (1999): 677–96.

Harjo, Joy. *In Mad Love and War*. Middletown: Wesleyan UP, 1990.

Hollrah, Patrice. *The Old Lady Trill, the Victory Yell; The Power of Women in Native American Literature*. New York: Routledge, 2003.

Irmer, Thomas. "An Interview with Leslie Marmon Silko." 12 April 2006. <http://www.altx.com/interviews/silko.html>.

Jacobs, Sue-Ellen, Wesley Thomas, and Sabine Lang, eds. *Two-Spirit People: Native American Gender Identity, Sexuality, and Spirituality*. Chicago: U of Illinois P, 1997.

Kingsolver, Barbara. *The Bean Trees*. New York: Harper, 1988.

Pridgeon, Alec. *The Illustrated Encyclopedia of Orchids*. Portland: Timber, 1992.

Roscoe, Will. Living the Spirit: Gay American Indian Anthology. New York: St. Martin's, 1988.

———. *The Changing Ones: Third and Fourth Genders in Native America*. New York: Macmillan, 1998.

Silko, Leslie Marmon. *Almanac of the Dead*. New York: Penguin, 1991.

———. *Gardens in the Dunes*. New York: Simon & Schuster, 1999.

———. *Yellow Woman and a Beauty of the Spirit*. New York: Simon & Schuster, 1996.

Tohe, Laura. "There is No Word for Feminism in My Language." *Wicazo Sa Review: A Journal of Native American Studies*. 15.2 (2000): 103–10.

Tong, Rosemary. *Feminist Thought: A Comprehensive Introduction*. Boulder: Westview, 1989.

Udel, Lisa. "Revision and Resistance: the Politics of Native Women's Motherwork." *Frontiers* 22 (2001): 43–64.

WATER AS LEITMOTIF IN SILKO'S
GARDENS IN THE DUNES

John Purdy

The title of Leslie Marmon Silko's third novel subtly suggests central elements of her entire canon. This suggestion is contained in the wonderfully evocative image of gardens in dunes. Since dunes are hills of sand, they possess very little natural vegetation, if any vegetation at all, and plants that grow there are sparse and stunted. It is a tentative existence, to say the least, and given the desert setting of the novel, this aspect of the title, therefore, possesses a literal sense, but there are other levels to the image as we interact with it.

Conjoining gardens with such a barren landscape immediately produces a conflict; one image of plush greenery collides with one of wind-swept sands void of water and thus life. There are other conflicting senses of the terms individually: gardens suggesting the presence of humans as caretakers (as with the Garden of Eden) and dunes the absence of humans, and presence/absence is one of the structuring devices of the novel. Furthermore, the sense of oasis/refuge surrounded by threat/danger also frames the events of the narrative. Finally, the ways societies often value gardens for the life they contain (and sometimes their utility) but devalue the "wilderness" that is not "settled" are consistently revealed throughout the novel.

In her earlier works, Silko challenged readers' easy dismissal of the deserts of the American southwest as lifeless voids. After all, these deserts, like those into which the prophets of Christendom journeyed for visions, are places where fundamental forces of the world are brought into stark and clear relief. As anyone who has lived in them will tell you, they are actually full of life and operate on seasonal cycles much like other climatic zones. Here, as elsewhere, these cycles and this life are reduced to one fundamental necessity, to water. Without it, there is no life, so it is one central, foundational fact of existence. Its sources are also, therefore, a central, converging point of connectivity that cuts across all life, all flora and fauna. In locations so intricately tied to the presence or absence of water, all life forms are most closely aligned with water and its cycles: seasonal rains and runoff that keep streams and springs alive.

It makes sense, then, that water should also operate throughout the stories of all cultures, providing a universal leitmotif across literary canons; from those of the great flood to those of earth diver, stories tell of great things that transpired in the presence or as a result of water. However, unlike other contemporary Native writers—Louise Erdrich, for example, who uses water as a point of connectivity between her Catholic and Anishinaabe heritages—Silko used water in her earlier works as a motif to enlighten some fundamental differences between cultures, and thus it operates as an investigation of European values as revealed by colonialism. In her canon, colonialism in the Americas worked in concert with Christian and Capitalist ideologies to demonize and objectify the "natural" world, and this included water. In effect, this objectification allowed for the colonists' manipulation and control of their environment, while it disavowed the central place it inhabits in the ancient, "primitive" cultures they moved to displace. The life implicit in the term "environment," however, exists only where water is found.

A deployment of water as a literary motif can be found very early in Silko's writings, and throughout her canon it places her readers, time and time again, on the cusp between differing, sometimes contradictory, value systems. As one considers the high respect for water displayed by the indigenous characters in her narratives, one must attempt to reconcile this regard with those of the industrial/postindustrial world in which we reside, a world that in Christian belief is doomed to an apocalyptic future. One celebrates life, one anticipates destruction, and she brings both into her narratives to act out their respective visions, often using water as a point of contention. Her short story "The Man to Send Rain Clouds," for example, draws heavily upon Pueblo belief systems about water, as the title reveals. In this story, the dead—if properly handled—will bring rains to the people of Laguna Pueblo, and thus survival in the future. This understanding provides the simple plot for the narrative.

A Laguna elder who has been tending his family's sheep on a remote ranch dies. His kinsmen travel to the ranch and retrieve his body. After the family and community have paid their respects and performed their obligations to the dead, and as Leon prepares to carry old Teofilo to the cemetery for burial, however, Louise suggests that they send for the priest so that he can sprinkle holy water on Teofilo's grave. The priest at first refuses, since he was not called to perform the last rites—his belief system's own obligations to the dead—and thus feels slighted. Finally, reluctantly, he agrees to perform one part of those duties by sprinkling the water, and Louise's request for the action makes sense within the cultural frame of reference the story constructs. In this event, two belief systems have a moment of productive connectivity but the belief system brought by colonial powers does not have superiority, nor does it supplant in its entirety the indigenous belief. Instead, one aspect of it is borrowed to supplement and complement the ancient ways: the water with its inherent connection to life and its transcendent connection to the afterlife, to other worlds.

The short story provided the title for one early anthology of American Indian fiction, and in the same collection Silko's "Yellow Woman" also ties people and water in a sacred, but also a literary, cycle. As the title suggests, this story derives from the Kochininako stories of Laguna tradition. In it, Silko's protagonist, Kochininako's modern incarnation, meets a man, a stranger, near the river on the outskirts of the pueblo. They make love there, and then he takes her with him into the mountains. After a series of events, she returns and on her trip back into the pueblo she stops at a place that now has new levels of signification for her and the reader:

> The river water tasted good, and I sat in the shade under a cluster of silvery willows. . . . I came back to the place on the river bank where he had been sitting the first time I saw him. The green willow leaves that he had trimmed from the branch were still lying there, wilted in the sand. I saw the leaves and wanted to go back to him—to kiss him and to touch him—but the mountains were too far away now. And I told myself, because I believe it, he will come back sometime and be waiting again by the river.   (Rosen 45)

The plot of "Yellow Woman" resonates with the earlier Yellow Woman stories, and like them, it begins and ends with the river, with water. This is a place of primal importance in the Laguna mythos, as Silko tells us in the film *Running on the Edge of the Rainbow*. This is where the mundane meets the extraordinary, the sacred, and where individuals transcend through their actions. These actions are not symbolic, nor are they imaginary, as the wilting willow leaves show; physical and mythical realities converge and coexist in this place in this story.

It is no wonder, then, that the river near Laguna became a point of cultural reference in Silko's first novel, *Ceremony*, a few years later. In this narrative, the river provides a subtle connection between the protagonist, Tayo, and his heritage. At one point, his aunt tells the story of once watching his mother (her sister) return home at dawn. She is naked, and crosses the river at a point that comes into the narrative later when Tayo—after a night of love making with a mysterious stranger—remembers, at dawn, the ceremonial coming of the Ka't'sina to the river crossing and pueblo. The suggestion ties this spot on the river to Tayo and the Yellow Woman visitations, and marks the place, once again, as one of religious significance. It also ties his story to the Laguna literary canon, which describes the place's relevance to both the ancient and modern worlds, but also the future.[1] In the mythos Silko describes, the cultural information about water can be evoked simply with the utterance "river."

In *Ceremony*, Silko brings other manifestations of water into the cosmology of her readers: the sacred spring that Tayo visits at several points, including one time with the mysterious woman, Ts'eh. The spring never dries up, despite times of severe drought such as the one Tayo returns to after World War II. In this place, several strands of Laguna culture merge, and Silko layers them into the descriptive details of the place itself: the colors, the "insect" life (including Spider Woman), the life the spring supports and perpetuates. Other scholars have unpacked some of the significance of this spring,[2] so I will not do so here, but I will note that the novel also brings in the rains, once more—through the drought and its conclusion after Tayo begins his quest, where his relationship with Ts'eh provides the first step—and through Tayo's earlier cursing of rain in the Philippines during the war. Thus, the novel covers three levels of water to be found throughout Silko's canon: the rains, the river, the spring.

These sources of life are explored in detail in her self-published collection, *Sacred Water: Narratives and Pictures*. Here, the Laguna, transcendent connection between people and water is carefully mapped out with visual images tied to commentaries that consider water and the life forms that depend or interact with it. For instance, there is a sequence early on that provides some of these fundamental realities. On page twenty we find a brief statement: "The old-time Pueblo people believe that natural springs and fresh-water lakes possess great power. Beneath their surfaces lie entrances to the four worlds below this world." On the facing page is a close-up photograph of water lilies in a pool. On the next page, there is a wide-angle shot of the lily pool, with two snakes swimming; facing this page there is another statement:

> At one time there was a beautiful lake west of Ka'waik, Laguna village. The word 'Ka'waik' means 'beautiful lake'; the Spanish word for 'lake' is 'laguna'.
> A giant water snake named 'Ma'sh'ra'tur'ee['] lived in the beautiful lake which was connected to the four worlds below and which allowed the gentle snake to travel down below. Down there, clear streams run year round, and flowers are everywhere because the Mother Creator is there.   (20–23)

In very short order, visually and verbally, she explains some elemental connections between beliefs and stories, people and place, people and other life forms, colonialism and the survivance of ancient beliefs despite its tragic consequences. And at the center of them all is the sacred water, which is tied directly to the life-giving force of Mother Creator. Water connects this world to primal, generative, universal forces.

Sacred Water's positive, optimistic images of water and life, however, are balanced in her second novel, *Almanac of the Dead*, with the negative, horrific visions of colonial forces arrayed to co-opt the life-giving powers of water and, literally, suck the land dry for commercial profit. From the deep wells proposed in the Tucson area to draw the remaining water table to provide water for swimming pools, lawns and expensive homes, to the dams built on the Colorado River and myriad other western streams to provide those same homes with electricity, the destructive presence of modern capitalism born of colonialism is explored in depth and detail.[3] Moreover, this short-sighted utilitarianism is internalized by some characters who are modern descendants of the indigenous peoples of the hemisphere so, much as in *Ceremony*, Silko blurs the simple cultural/ethnic binaries to be found in other authors' works, and emphasizes, instead, that the true binary in issues such as ecological ones is in the ways individuals value their world, water included: either as a life-giving force to be revered, or as a commodity to be exploited. In *Almanac*, the deaths from thirst of people trying to cross the Sonora Desert from Mexico to the U.S. provide one straightforward lesson on values in this regard; these characters do not find a garden in their dunes, only death in their quest for inclusion in the affluence of the capitalist society north of the border.[4]

This brings us back to *Gardens*, which, stylistically at least, appears to be quite a departure from Silko's earlier narratives. A novel in the Jamesian tradition in ways, *Gardens* nonetheless extends Silko's earlier issues back into history (the late nineteenth century), but also into other landscapes and into other cultures. This engagement with other colonized indigenous traditions can be found in *Almanac*, where Dhambala (the snake) of African stories is evoked in connection with Ma'sh'ra'tur'ee of Laguna. However, in *Gardens*, this type of connection is much more expansive; here, water is used not only to provoke a comparative assessment of Native and non-Native ideologies and cosmologies, but also as a point of resistance to the globalization of European, colonial values. In this way, the narrative's concerns are very closely tied to her earlier works, but *Gardens* extends them through her deployment of water as leitmotif. Rain, springs, streams and the life they support once again are used to valorize indigenous life beliefs and to critique the effects of European colonialism upon them and upon the land. However, here Silko explores several generations of colonial movements, and, in a way much like Carter Revard in his wonderfully humorous short story "Report to the Nation: Repossessing Europe," turns the colonial gaze back upon itself. In *Gardens*, water, therefore, becomes a shared signifier for the cultures of indigenous characters in the U.S., but also other societies the novel discovers as its central characters, Sister Salt and Indigo, quest for safety and security in an increasingly hostile world.

The novel begins and ends in the gardens that rely upon water to survive in the dunes: on the spring and the rains. The opening paragraph clearly establishes an edenic baseline for the sisters' values and for their quests.[5] In this remote, ancient garden, the two young children frolic naked in the rain. "The rain smelled heavenly. . . . She took a deep breath and ran up the dune, where Sister Salt was naked in the rain. . . . The rain she swallowed tasted like the wind. . . . They lay side by side with their mouths open and swallowed raindrops until the storm passed. All around them were old garden terraces in the dunes" (15). The pure bliss Silko describes is stripped (no put intended) to bare essentials: life, earth, rain, garden. The sheer joy and celebration of these fundamentals do not change throughout the book, despite the ways history has shaped our understanding of them.

In effect, there is little to place or mark this paragraph's description to establish place or time or culture; it provides, instead, an image that is transcendent. However, the exposition that follows locates the narrative quite quickly in the colonial history of the Americans, with "Indian police," yet it complicates that placement as well, since the police are ordered to arrest "the Messiah" (15). For a reader trying to situate the novel within historical and geographical frameworks, the conflation of North American societies and those of "the Holy Land" at first appears incongruous.[6] However, if one recognizes that the history of one resonates with the history of the other, this confusion is reconciled in a concept that permeates the remainder of the narrative's plots: the story of the Messiah *is* a story of colonialism through the Roman occupation and subjugation of the nation of Israel. It is a story of resistance and transcendence against forces with very different sets of beliefs and values, and this difference is, once again, often enacted in sites where water factors prominently. Silko's narrative recovers the early history and beliefs of Christians, but also the layers of ideologies that have buried them for millennia.[7]

After the locale of the gardens is established, the next watered event of prominence is on the Colorado River near the town Needles, where the two sisters, their mother, and their grandmother live as they participate in the new, capitalist economy brought by the Americans; they sell crafts to the tourists who travel through by train on their way to or from Southern California. Thus, the image of the desert as an intermediate, uncivil landscape one must endure to reach one's destination is established and the convention of the "frontier" is evoked—wherein indigenous and non-indigenous meet and, sometimes, trade—but this is filtered through an indigenous point of view. It is also in Needles that the family learns of the Messiah and that he and his followers are to visit, bringing with them a vision of the future and a means to combat colonial power: the Ghost Dance. This, too, is connected to water.

> The dance was a peaceful dance, and the Paiutes wished no harm to white people; but Jesus was very angry with white people. As the people danced, great storm clouds would gather over the entire world. Finally, when all the Indians were dancing, great winds would roar out of clear skies, winds the likes of which had never been seen before; . . . [the] winds would dry up all the white people and all the Indians who followed the white man's ways, and they would blow away with the dust.   (25)

Silko's description of the dance the Paiute visionary Wovoka brought to the western nations emphasizes the connections between death and dust, life and water (absence/presence), and the dance the family participates in is set on the river. As they dance, they sing: "The black rock is broken and from it pours clear fresh water that runs in little streams everywhere" (29).[8] With their efforts the absence/presence is reversed and the scene is moistened by a wet snow. Before they can complete the dance cycle, however, the Army and Indian police intervene and destroy the dancers' camp (much as they did at Wounded Knee) in fear of the dance's power to unite the peoples their society has marginalized: the Natives and Mormons. The attack fragments the family, sending the sisters for safety to the river and then the gardens. Thus, the river provides safety and a promise for the future, but also the threat of discovery and capture, as does the garden. As sources of life, we are drawn to them and so are those who seek to prey upon life, so places of water are contact zones where people from diverse backgrounds interact, for good or ill.

From this initial event in the sisters' journeys forward, the narrative alternates between two main story lines: those of Sister Salt and Indigo, with the latter alternating at times between the points of view of Indigo, Hattie, and Edward, well-to-do easterners who become her custodians after Indigo escapes the federal boarding school in, appropriately, *Riverside*, California. In each storyline, however, events that transpire with water as a central actor provide the means of understanding Silko's expansive global perspective of the history of colonial eras and their extractive, exploitative mentalities.

For the most part, Sister Salt's story after she and Indigo are forcefully separated centers on the Colorado River, the water source that weaves throughout her attempts to survive and to find her family. First, she is sent to the reservation at Parker and forced to work in a laundry, where water is harnessed and altered for financial purposes. However, she and her Chemehuevi friends — the twin sisters — start their own business to rival the superintendent's laundry, and ultimately turn it to profit by locating it near a worker's camp on the river.

The workers have been brought to the river to dam it and to divert its water into a canal destined for Los Angeles. Much like the Central Arizona Project today, this turns a fundamental element of life into a commodity, an object to be controlled and utilized for financial gain and not revered as a sacred force that operates of its own volition and benefits those who understand that imperative. Capitalists do not and the results strike Sister Salt: "Now the river was unrecognizable—rechanneled and trapped into narrow muddy chambers outside its old bed. The poor cottonwood trees and willows were ripped out and plowed into mounds of debris, where their roots reached out plaintively like giant skeleton hands" (218). Indigo reiterates this vision when she returns late in the novel and sees the same changes, which she also equates with skeletons and death. The river—like the indigenous people who have lived near it and drawn life from its waters for eons—is now feeling the same demands and restrictions placed upon those people by the federal and local governments and their economies; reservoir and reservation derive from the same Latin roots.

However, from Sister Salt's point of view, the river offers potential of other kinds: for food, of course, and shelter, but also as a site beyond the restrictions of reservation and American society. Here, she and the twins take their men; here, she lives apart from the noise and dangers of the camp. Although she works for Candy—the man of mixed African-Native American descent who fathers her son—she inhabits the margins of the camp where he turns the capitalist economy to his profit and, he thinks, independence.

In essence, Candy runs a casino where he sells the beer they make, yet another alteration of water. The money he and his partner make, however, is in constant danger from local politicians and other thieves, so Candy buries their funds in the sand along the river. It is significant that he uses the riverbank to hide the material symbol of the capitalist ideology that is destroying the river, and that Candy's plan does not work. They lose their money to a Native woman who uses it to buy arms to fund a revolution against colonial forces in Mexico; however, during a long, nearly deadly trek through the desert in search of the thief, as in many traditions, Candy comes to a new awareness of life and economies. As he lay dying from thirst, he realizes that all his adult life has been spent in quest of money, that he has not fulfilled obligations to his ancestors, and that he "abandoned the little grandfather, his son, to chase after money. That's how he got himself into this predicament in the first place—so crazy over the money he did not carry enough water. Any human that weak might as well be dead" (446). The revelation saves him, though; a thundershower rejuvenates him, he is found, and he is taken to Tucson where, tellingly, he hires out to drive one of the wagons full of arms southward.[9] His revelation resonates with the understanding the Sand Lizard people—Sister Salt and her family—possess of water's signification. In the desert of this story, the trappings of "modern" society and its affluence are revealed for what they are: illusory and life threatening.

Sister Salt's sojourn near the river comes to an end when she and Indigo are reunited. This takes place on property the twins purchase from an elderly aunt. From this property they watch as the waters of the river back up behind the new dam, flooding the farms of the Christian Chemehuevi who persecute the twins and Sister Salt for their "wanton" ways.[10] On this farm, Indigo also plants some of the flowers she has brought home from her travels, so this section of the novel resonates with some of Silko's earlier work. Once again, water and the Mother Creator are intricately tied. For a condensed exploration in her fiction of the connections between ownership of land, the primacy of water, perceptions of beauty and morality, see her short story "Private Property." In *Gardens*, however, the beliefs and values exposed in the short story find expansive, transatlantic consideration, and this is accomplished by Indigo's journey back along the paths of colonial history.

Her journey begins with her capture and train ride to the school in Riverside. While the train trips she takes reflect a common mode of transportation in the era, they also represent the historical reality that the west was opened to mass immigration and exploitation by the railroad, in effect removing long and arduous journeys across the plains or by sea for people and products alike.[11] When she accompanies Hattie and her husband Edward on the train trip east, they retrace the movement of Manifest Destiny across the continent.[12] From Long Island, they follow that salt-water pathway back to roots in England and Italy. It is this journey and the connections Indigo provides that mark Silko's growing engagement with issues of global concern and her expansive understanding of historical forces that operate to determine current events.

The character Edward provides a compacted version of the colonial history and psychology she investigates. Also in the Jamesian tradition, he is a member of the leisure class described in the economic study Thorstein Veblen published in 1899. Descendant of the generations that provided the title "Robber Barons" to several prominent American families, Edward is a nineteenth century caricature: a well-to-do naturalist. This characterization is complicated by the ways his natural curiosity and interests are turned to capitalist enterprises, resulting in his gradual decline and death. He symbolizes the elemental colonial urge: to exploit the remote (and often "exotic") for personal gain. His expedition to the Pará River in the Amazonian rain forest is both a fitting example of his motivations and the turning point in Edward's "fortunes."

His trip's purpose is simple. He and his comrades are to travel to a remote site in the rain forest, collect several species of orchids, and sneak them out of the country, in effect profiting from colonial governments as they attempt to reserve a monopoly on the resources they have taken from indigenous people and lands. This irony is given further force by the ways Edward's plans are constantly thwarted, oftentimes in proximity, or through the intervention, of water. For instance, his spoils are claimed, on one trip, by the sea. His orchids also must be tended to avoid rot, the result of moisture different from that of the flower's place of origin. To underscore the diabolical and deadly nature of this exploitative psychology, Silko has Edward's comrades destroy a unique garden of orchids after they collect their "specimens," and thereby "cornering the market" for this one species. As the hillside burns, Edward nearly dies in the flames; he breaks a leg as he tries to return to the safety of the river and the canoes that they used to access this garden. Left for dead, he drinks from the river and has dreams and hallucinations. Ultimately he is rescued, and returns home, without his spoils, to face a lawsuit over the failed mission.[13] However, unlike Candy and his near-death experiences in the desert, Edward fails to learn from his experiences on the river. His quest does not provide a new pattern of understanding about water and the life with which it is intricately connected; he continues with his capitalist and colonial ideology, sinking further and further into the western mythology of easy riches and empire, and it kills him. That he dies relying upon a "new technology," on progress, to save him is both ironic and prophetic.

One should note also that the orchids are collected and sold for the purposes of hybridization to fulfill the fancies of the leisure class and its predilection to alter nature to suit its own purposes. The Masque of the Blue Garden (a veiled allusion to Poe's "The Masque of the Red Death"?) is one of the most damning illustrations of this propensity. It exemplifies Veblen's concept of "conspicuous consumption" very clearly. Edward's wealthy sister, Susan James (an allusion to Henry James?) has a tradition of an annual party that has as its centerpiece a garden, but one diametrically opposed to the gardens of Indigo's experience. Susan's is not dedicated to the life and waters it holds, but to an artificial construction of her individual psyche. Rather than nurture the indigenous, she uproots and remakes her garden, ad nauseam, by transplanting and transforming this one place in Oyster Bay time and time again to fit a "theme." At once a display of her wealth and the power it brings, it is also a sign of her class and its need to confine and control the world around them for their own sense of self. With Indigo as lens, Silko takes her readers behind this hubris and its illusions.

As she walks the gardens, Indigo finds the pools placed for effect, but also that they sustain life that operates beyond Susan's attention. She also finds that Susan is having an affair with her gardener; they make love in the seclusion of the gardens. And, when Indigo is once more captured by white men, she finds that beyond the manicured lawns and gardens of the Americans, the indigenous Other survives in the dunes and on the gardens of the sea, despite the fact that the Matinnecock Indians are invisible to the rich people who have taken and altered their lands. Here, on the far edge of the continent where English colonialism came ashore, where the offices of American economic power reside, and where the ruling elite—born of revolution against the colonial power of England—now directs the transformation of the U.S. into a modern colonial power, Indigo finds a kindred people who share many of her own values and who possess a resilience as a result.[14] It is a lesson she finds elsewhere on her journey, specifically in her interactions with two springs: one during their visit to Hattie's Aunt Bronwyn's home in Bath (and thus "The Wife of Bath"?) and the other in their stay with her friend Laura in Lucca.[15]

The landscape Indigo finds at Bronwyn's is in many ways the antithesis of her own home in the desert. She is "amazed at how damp and green the air smelled in England. Water, water everywhere, it seemed—in little ponds and lakes along the river" (235). Bronwyn's house is an old cloister that many locals consider to be too close to the river for safe human occupation. She, however, knows otherwise, and recognizes that this place has an inherent power. Her gardens, like those of the Sand Lizard people, have at their center an ancient spring. This placement of water is significant for an understanding of Bronwyn's character, for she is clearly tied to ancient belief systems with her reverence for rocks, water, and the non-human life that surrounds her, but also the mythic stories that describe the significance of each.

Like Indigo, Bronwyn inhabits the Industrial Age, but these two characters' values are most definitely at odds with those the era valorizes and this contention is revealed with the ways places of water are deployed in this section. Here, the Avon has long ago suffered the transformation the Colorado is undergoing: "the Avon's waters appeared almost sluggish, due no doubt to the construction of weirs, built since medieval times to control flooding" (236). The belief that one can and should control the natural forces of the world for one's use is pervasive and its roots are found on their visit to Europe. However, although popular belief holds that, once controlled, these natural forces reside only in ancient history, the narrative suggests otherwise. Flooding continues, and as Hattie learns in her night in Bronwyn's garden, primal energies are at work here despite the attempts of modern societies to objectify, contain and thus deny them.[16]

One would think that such abundance would diminish the importance of water in this place, but this is not the case, at least for the ancient cultures that once inhabited Bath. The excavation of the baths provides Silko's understanding of the primacy of water in these cultures and through it their ties to the indigenous cultures of the Americas, but also the ways colonization works to subvert indigenous beliefs.[17] The excavations expose the layers of human history at the springs and take Silko's readers to the urquelle, the origins of the baths and the fundamental reverence the indigenous Celtic culture has for water: "On gravel terraces of an ancient floodplain, hot springwater bubbled to the surface with medicinal and magical properties" (236). Much like the springs of the Sand Lizard people, this spring provided a focal point for belief and identity, so it is also the place where subsequent colonial forces directed their energies for the remapping of the physical and cosmological landscape. "The Romans, always wary of offending powerful local deities, prudently named their town Aquae Sulis. But the Romans could not permit Sulis [the Celtic deity] to rule supreme any longer, so they built a temple with a great pool over the springs, dedicated to Sulis and to Minerva as well" (236). And on top of the ruins of Roman colonization one finds the history of England written again and again as the spring's baths were turned to the use of, primarily, the elite of a series of societies. Unlike the Romans, though, subsequent Christian cultures — the Normans included — were not wary of Sulis; like the Romans, however, their churches and cathedrals were built on or in proximity to the ancient places of power, thus attempting to co-opt and supplant them.

This history is reflected in the gardens Indigo finds in Lucca as well. At once, their visit exposes both ancient and contemporary colonial movements. Laura's gardens hold their own ancient spring where statues of ancient deities are found in a grotto, hidden under the detritus of subsequent colonial invasions. These are signified by Laura's "Moorish fountain" (285), the previous owners who were part of Napoleon's occupation of Italy, and Laura's husband's activities in the failed Italian colonial efforts with the incursion into Abyssinia, to name a few. The colonial urge is an ancient one in this landscape, so Laura's interests in the ancient peoples echoes those of Bronwyn's and both characters attempt to exhume the primal, indigenous beliefs that are buried under the layers of colonial occupations. In this way, they become the new guardians of life, of the gardens.

With the spring in Laura's garden, Silko makes overt connections between indigenous beliefs in Europe and the Americas, and these once more tie the life-giving force of water to gender. This tie is brought forth with statuary at first; near the springs, a Medusa head is found. This Gorgon from Greek mythology provides the connection between the power of women and its connectivity to water, but also other life forms, such as snakes. Later in their tour of the garden, snakes and water are prominent and in the unique gladiolus garden—the seeds of which survive Indigo's trip home—we find Laura providing the lesson for the disoriented Edward and her readers: "'How odd this black garden is!' Edward whispered to Hattie. The sight of the breasts on the waterbird pitcher recalled the designs incised on the egg-shaped rock yesterday. . . . 'I assume black is symbolic of night and death,' Edward said; Laura broke into a smile. To the Old Europeans, black was the color of fertility and birth, the color of the Great Mother" (298). In Edward's utterance resides a philosophical orientation central to the colonial ideologies of his people. His valued binary white/black resonates with the construction of race to facilitate and validate the supplanting of indigenous beliefs, the subjugation of the people and their lands, not to mention the institution of slavery, and the Victorian suppression of sexuality goes hand-in-hand with the attempts to constrain and control nature, human or otherwise. In Laura's gardens the man/woman and the human/animal binaries are strategically resolved through the connection between life and life-giving water, between womankind and the generative power of nature: Mother Creator. This configuration is clearly formulated through the artistic productions of the past that speak of the reverence the "Old Europeans" had for the life that women and water produce. Each strand of connection resonates with the gardens and spring where the novel began.

The conclusion of the novel brings these strands together. During the sisters' absence, the gardens have been vandalized:[18] the apricot trees Grandmother Fleet planted have been hacked down; the old snake has been killed.[19] However, from the trunk of one tree, a green shoot springs, and Indigo watches as the old snake's "beautiful granddaughter" drinks from the spring (478–79).

There are other changes as well. The seeds Indigo brings grow into a colorful celebration of life. Despite the incursion of people who defile the spring, the gardens and the life they hold, Silko paints an image of resilience, of survivance. The two sisters' guests have paid off, in a reversal of the colonial movements of the past. Much as in "The Man to Send Rain Clouds," the indigenous characters select elements of the "other" to transplant, and to complement what they already possess. These include Indigo's seeds, of course, but also Sister's son, as well as the monkey and parrot Indigo picked up along her way. This is true of the other two springs and gardens as well: Hattie returns to live with Bronwyn and they will visit Laura, and in each of their gardens the plants indigenous to the Americas are tended and watered by women who have an affinity with a life that transcends and resists the deadly forces that would deny it. The three springs are connected to the same source: the "Mother Creator" who resides in a world of plentiful and clear waters, and who can be connected to through the springs she sends into this world.

NOTES

1. For an extensive look at this level to the story, see my article, "The Transformation."

2. See the first chapter of Robert M. Nelson's *Place and Vision*.

3. This includes the evil character, Trigg, who, like monsters in Laguna stories, drains his victims' blood and harvests their organs for the global trade in transplants.

4. I will discuss this further, later in the essay; in *Gardens* a very similar event takes place when the quintessential capitalist, Candy, nearly dies in the desert.

5. Quests are more often than not structured like the novel: a person leaves "home" and returns with something of value for the place to which she/he returns. Many times, Yellow Woman returns to the pueblo pregnant with the twin heroes, who will help the people survive.

6. A. M. Regier discusses the role of the Ghost Dance in the novel, as well as the ways hybridity operate. However, in "Revolutionary Enunciatory Spaces" the central figure in Wavoka's vision is referred to as "a" Messiah, while Silko refers to him as "the," and thus brings East and West together.

7. This recovery is most overtly expressed in the novel through Hattie's thesis: a study of ancient Christian texts that provide a window into the earliest days of Christianity.

8. The centrality of rocks to the novel is quite obvious. From the meteor rocks Edward covets, and Natives revere, to the rocks in England that travel to drink from the Avon River, they play a role similar to the water itself: to compare differing concepts of life. Silko has written about rocks in *Yellow Woman and a Beauty of the Spirit*.

9. Placed against Silko's other works, this inversion of the arms dealing of *Almanac of the Dead* provides yet one more example of her north-south reconfiguration of the history of Manifest Destiny.

10. Interestingly, at the end of the novel the Christians are forced by the rising water to build a rustic structure to replace the church the waters claim, in a way taking them back to the earliest days of the religion, a time Hattie studied for her thesis on Gnostic texts that had women as central to the belief system.

11. Also, the trains of the era operated on steam, so their paths were determined at times by the presence of water as fuel, of sorts.

12. While it is true that this east-west configuration does not accurately represent the history of the west and erases the influences of Spanish, Russian, English colonialism on a north-south axis, it is the popular movement pattern found in much of the literature of the U.S., a pattern Silko often problemtizes.

13. Silko's humor is subtle here: Edward is rescued by the monkey, Linnaeus. One assumes this is an allusion to Carolus (aka Carl) Linnaeus, the eighteenth century, Swedish naturalist who created the taxonomy Edward and his ilk use throughout the text, a classification system that has its roots in Latin.

14. After all, the war with Spain resulted in the U.S. acquiring former Spanish colonies, such as the Philippines and Cuba.

15. This character is a nod to our dear editor, no doubt.

16. The literary irony for the age Silko describes is that it produced Naturalism with its attempt to complicate the belief in humankind's mastery of the world.

17. This cross-Atlantic connection is strengthened with the plant life Indigo finds in Bronwyn's gardens: the indigenous North American species—corn, tomatoes, potatoes, and so on—that were brought to England from their colonies and thus transformed the lives of the colonizers.

18. This is an interesting term in the context of this discussion of indigenous/colonist histories.

19. Although I have not discussed the significance of the snake, it should be noted that Silko deploys snakes throughout her canon, and here, in this garden, the snake functions much as water to underscore the differences in values between indigenous and colonial societies. The snake in versions of the Garden of Eden story functions very differently than the old snake in the Gardens in the Dunes, and his death signifies the Christian interpretation of Genesis: to harm snakes in retaliation for humanity's fall from grace.

WORKS CITED

Nelson, Robert M. *Place and Vision: The Function of Landscape in Native American Fiction.* New York: Peter Lang Publishing, 1993.

Purdy, John. "The Transformation: Tayo's Genealogy in *Ceremony.*" *Leslie Marmon Silko's Ceremony: Casebooks on Contemporary Literature.* Ed. Allan Chavkin. New York: Oxford UP, 2001.

Regier, Ami M. "Revolutionary Enunciatory Spaces: Ghost Dancing, Transatlantic Travel, and Modernist Arson in *Gardens in the Dunes.*" *Modern Fiction Studies* 51.1 (Spring 2005): 134–58.

Revard, Carter. "Report to the Nation: Repossessing Europe." *Family Matters, Tribal Affairs.* Sun Tracks 36. Tucson: U of Arizona P, 1998.

Rosen, Kenneth. *The Man to Send Rain Clouds.* New York: Viking, 1974.

Silko, Leslie Marmon. *Almanac of the Dead.* New York: Simon and Schuster, 1991.

———. *Ceremony.* New York: Viking, 1977.

———. *Gardens in the Dunes.* New York: Simon and Schuster, 1999.

———. "Private Property." *Earth Power Coming: Short Fiction in Native American Literature.* Ed. Simon J. Ortiz. Tsaile, AZ: Navajo Community College P, 1983. 21–30.

———. *Running on the Edge of the Rainbow: Laguna Stories and Poems.* Larry Evers, Producer; Denny Carr, Director. New York: Norman Ross Publishing Inc., 1978.

———. *Sacred Water: Narratives and Pictures.* Tucson, AZ: Flood Plain P, 1993.

———. *Yellow Woman and a Beauty of the Spirit.* New York: Simon & Schuster, 1996.

Veblen, Thorstein. *The Theory of the Leisure Class: An Economic Study of Institutions.* New York: Macmillan, 1899.

BIOLOGICAL INVASION DISCOURSE AND LESLIE MARMON SILKO'S *GARDENS IN THE DUNES*

James Barilla

To experience the anxiety over exotic invaders, you don't have to pore over obscure scientific journals. Biological invasions are hot, as a recent full-page ad in the Sunday newspaper insert *USA Today* attests. The Nature Conservancy, once known for its appeals to save land from development through the purchase of easements, is now appealing for membership and donations to help fight the growing plague of invasive species. Interest in biological invasions has grown exponentially, not as a direct result of the events of September 11, but certainly in tandem with the growing concern over the permeation of our borders and the unease over the possibility that malign forces have taken up residence in the place we call home.[1] The scientific phenomenon has become a recognizable cultural phenomenon, even if biological invasions were from the start a projection of cultural disquiet. In the midst of anxiety over globalization and genetic engineering, the invasion phenomenon has spawned its own discourse, an interdisciplinary corpus of definitions, debate and emotions, in which biological invasions figure as an ecological symptom of cultural disease.

What is an invasive species? The definition remains a source of contention, with a plethora of competing definitions suggesting the multidisciplinary nature of the discourse and the pervasiveness of concern. However, most attempts manifest the same fear of monoculture, of the power to "take over," of the innocuous transformed into the monstrous and threatening. Ecologists tend to define any species that spreads outside its natural range as invasive, but this term by itself does not capture the extent of the problem.[2] Other definitions, like that provided by the Convention on Biological Diversity or the Global Invasive Species Programme, refer to alien or non-native species, and also require that the intruder cause measurable harm. The definition offered by the Invasive Species Specialist Group includes two additional characteristics, that the species is transported by humans, and that it overcomes an otherwise intact native ecosystem. The ecologist Mark Williamson defines it as an event rather than a state of being or identity: "Biological invasion happens when an organism, any sort of organism, arrives somewhere beyond its previous range" (3). Ultimately, biological invasion discourse is not strictly focused on the act of invading, nor is it fixed upon the characteristics of the invader, or even the event itself. All of these are important, but paramount is the concern over the disruption of order and stability and the repercussions this might bring. The definitions share a sense that a pre-existing state of order has been violated, that an agent from an external location has come into a place where it does not belong.

Leslie Marmon Silko's *Gardens in the Dunes* shares this anxiety over the disruption of order brought about by globalization. Silko's narrative, however, considers contemporary concerns over invasion within the context of the (European) colonization of the Americas. The novel exoticizes the human invaders who are taking over the native landscape and extinguishing indigenous cultures. Unlike most bioinvasion narratives, however, Silko does not pathologize movement as a harbinger of exploitation: her central figure, a young Sand Lizard girl, travels the globe, collecting seeds and experiences. Yet Silko is careful to suggest that this freedom of movement and cultural cross-pollination can only occur when it does not violate a global order that is based on indigenous territorial integrity rather than colonial relationships. In such a narrative, reconfiguring the terms of glocalized trade and consumption becomes the paramount concern rather than erecting barriers to movement. While one might argue that species are not like cultural artifacts, it is Silko's clear intention to blur those distinctions by imbuing the artifact with spiritual life, and by making artifacts and species subject to the same consumption pressures. Ultimately, the novel connects biological diversity to cultural diversity as dynamic and mutually dependent features of the same ecosystem, but the management and preservation of diversity becomes an expression of local sovereignty instead of colonial appropriation of the local as a fetishized consumer item.

Globalization stimulates broad cultural anxiety over the loss of unique identity markers that might result in a monoculture, such that bio-invasive discourse might be viewed within a long tradition of vanishing natives, disappearing cultural and natural diversity, and attempts at preservation and rescue. Yvonne Baskin, for example, argues that the "same forces that are 'McDonaldizing' the world's diverse cultures are also driving us toward an era of homogenized, weedy, and uniformly impoverished plant and animal communities" (6). In this worldview, uniqueness is what separates one culture or species from another. Species exist as discrete units in a categorical system whose members are always in a certain state of flux, but in which change occurs at a glacial pace. That two congener species, like coyotes and wolves, can produce fertile offspring suggests an incomplete degree of speciation within the same taxonomic category—they have not lived in isolation long enough to completely establish their separate, unique identities. The narrative of speciation occurs, then, within an all-encompassing continuum of uniqueness, which in turn creates a sense of temporal security and global diversity.

Uniqueness of this kind comes from isolation, from the state of solitude and order created by impermeable boundaries. It is hardly surprising, then, that the anxiety over invasive species reflects a greater fear of the loss of this isolation-based order that in biological invasion discourse is known as beta diversity (or gamma diversity at larger comparative scales). As Jason and Roy Van Driesche write, "the loss of isolation is one of the major factors disrupting native communities worldwide" (34).[3] This linkage of isolation and uniqueness creates anxiety because it is always threatened by disruption. Ironically, although the sense of uniqueness relies upon isolation for its existence, it also stimulates the desire to consume that leads to the loss of isolation through the gathering, reproduction and widespread distribution of the unique resource.[4] If you don't have the authentic object or species already, the opportunity exists for you to desire it, and to pay someone to provide it. Alpha diversity, or an increase in the number of species in a particular local area, increases as a result, at least in the short term.[5] The isolated species, like a unique cultural object, possesses a novelty value based on its beta diversity characteristics that gives it currency in the global marketplace. So long as it remains localized and rare, it serves in the market as an emblem of what must be protected from the market's appetite, while at the same time whetting that appetite. The endangered bird's innocent face seems to be outside the commodity system, when actually as an image, if not a material item, it is already a part of it.

The invasive species, on the other hand, reveals the stain of human tampering from the outset of its narrative, since invaders almost always travel with human cohorts. Once introduced, they proliferate without human assistance or control, and are then guilty of forcing human intervention in the landscape. In biological invasion discourse, they are pathological consumers of novelty, overabundant competitors not just with other species for resources but also with human desires to consume the novelty value of the unique species they threaten. Ironically, although they are recognized as new to the landscape, they are accorded no novelty value.

Gardens explores this contemporary anxiety in the context of prior period of cultural flux, the conquest and colonization of indigenous cultures and biota that occurred at the end of the Victorian era. Edward, a professional collector, epitomizes a certain exploitive form of globalization: he hunts for unhybridized, rare local plants so that he can trade on their uniqueness and ultimately render them ubiquitous. Rather than condemn the collecting impulse entirely, however, Silko proposes that the value of collecting, and appropriation more generally, depends upon the status of the trader. Edward's collecting impulse runs parallel to the equally avid collecting of his ward, the Sand Lizard girl Indigo. Yet because he attempts to claim the original material, to name a new species after himself instead of acknowledging the plant's origins elsewhere and respecting its biological sovereignty, his collecting becomes piracy, the theft of natural and cultural capital, and the transfer of indigenous knowledge and material into a monetary system of exchange at unfair rates. "Was it possible to see the artifacts that were for sale?" Edward inquires almost continuously (258), even as he encounters a series of people who value the objects for their transcendent spirituality and their in situ value. Citron and rubber are just two examples Silko provides of the movement of natural capital that does not result in greater benefit for both parties in the exchange.[6] Posing as an artist, secreting lemon tree cuttings among his paintbrushes as a ruse, Edward's aim is to wrest the local product from local control. Citron will no longer be a Corsican resource-it will grow everywhere. Yet these are cuttings, not seeds, a key distinction when it comes to the interests of the plant itself. Seeds are symbols of biological sovereignty and wildness; cuttings represent the transformation of the plant into commodity. Indigo collects seeds on her travels, but Edward is interested in cuttings.

In the face of Edward's all encompassing desire, Indigo herself trembles on the verge of becoming a rare collector's item, since Edward is "intrigued with the notion that the child might be the last remnant of a tribe now extinct, perhaps a tribe never before studied by anthropologists" (113). Edward's adventures in exploitation illustrate the two dangers of injustice in trade: first, the novelty value of the species increases as it becomes more rare, a fact that Edward's orchid collecting competitors exploit by scorching the Amazonian ravine that is the only known source of a rare orchid after they have gotten their own specimens for sale. Secondly, this rarity inspires the desire to propagate copies and fakes, to wrest the authentic object/species out of its local situation and make something similar available everywhere, as Edward attempts to do by smuggling bergamot cuttings out of Corsica. As often happens, the localized species loses genetic diversity through the extermination of the wild population that makes it a rare, human-dependent commodity.[7] The human dependent version may spread through propagation across the globe, but it is no longer the unique, localized and genetically diverse species that made it desirable in the first place.

While critics like Baskin thus contend that "our desire for novelty has become a homogenizing force" (17), the power of such a desire cannot be easily dismissed, since it may also underpin our actions to save rare endemics from obliteration. How else to rationalize the disproportionate resources devoted to saving rare bird species in places like Hawaii, except to note that rarity intensifies the desire to preserve? Consumption is an ambivalent force, and as such it produces a number of ironies. The fact that we crave the experience of novelty may in fact inspire restoration narratives that recuperate consumption into a celebration of diversity and dynamism. As we see in *Gardens*, novelty, if we define it as something new or different that generates an experience of pleasurable consumption, can actually serve as a focal point for reconciling two very different visions of what newness means and how it should be experienced.

The chief proponent of novelty as a beneficent force was the philosopher and theologian Alfred North Whitehead, who viewed novelty as the highest source of inspiration. By novelty, Whitehead meant the forces of creativity and inspiration and intensity of feeling that bring something new into being, as opposed to the systematic, habitual or routine ways of existing. The craving for the experience of novelty, he believed, mirrors that of the divine—it is the way that the universe develops. Such a vision hardly seems destined to inspire a community-based, ritualized practice, since it seems more like an invitation to wanton consumption and individual desire fulfillment. Yet Whitehead's vision is important to biological invasion discourse, and to Silko's desert garden, in its emphasis on the experience of things instead of the things themselves, its focus on process instead of stasis, and its attempt to reconcile the desire for newness with the equally powerful desire for stability. As Whitehead contends, "The world is thus faced by the paradox that, at least in its higher actualities, it craves for novelty and yet is haunted by terror at the loss of the past, with its familiarities and its loved ones" (516).

The postmodern view of novelty value is epitomized by Salman Rushdie's "hotchpotch, a bit of this and a bit of that," with its emphasis on blurred boundaries, hybridity and the jarring experience of the familiar face in the unexpected context. Preservation advocates, on the other hand, prefer novelty as the form of uniqueness derived through isolation. This preservationist view of novelty both reflects and is a reaction against the narrative of modernity, in which progress serves to uncover the unique so that it can be erased or built upon with something new.[8] Both are valid, for novelty represents a spectrum of experiences that range from the unique to the unexpected. What matters is not entirely the tangible object itself, but the experience of it, or the narratives constructed around it.[9] The garden in the dunes is a metaphorically rich space partly because of its narrative status as a biological and cultural oasis, a refuge for the rare that produces novelty as a narrative experience that can be consumed without visiting the physical location. Yet to enter this garden narrative is to experience novelty at its most intense in both the postmodern and the preservationist sense, since the garden is both remote from murderous Euramerican settlers, and an incorporation of their ideas and genes. Newness has invaded the oasis. The desire for novelty demands that the process of maintaining native species and controlling invasives offer opportunities for newness and creativity to enter while also preserving a sense of the past, and it is this ambivalent, postmodern preservationist impulse that shapes the narrative of the garden space.

Change in preservationist narratives usually occurs as a by-product of consumption-induced trade, where it often borders on vice. At the root of every vision of environmental apocalypse, it seems, is not only wanton violence, but gluttonous consumption. Yet if we consider the way consumption often figures in such restoration narratives as *Gardens*, what we find is not a refutation of novelty value so much as a reassessment of the terms by which novelty is consumed. Resistance to colonial appropriation lies in a refusal to participate in exploitive trade. Silko's indigenous merchants, for example, refuse to sell novelties they know will be expropriated and exploited. Much to Edward's confusion and dismay, for example, a "black Maya" recognizes him for the cultural predator he is and refuses to sell him the meteorites he desires. The refusal does not diminish the pressure to participate, however; in fact, it increases the novelty value of the object and thus the desire to collect it. Edward's deathbed dream finds him lying in thrall in the Maya's lap, unable to dispel the vision of the meteorite he couldn't buy and the woman who resisted his advances (429). Stimulating desire in the hegemonic consciousness does not lead to change; Edward dies as unrepentant a bio-pirate as he was in life, filled with desire, not remorse.

The shape of this postmodern preservation narrative is still being forged in the scientific discourse. One current focal point, for example, is the normalization of terms for the processes and actors involved in the narrative of invasion. Richardson et al attempt to categorize the process by suggesting that naturalization "starts when abiotic and biotic barriers to survival are surmounted and when various barriers to regular reproduction are overcome," whereas invasion demands that the introduced species actually spread to form other colonies (97). The ultimate invasive species, Richardson et al suggests, one capable of changing "the character, condition, form, or nature of ecosystems over substantial areas" should be called a "transformer," to distinguish it from less robust invaders (93).

These are the narrative parameters for biological agents, but what Silko offers is the corollary narrative of cultural invasion, the narrative of the human colonization that led to the introduction of the starling and the roof rat in the

Americas. Narrating that portion of the invasion story in which humans are the ultimate transformer species, reveals some disturbing extensions of current thinking on invasive species.

Silko's postmodern vision of localized space suggests a mosaic of habitats with varying degrees of border permeability, a vision of a postcolonial world order that challenges the rhetoric of biological invasions by pathologizing colonization rather than consumption as the underlying, human-inspired threat to indigenous existence. The biological critique of migration is not, one might argue, a reaction against novelty *per se*, but to novelty outside of certain parameters that threatens to create monotony instead of diversity. The biological invader is a wild form of novelty—it has escaped the boundaries of expected behavior and location. Simberloff has suggested that it is the very newness of the invasive species that creates the problem for endemics—the invader exploits a niche in the new system that was not previously occupied and expands from there. Silko's vision of a non-invasive cultural hybridity reflects a similar concern for the invasive potential of unrestricted novelty, since cultural exchange in the novel only takes place within the context of a fixed topographic identity. The topographically and climactically restricted boundaries of the garden in the dunes define the parameters in which cross-cultural experimentation can occur without the threat of cultural loss.[10] The ancestral dynamics of the place offers the girls a sense of sovereignty that in turn confers the power to borrow and weave without the risk of being appropriated and subsumed.

This liberating connection to an ancestral place, however, is unavailable to those who are outside their proper territory and seeking to become native to new places, a position that conflicts with the vision of native identity offered by American restoration advocates like Wes Jackson. Jackson, who has attempted to revitalize prairie communities by developing new agricultural strategies that take advantage of local, wild plants, advises would-be natives "to build cultural fortresses to protect our emerging nativeness" that are "strong enough to hold at bay the powers of consumerism" (101). "Homecomers," he argues, are searching for a place "to dig in and begin the long search and experiment to become native," rather than remaining homeless, or returning to some ancestral home. The global order of *The Garden in the Dunes*, by contrast, rejects the notion that indigeneity can be created: Silko does not incarcerate the native in a single space, because there is no need to develop a sense of native identity—the girls' Sand Lizard identity is inherent, and their fortress, the garden, already exists. Instead, Silko's Sand Lizards harness the power of consumerism to energize experiments in syncretic identity and cross-cultural trade in novelty. Rather than building walls, they cross barriers that already exist.

The irony of Silko's vision is that it accepts the traditional biological naturalisms of place while shifting the focus to the validity of human cultures moving permanently out of their appropriate geographic ranges. It applies biological naturalisms to human migration: the transformers cannot become homecomers in the American West. Just as Indigo and Sister Salt return to the touchstone of their Sand Lizard garden, their spiritual and cultural home, so Euramericans can assuage their feelings of anomie with a return to their European homeland where "the damp cool air" and "abundant shade" have resulted in "light pink skin, light blue eyes, and light brown, thin hair" (234). The appropriate place for Aldo Leopold's ecological restoration and recovery efforts, Silko suggests, is in Europe, not the Sand Counties of Wisconsin. Aunt Bronwyn is Silko's vision of a Leopoldian figure at home; she has returned from America to the Celtic and Roman center of Bath, set about restoring a derelict Norman estate, and organized local resistance against the destruction of spiritually important stones and artifacts. Her resistance is both ecological and spiritual—as a homecomer, she has "gone native" (254), and fights against the housing development that results in "ancient oaks preserved since the times of Celtic kings, only to be cut down now as earthmoving teams carved wide scars in the bellies of the hills overlooking the river" (237). Locating a homeland for the erstwhile colonizer allows the topographically limited hybridity of the garden in the dunes to become a universally applicable means of global organization. Like Indigo, Aunt Bronwyn is a seed collector-she has plants in her garden from all over the world. In her proper geographic place, Silko implies, Bronwyn can safely collect without colonizing other people's land, something she could not do in America.

The American return journey, then, is back to the originary homeland of Europe, and restoring the ecological community in the Midwest, or even joining the Sand Lizards in the garden in the dunes, cannot complete it. Hattie, Indigo's fellow traveler, cannot join the Sand Lizard family, despite her longing to do so, because the source of her spiritual visions is across the ocean. Her attempts to exist on the borders of the garden community lead only to personal disaster as she is beaten, raped and ostracized by members of the white community. Her final act in the American West, before she returns to Europe, is to burn down the town of Needles, an act of cathartic destruction akin to erasing the traces of Euramerican presence. She finds the solace of home with Bronwyn, a place from which she can communicate with Indigo via the mail, and possibly even visit with her in the garden in the dunes, without abetting the unresolved offense of lost sovereignty. Thus are the connections between genetics and territory that underlie bioinvasion discourse, the otherwise unspoken part of the invasion narrative, exposed.

Mark Sagoff has portrayed biological invasion rhetoric as rife with xenophobic references, and Silko's novel would seem liable to the same critique, unless one notes the frequent centerpiece of Sagoff's argument that most of "us" are not native to the continent and therefore don't have the right to critique the movement of other species without critiquing our own presence.[11] Silko's novel provides a native human perspective on invasion and colonization that intensifies this irony while also providing alternative forms of movement and exchange between species and cultures. The novel defines the terms of cultural and biological glocalization with less concern for maintaining an isolation-based beta (or gamma) diversity than augmenting and maintaining alpha diversity through trade based on local sovereignty.

Setting the novel during a moment of colonial expansionism and high modernity does not diminish Silko's clearly postmodern ambitions for this space. The sand garden is as postmodern a space as its urban, European counterparts, even as it exists simultaneously within pre-modern and modern narratives.[12] Novelty, this narrative suggests, can come from an encounter with native plants as easily as with biological invaders. What could be construed as an invasion of a pure native space, then, becomes a celebration of a non-invasive hybridity, of the pre-modern and modern as fibers in the same postmodern fabric. Through mutually respectful trade, the foreign element is woven into the local tapestry, making it brighter and more useful by comparison with the old and increasing alpha diversity. Sand Lizards are collectors and traders, willing to integrate any possibility into their culture:

> Grandma Fleet always advised the girls to collect as many new seeds as they could carry home. The more strange and unknown the plant, the more interested Grandma Fleet was; she loved to collect and trade seeds. Others did not grow a plant unless it was food or medicine, but Sand Lizards planted seeds to see what would come; Sand Lizards ate nearly everything anyway, and Grandma said they never found a plant they couldn't use for some purpose. (85)

The girls' grandmother is a master of appropriation, turning the trash of colonialism into the sustenance of life outside it. Her living memorial, in fact, is the apricot trees whose seeds she has gleaned from the trash mounds of Needles, which grow over her grave (24). Her practice inspires Indigo's own passion for collecting horticultural oddities from all over the world and carrying them back to the garden. Like Grandma Fleet, however, Indigo never steals seeds—she collects those that nobody wants, or receives them as gifts. Collecting seeds, then, can be a form of cultural interaction as much as appropriation, a trading of knowledge and capital, as in the instance when Grandma Fleet gathers a bag of roots and seeds to bring to her Mormon friend in gratitude for the food and information the woman has given her (40).

Yet the seeds the Sand Lizards carry and plant are, in the discourse of biological invasions, often weeds whose wildness comes from the refusal to be native only within certain territorial parameters. Their spread causes a loss of beta diversity, even if they help sustain the localized culture.

On the most literal level, Indigo's collecting would render her an ecological pariah — she introduces exotic species into a niche previously inhabited only by "sand food," a cohort of species she recognizes as unable to reproduce elsewhere: "Sand food could never grow in England or New York or even Parker. Sand food needed sandstone cliff sand and just the right amount of winter snow, not rain, to grow just under the surface of the sand" (246). The hybrid gladioli flourish in the sand garden, as they do in Parker, along with the apricot trees and the other nourishing crops from other regions. That these exotic species might crowd out the sand food never occurs to Indigo, and it never appears in the teachings of Grandma Fleet. Gladioli never become the ecological disaster of cheat grass or tree snakes in Silko's narrative, perhaps because the forces of native appropriation and assimilation are too powerful. Gladioli, like squash and beans, become native plants through indigenous human tending and management. Few moments could be more jarring for the committed ecological restorationist, however, than the vision of rows of gladioli growing in a rare desert garden, introduced by an indigenous girl who extols their beauty and the fact that they taste good, too.

NOTES

1. Cf. Robert Devine and Heather Millar.

2. See Rejmanek et al.

3. It is primarily the exoticism of invasives in the landscape, their being "out of place," as the provocative title of Van Driesche's work describes it, or "out of bounds," as another recent title suggests, which makes their presence a threat. Cf. Van Driesche and Chris Bright. Whether the argument that bio invaders are disrupting native human communities is in fact universally valid is a different question-the Van Driesche's highlight the invasive pig problem on Hawaii, where hunting the invasive animals has developed into a popular cultural practice among native Hawaiians.

4. James Clifford describes the paradox of the authentic novelty: the desire for a refuge from change serves as the motivation for acquiring collections of authentic objects.

5. For a discussion of alpha, beta and gamma diversity, see R. H. Whittaker.

6. Michael Pollan makes a similar point in *The Botany of Desire*: the apple benefits greatly from human exploitation of it, so long as trade occurs in the seeds that spread a broad range of its genetic

material around the globe. With the arrival of regimented monoculture and the genetic uniformity achieved through cuttings, however, benefits to the species disappear.

7. The point of origin of a species often represents the locus of greatest genetic diversity. The apple, for example, displays tremendous diversity in the Eastern European forests from which it was originally domesticated. Cf. Gary Paul Nabhan and Michael Pollan.

8. Cf. Arran Gare.

9. This is not so different from the argument Silko makes in "Landscape, History and the Pueblo Imagination," in which certain geographic features take on significance through narratives constructed around them.

10. Unlike Gloria Anzaldua, who is careful not to respond in kind to those who call *tejanos* invaders in *Borderlands*.

11. Sagoff's characterization of bioinvasion rhetoric, much of which harkens back to Charles Elton's 1958 work, has met with controversy in biological circles, but it has also led to efforts to standardize terms and avoid pejorative phrases.

12. See Frederic Jameson's description of the postmodern condition in "Third World Literature in the Era of Multinational Capitalism."

WORKS CITED

Anzaldua, Gloria. *Borderlands/La Frontera: The New Mestiza*. San Francisco: Aunt Lute, 1999.

Baskin, Yvonne. *A Plague of Rats and Rubbervines: The Growing Threat of Species Invasions*. Washington: Island P, 2002.

Bright, Chris. *Life Out of Bounds: Bioinvasion in a Borderless World*. New York: Norton, 1998.

Clifford, James. *The Predicament of Culture: Twentieth Century Ethnography, Literature and Art*. Cambridge: Harvard UP, 1988.

Convention on Biological Diversity. 10 Jan. 2006 <http://www.biodiv.org/default.shtm>.

Devine, Robert. *Alien Invasion: America's Battle With Non-Native Animals and Plants*. Washington: Natl. Geographic Soc., 1998.

Drake, James A., Harold A. Mooney, and Francesco Di Castri. *Biological Invasions: A Global Perspective*. New York: Wiley and Sons, 1988.

Elton, Charles. *The Ecology of Invasions by Animals and Plants*. Chicago: U of Chicago P, 2000.

Gare, Arran. *Postmodernism and the Environmental Crisis*. London: Routledge, 2001.

Global Invasive Species Programme. 12 Feb. 2006 <http://www.gisp.org/>.

Invasive Species Specialist Group. 20 Dec. 2006 <http://www.issp.org/homepage.html>.

Jackson, Wes. "Matfield Green." *Rooted in the Land: Essays on Community and Place*. Ed. William Vitek and Wes Jackson. New Haven: Yale UP, 1996. 95–103.

Jameson, Frederic. "Third World Literature in the Era of Multinational Capitalism." *Social Text* 15 (1986): 65–87.

Leopold, Aldo. *A Sand County Almanac, and Sketches Here and There*. New York: Oxford UP, 1987.

Millar, Heather. "When Aliens Attack." *Sierra* (July/August 2004): 31–63.

Nabhan, Gary P. *Enduring Seeds: Native American Agriculture and Wild Plant Conservation*. Washington: North Point P, 1989.

Pollan, Michael. *The Botany of Desire: A Plant's-Eye View of the World*. New York: Random, 2001.

Remanjek, Marcel et al. "Ecology of Invasive Plants: State of the Art." *Invasive Alien Species: Searching for Solutions*. Ed. H. A. Mooney et al. Washington: Island P, 2002.

Richardson, David M., Petr Pysek, Marcel Rejmanek, Michael G. Barbour, F. Dane Pannetta, and Carol J. West. "Naturalization and Invasion of Alien Plants: Concepts and Definitions." *Diversity and Distributions* 6 (2000): 93–107.

Rushdie, Salman. *Imaginary Homelands: Essays and Criticism, 1981–1991*. New York: Penguin, 1992.

Sagoff, Mark. "Why Exotic Species Are Not As Bad As We Fear." *Chronicle of Higher Education* 23 June 2000: B7.

Silko, Leslie Marmon. *Gardens in the Dunes*. New York: Simon and Schuster, 1999.

———. "Landscape, History and the Pueblo Imagination." *The Ecocriticism Reader: Landmarks in Literary Ecology*. Ed. Cheryl Glotfelty and Harold Fromm. Athens: U of Georgia P, 1996. 264–76.

Simberloff, Daniel, ed. *Strangers in Paradise: Impact and Management of Nonindigenous Species in Florida*. Washington: Island P, 1997.

Van Driesche, Jason, and Roy Van Driesche. *Nature Out of Place: Biological Invasions in the Global Age*. Washington: Island P, 2000.

Williamson, Mark. *Biological Invasions*. London: Chapman, 1996.

Whitehead, Alfred North. *Process and Reality: Gifford Lectures Delivered in the University of Edinburgh During the Session 1927–28*. New York: Free P, 1979.

Whittaker, Robert H. "Evolution and Measurement of Species Diversity." *Taxon* 21 (1972): 213–51.

WALKING IN BALANCE: THE EUROPEAN-BASED SPIRITUAL JOURNEY IN LESLIE MARMON SILKO'S *GARDENS IN THE DUNES*

Annette Van Dyke

In an interview, Leslie Marmon Silko acknowledges that what all three of her novels have in common is that they are about "a kind of trying to find a way to deal with the . . . grief of being human beings in a world like this." They are "about transformation and transcendence, each one of them, in some way" (Perkins 124). About *Gardens in the Dunes* she says, "I was writing for the seekers without knowing it" (Arnold 184). She explains that her work is inclusive: "[I]t's not valid to use race or skin color. . . . [W]hat matters is how you feel and how you are and how you see things, and not how you are on the outside" (Arnold 188).

In *Ceremony*, Silko delineated a curing ceremony for her readers and for herself through her character, Tayo, but especially for her Native American readers. In *Gardens*, she delineates a Euro-American spiritual journey through her character, Hattie, to give her Euro-American readers a spiritual model, firmly illustrating her belief that what matters is "people of like hearts and minds" (Silko qtd. in Arnold 188). As she did in *Ceremony*, Silko's story attempts to counter the Euro-American view that elevates one part of creation above others: men over women, humans over plants, animals, and earth; and mind/spirit over the physical in order to bring her character back to balance. In *Gardens*, Silko shows on a personal level rather than at the global level of *Almanac of the Dead*, that the Native American perspective of the interconnectedness of all things without hierarchy must be constantly maintained in order for humans to continue.[1] In *Gardens*, through her character, Hattie, Silko shows "another way to see things and possible ways to connect up, in a spiritual way, to withstand" (Arnold 183)—a way to balance Euro-American ideas with Native American ideas.

Like Tayo's, Hattie's story is a journey to claim an identity and a home.[2] Like Tayo, she is an outcast, "the heretic of Oyster Bay" (*Gardens* 79). By making her character an outcast, Silko gives her the potential to belong to the category of "people of like hearts and minds" (Arnold 188). As a woman of the Victorian era, Hattie is an intellectual rebel. Schooled at home by her father she is urged to go "beyond the narrow interests of current feminists . . . and look to the greater philosophical questions about free love and God" (95). She attends

Vassar and then Harvard Divinity School where she attempts to write a thesis on the "female spiritual principle in the early church" (102). Not only is her thesis rejected, but her moral character is called into question when her classmate, a Mr. Hyslop, attempts to assault her, assuming that a free-thinking woman would endorse free love. Although Hattie becomes ill after these events and is driven to marry because of the personal support she feels from her husband Edward, Silko has not made her a bookish, shrinking violet. We learn that she had a pony that she rode alone as a child, she did not want marriage or children and wanted to travel.

After setting up the character Hattie as an unusual Euro-American woman of her time, Silko next sends her on a journey to recover her Celtic tribal roots. In order to balance Euro-American ideas and Native American ideas, Silko sees it as important to be able to get back to pre-Christian perspectives and believes these are still available to Euro-American seekers from their own heritages: "Europe is not completely Christianized. . . . There is a pagan heart there, and the old spirits are right there" (Arnold 166). To further aid Hattie in this task, Silko gives her a Native American guide, Indigo, the girl from the fictional Sand Lizard People. Indigo allows Hattie to begin not only to see the world with the fresh eyes of a child, but also with a Native American perspective while bringing in the important concept of Hattie's responsibility to others.

As she gathers seeds and bulbs from the gardens of England and Italy, Indigo becomes Silko's example of how "to eclectically take things that have meaning from place to place and somehow bring it and include it, incorporate it and bring it back to our place so that there's this ongoing exchange" (Perkins 118). This is an important message about how culture grows and changes and even about constructing and reconstructing one's worldview. Another example of this is Aunt Bronwyn's cloister gardens that appear in the center of the novel. The gardens are divided into quadrants: north for indigenous English plants; east for plants introduced by Romans and Normans; and south and west, plants from the Americas, Africa and Asia. This garden contrasts with the gardens which Hattie's sister-in-law grew in Oyster Bay which are examples of excess and extravagance: lilies that "required special care in the winter in the glass house" (163) and full-grown sixty-foot trees which are planted just for a party.

As foil to Indigo and as an example of a Euro-American who refuses to change, Silko uses Hattie's husband, Edward, the botanist. While Indigo and Aunt Bronwyn are examples of a respectful cultural exchange, Edward collects plants to classify them and to sell them, an attitude that illustrates his belief in the hierarchy of men over the animate and inanimate and a disrespectful attitude toward plants and animals. Throughout the novel, he is given many opportunities to change, but he refuses to do so. This is the reason that Hattie eventually leaves him.

However open to new ideas Hattie might be, she does not readily accept the view of her ancestors and of Native Americans that everything has a spirit and is sacred. Hattie reconnects to her Celtic spiritual heritage through her Aunt Bronwyn, who although, born in America, has settled in Bath near the grave of her English grandfather, part of a group who revered stones. The dream that Hattie has back in Oyster Bay that her Aunt Bronwyn was urging her to slide herself down the length of a flat altar stone, but her dress catches and rips seems to foretell the difficulties she will face—a needed shedding of outward trappings of a Victorian woman in order to proceed.

During her visit to Bath, Hattie remembers the lush landscape she has not seen since she was a child. She finds the altar stone of sun and moon deities that appeared in her dream. In what seems to be the beginning of a healing ceremony, she has a vision of light in Aunt Bronwyn's garden and hears knocking: "It was as if starlight and moonlight converged over her as a warm current of air enveloped her; for an instant Hattie felt such joy she wept" (250). Later, thinking of the light, "[w]ords from her thesis notes cascaded before her mind's eye, then suddenly scattered as if . . . the words were dry leaves blowing away in the wind: poor judgment, bad timing, late marriage, premature marriage, dread of childbirth, sexual dysfunction" (251). The light scatters her worries and turns her search inward away from the prescriptions of her Victorian culture—allows her to think about new ideas unmediated by institutional structures such as the Academy or the Church and opens her up further to the mystical.[3]

The next phase of Hattie's journey does not come easily. While Aunt Bronwyn and Indigo have an instant rapport and share commonly-themed stories, Hattie resists Aunt Bronwyn's stories that stone, trees, and plants have souls and could take retribution for harm done to them. Everything was cyclically connected; people were food for plants. Aunt Bronwyn has an affinity for white cattle. About this Silko says, "As hard as Christianity tried . . . to break that connection between the Europeans . . . the earth, . . . the plants and animals . . . that connection won't break completely. . . . I wanted to acknowledge it a little" (Arnold 167).

Another way to shift the perspective in which Hattie is raised is to acknowledge the power and sacredness of the feminine. *Gardens* abounds with Goddess symbols that connect with the Laguna belief in the "creative and life-restoring power" (Allen 48) of the feminine earth spirit or Thought Woman. The healing baths have altars dedicated to goddesses. "The eyes of the original Mother, the Mother of God, the Mother of Jesus" (267) are carved into the standing stones; "carved and ceramic figures of toads" are seen "as incarnations of the primordial Mother" (243). Old Europeans see a "link . . . between raindrops and drops of breast milk" (303). When Hattie and Indigo visit Laura's gardens (another unconventional academic) in Italy, they view many sculptures of the Goddess in different forms: as snake, as bird, as bear. They discover that the black gladiolus gardens were meant to recall "the color of fertility and birth, the color of the Great Mother" (298). When Hattie's husband, Edward, tried to protect Indigo from seeing some of the sculptures because "the child was from a culture of snake worshipers and there was no sense in confusing her with the impression the old Europeans were no better than Red Indians or black Africans who prayed to snakes" (306), that is exactly Silko's point. These cultures were very similar. However, Hattie begins to open up to the idea that what she has been taught had an earlier meaning that was corrupted: She thinks of the "statues of the Blessed Virgin standing on a snake," noting that she was taught that "Mary was killing the snake," but if the statue "was based on a figure from an earlier time," perhaps not (306).

The viewing of the vision on the whitewashed wall by Hattie and Indigo is an important part of the book. Hattie sees the luminous glow she had witnessed in the English garden on the wall in Corsica and is somewhat restored to a pagan or pre-Christian view of the world. She now believes in miracles—in magic. Hattie tries to offer this insight to Edward, but he "wisecracked about 'religious hysteria'" (322) and only has thoughts about machines that could be used for mining and destroying the earth. Indigo's search for the Messiah across Europe and the Americas and her acceptance that what she sees on the wall are the same spirits for which she has been searching reinforces the idea that spirits belong to the people everywhere. The spirits cannot be circumscribed by the Church officials as the Monks attempt to do—another support for pre-Christian ideas. Silko says of the appearance of the Messiah in *Gardens*, "I really wanted to show that Jesus Christ doesn't belong to any given group or religion or continent. . . . So I wanted to add . . . a Native American Jesus" who is part of a "pantheon" of "good spirits" (Perkins 120–21).

A next step for Hattie is to shed her husband who ties her to Euro-American scientific ideas and greed. Denise Cummings argues that Edward's "very use of the camera and his obsession with the classificatory system of botany identify him with Western modernity. The epistemological failure of Western science and technologies renders Edward blind; he can never 'see' and consequently, dies trusting in a quack's scientific cure for an illness he endures" (85). The incident of Edward trying on the tin mask in Bath is a telling one: "He supposed it was self-consciousness that caused the odd sensation when he looked through the eyes of the mask; more distance seemed to lie between himself and Hattie and other people, though they did not move" (259).

Obsessed with his purchases from the Celtic sacred spring, Edward does not wish to attend the picnic that Aunt Bronwyn has prepared. He has bought a lead curse tablet that actually describes his failure to understand how modern culture has deadened him: "To the goddess Sulis. Whether slave or free, whoever he shall be, you are not to permit him eyes or health. He shall be blind and childless so long as he shall live unless he returns . . . to the temple" (260). Science has become his god; he has no place for stories or a new way of seeing.

Later, Hattie has a dream about the light from Aunt Bronwyn's garden. The light becomes the tin mask that "cover[s] the face of the figure in the shadow" (274). Hattie believes the figure in the shadow to be Edward and she wakes up alarmed. For Hattie, who is open to the power that the light represents, it is comforting. For Edward the light is threatening and further encases him in his inability to "see" as the curse predicted. When Edward asks about the dream, Hattie does not believe Edward can understand and she tells him nothing.

For Hattie, "[t]he glowing light in Aunt Bronwyn's garden and the disembodied mask she dreamed" become "more real now than her manuscript or her marriage" (374), signaling her move into a new way of perceiving. As she makes plans to return Indigo to her sister in the southwest desert, she continues to be comforted by the lovely light in her dreams. Once Indigo is settled with her sister, Hattie continues to bring household items and groceries to them. Hattie has disavowed the greedy perspective of many Euro-Americans, enduring ostracism from the little town in which she buys her supplies.

Although Hattie is one of the "people with like hearts and minds" who does not care about race or skin color, the people in the town are another matter. On a supply gathering trip, Hattie, who is seen as "white squaw" (415) by the town, is raped, robbed, beaten with a rock and left for dead in the road. Found by Indians who take her back to the town where the barber and his wife tend to her, Hattie is told that there was "no record of a fare from the hotel on the day of her attack" (461) so nothing could be done. "You and the Indians. . . . People here don't welcome outsiders who meddle" (461).

Still in terrible shape, Hattie finally makes it back to Indigo and her sister who are camped along a nearby river where the dance for the Messiah is being held. Very ill, Hattie is made stronger by seeing "the luminous glow streaming in all around her" (470) during the third night of the dance for the Messiah. Hattie believes that "[t]he dancers' prayers saved her life—each night of the dance she recovered a bit more as the Messiah drew nearer" (473), signaling her change of worldview.

When Hattie's parents come for her with the soldiers, disrupting the last night of the dance, Hattie realizes that she does not belong with her parents, nor with Indigo or buying land and settling near the racist townspeople who have used her presence to shut down the dances. Her home is with Aunt Bronwyn back in England, continuing to explore Old European belief systems. However, in a fit of revenge or, perhaps, retribution reminiscent of *Almanac of the Dead*, before Hattie leaves she sets fire to the town that sheltered her rapist and that torments and cheats the Indians.

True to Silko's idea that *"Gardens in the Dunes* is meant as a reward, something less rigorous for the reader,"* (Arnold 168) the novel ends happily with Hattie finding her home and identity in England while Indigo and her sister return to the old gardens in the dunes. From England, Hattie's continued generosity allows Indigo and her sister prosperity with the purchase of livestock. Indigo's seed collection and gladiolus bulbs ultimately make them popular with their Christian Indian neighbors, and Indigo discovers the bulbs make tasty vegetables in a stew, examples of the usefulness of Silko's idea of "ongoing [cultural] exchange" (Perkins 118). The book ends with the Indigo and her friends watching "Old Snake's beautiful daughter" at the pool near the old gardens in the dunes, signaling restored fertility. As Brewster Fitz points out, it is "a vision of the return of the matriarchal spiritual principle to the garden. It is the paradoxical vision of luminous darkness filled with grace. It is a vision" (231) of the Native American Coatlicue, the Serpent goddess. Coatlicue is the "consuming internal whirlwind . . . the symbol of the underground aspects of the psyche . . . the mountain, the Earth Mother who conceived all celestial beings out of her cavernous womb . . . Goddess of birth and death . . ." (Gloria Anzaldu'a qtd. in Fitz 231). Further, "it is the vision of Mother Earth wrapped in a healing blanket of transplanted and indigenous flowers"—the gladiolus intermingled with the native datura" (Fitz 231), and it echoes the story Laura told Indigo in Italy of a white snake goddess.

In *Garden*, Silko has shown her readers how we have more in common than we realize if we care to see. About the novel Silko says, *"Gardens in the Dunes* . . . is really about now. It all connects together and it gives you a psychic and spiritual way to live . . ." (Arnold 183).

NOTES

1. See my "Curing Ceremonies: The Novels of Leslie Marmon Silko and Paula Gunn Allen" (12–31), for a discussion of this perspective and application in *Ceremony* and "From Big Green Fly to the Stone Serpent: Following the Dark Vision in Silko's *Almanac of the Dead*" (39–47), for *Almanac of the Dead*.

2. For a brief discussion of this see Denise Cummings 84–85.

3. In the interview with Arnold, Silko discusses the worth of the Gnostic tradition, for instance, as being unmediated. She says, "And that's why ultimately I hope this is a gnostic novel" (186).

WORKS CITED

Allen, Paula Gunn. *The Sacred Hoop: Recovering the Feminine in American Indian Traditions*. Boston: Beacon P, 1986.

Arnold, Ellen L. "Listening to the Spirits: An Interview with Leslie Marmon Silko." *Conversations with Leslie Marmon Silko*. Ed. Ellen L. Arnold. Jackson: UP of Mississippi, 2000. 162–95.

Cummings, Denise K. "'Settling' History: Understanding Leslie Marmon Silko's *Ceremony, Storyteller, Almanac of the Dead*, and *Gardens in the Dunes*." *SAIL* 12.4 (Winter 2000): 65–90.

Fitz, Brewster E. *Silko: Writing Storyteller and Medicine Woman*. Norman: U of Oklahoma P, 2004.

Perkins, Owen. "An Interview with Leslie Marmon Silko." *High Plains Literary Review* 14.2–3 (Fall-Winter 1999): 80–124.

Silko, Leslie Marmon. *Almanac of the Dead*. New York: Simon & Schuster, 1991.

———. *Ceremony*. New York: Viking Penguin, 1977. New York: Penguin books, 1986.

———. *Gardens in the Dunes*. New York: Simon & Schuster, 1999.

Van Dyke, Annette. "Curing Ceremonies: The Novels of Leslie Marmon Silko and Paula Gunn Allen." *The Search for a Woman-Centered Spirituality*. New York: New York UP, 1992. 12–40.

———. "From Big Green Fly to the Stone Serpent: Following the Dark Vision in Silko's *Almanac of the Dead*." *SAIL* 10.2 (Summer 1998): 36–48.

THE GARDENS OF MEMORY BETWEEN THE OLD AND THE NEW WORLD: "ALL WHO ARE LOST WILL BE FOUND"

Laura Coltelli

For Francesco Gozzi

"There is nothing more political than what's in your gardens" (Cohen 56). This concise concept (but "political" should be understood in its widest possible extension) by Leslie Marmon Silko embodies the theme that guides us through her most recent novel, *Gardens in the Dunes*.[1] A memory that lives in the garden interprets it not as creation of space, but as reception of a culture and, even more, as an artistic transfiguration of the human condition. Living while letting oneself be permeated with the life of the garden implies sharing it with whoever lives therein. It signifies an invention of new forms on the part of those who have received and comprehended the heritage handed down, by living within those precincts, and living there with others.

In a broader cultural function, it expresses a mythic relation with the environment in order to anchor existence itself to a mythic representation of the world. If it is a place where a cultural form is forged, above and beyond specific identities traceable in every land, then true gardens—at least those not conceived to strike the imagination as an expression of *grandeur*—are complex domains to be comprehended in a totalizing manner, fertile meeting grounds, where various culture coexist in the same place.

What is included, rejected, interpreted in a garden, thus becomes political discourse of acceptance or rejection, of hierarchical classification, or exegetic crystallization of meanings linked to a concept of immutable superiority and truth. Silko challenges and reformulates this vision in proudly alternative interpretations, which have their origin and are contextualized in a "feminine principle," intensely entwined with the pueblo tradition versus a western world grounded on the male role to which we are immediately introduced through the academic misadventure that befalls Hattie, "the heretic of Oyster Bay" (who in various ways during the course of the novel seeks a balance between western civilization and the Native American worldview), when the Harvard Divinity

School committee brands her thesis as "Gnostic heresy" because it asserts that Jesus had women disciples and Mary Magdalene wrote a gospel suppressed by the church.[2]

"Adam, live! Rise up upon the Earth" and "The Female Spiritual principle came in the Snake, The Instructor"—woman and snake, female guiding spirit, which restore life to Adam, while "the Arrogant Ruler cursed the woman and the snake" (102)—are passages that immediately herald the overturning of the orthodox Christian account of the creation of mankind. Not only is Eve endowed with creative power, but a matriarchal spirituality pervades the snake which, in turn, gives knowledge and discernment, transformative power, awareness and toleration of diversity. The concept of salvation or damnation dispensed by the Garden of Eden after the Fall is immediately set in opposition, in the first part of the novel, to the Ghost Dance where "In the presence of the Messiah and the Holy Mother, there was only one language spoken—the language of love—which all people understand, he [a Paiute man] said, because we are all children of Mother Earth" (34).

Thus the curse after the construction of the Tower of Babel is canceled by that single mode of communicating which perhaps also eliminates the language diversities that are variously heard (even if not fully understood) by Indigo during her journey, for they all converge into that "language of love" deriving from a common approach to life, which in turn springs from common roots.[3]

This rewriting (pre-Christian or heretical) of texts which incarnate the very foundations of the religious spirit of the Western world acts as a force which— although intertwined with syncretic resemblances—profoundly disrupts a vast array of beliefs the Europeans brought with them to America, beliefs that are also incorporated in a perspective of tribal experience. Naturally, in proclaiming this series of alternatives, above all the idea that all things derive from gendering the land with a female earth energy, the concept of "wilderness" or "virgin land" to be violated and subjugated is excluded: there can be no mobile frontier which was continuously expanding westwards at a particular time in history, because, as Grandmother Fleet says, "the old gardens had always been there" (16–17).[4] What is recounted is thus a story that goes back to the beginning of all things and to the same place from whence they *became* the Sand Lizard people.

It is in this very garden that the young Indian girl Indigo's journey has both its beginning and its end. Her discovery of Europe and also, in a sense, that of her "protectors," Hattie and Edward, overturns the traditional characteristics of the Grand Tour and by extension, also the characteristics of the massive emigration towards America which reached one of its highest levels precisely at the turn of the nineteenth and beginning of the twentieth century, the period in which the events of the novel are set.

In fact, Indigo's cultural and spiritual inspiration is fundamentally buttressed—through contrasts or similarities, presences or absences—by the native land she always bears within her. Yet this by no means implies sterility of vision or preconceived rejection of the new, but rather a profound knowledge, awareness and experience of "her" land that is a manner of being and a manner of comprehending life. The concept of hybridization, which pervades the entire novel—together with the growing and transplanting of plants, standing respectively for metaphors of civilization and migration—has a primary valence as a quest, as a possibility of interaction among different cultures, and above all as a legacy handed down to us from a past of shared beliefs even if experienced in different cultural contexts, pre-existing affinities that have been violently shattered and manipulated by economic and/or religious power structures.

A first garden, a "white" garden, namely that of Riverside, is the scene of the meeting between Hattie and Indigo, after Indigo has run away from the boarding school she was forcibly taken to after a police raid on the Ghost Dance, followed by the disappearance of her mother, the transfer of Sister Salt, her older sister, to the reservation and the death of Grandma Fleet, who passed away in her sleep, protected by the earth of their ancestors.

And it is precisely the contact with the earth, "the wonderful odor of the rich earth" (105) that embraces the young girl in this garden where she tries to hide after her flight. She is not at all surprised by the encounter with the monkey Linnaeus, with whom she initiates a veritable conversation in a most natural manner, significantly freeing the monkey from its cage, just as she had freed herself from her captivity by running away from the boarding school.[5] Later we learn that the garden had more or less become overgrown, and it was going to be redesigned according to Hattie's plans—an announcement that prefigures the way Hattie's life is likewise eventually destined to change. For she senses in the worlds of her husband's reply on the subject of Indigo "something disturbing about his impression of her—something she could not yet identify" (108). From these very first emblematic scenes in that Californian garden, Hattie's husband, Edward, a botanist by arid scientific training and a plant merchant by disposition, stands out as an alien presence, one that is particularly critical vis-à-vis Indigo, whom he proposes to take back to the boarding school immediately—and as proof of his intention he appears right away with a rope to capture her. Later, however, he acquiesces in Hattie's plan and condescends to take the child with them on their European journey where he will search for plants (officially to study them, but with the secret plan of making off with all possible sorts of cuttings), as he realizes that "the child would be an asset in Corsica; the natives adored children" (112). Signally, plants and seeds constitute virtually the only words intentionally pronounced by Indigo, despite having a good command of English, repeating "the names of the plants and shrubs after Hattie, but otherwise she spoke at length only to Linnaeus, when they played in the glass house together" (113). And it is plants, again, that she yearns to talk about with Mama, Grandmother Fleet and Sister Salt, in daytime reveries or in dreams, musing time after time on her experiences.

In Hattie's garden, Indigo's closeness to the plant world kindles intense reactions within her, springing from scents, the taste of pollen and petals, brilliant colors. Plants are never the object of mere ecstatic contemplation, but almost become one with Indigo's physical make-up: her body penetrates them and is, in turn, penetrated by the plants themselves, with the constant desire to share them with those from who she has been separated, as if their full enjoyment could not be completed on account of this separation. In these episodes the appeal to her mother, her sister and her grandmother becomes almost a refrain that directs the text towards that world as if it were a mirror in which all is reflected and by which all is captured.

But the "color of money" increasingly replaces that of the plants as the journey gradually moves from the gardens of the Southwest to those of the East Coast. The environment of Oyster Bay, Hattie and Edward's home area, is pervaded by the possession of money and by the social status to which it is indissolubly linked. Through frequent analeptic procedures, even before reaching the home of the Abbotts, Hattie's parents, we learn of Hattie's substantial dowry and we are made aware that her mother "talked about money almost incessantly—who had money, how they got the money, and who lost their money" (81). Furthermore, there are convivial conversations on the cost of the new garden to be put on show for the summer ball, on the luxurious lifestyle that Susan, Edward's sister, who lives in a property adjoining that of the Abbotts, lavishes on her daughters, on the problems surrounding the funding of Edward's expedition to Corsica after the failure of an earlier expedition along the Parà river and his consequent indebtedness, astutely monitored by his sister and brother-in-law who aim "to buy out his share of the estate entirely" (165). The exotic gardens of South America were explored by Edward for their "commercial potential," all species "fit for human consumption" (94), in a sort of international smuggling with the protection of conniving governments interested in assuring themselves of a monopoly over prized cultivations.

The fire that destroys the habitat of a rare orchid during that ill-fated expedition, with the result that only a small number of investors come to possess the few plants that had already been stored safely, is a proleptic passage that prefigures the parallel destruction of the valley of the Colorado River, whose course is deviated to carry water to Los Angeles: fire and water not so much as manifestations of a violent nature but as violated nature. Thus once again what is proposed is the paradigm of a wilderness which must be replaced, through destruction, with a different landscape, without any harmonic contact between nature and culture. In this sense the myth of America as a garden dissolves into a fully native perspective, proudly upheld:

> So long as the human consciousness remains *within* the hills, canyon, cliffs, and the plants, clouds, and sky, the term *landscape*, as this has entered the English language, is misleading. 'A portion of territory the eye can comprehend in a single view' does not correctly describe the relationship between the human being and his or her surroundings. (Silko, "Landscape" 84)[6]

The microcosm in both these places of the New World presents almost identical modes — profound divisions or occasional interminglings, almost always derived, if not indeed imposed, by the dominant culture and by a social fabric that creates itself in racial divisions as a technique of domination.

The Masque of the Blue Garden is the most important event organized by Susan. It consists in designing a new themed garden every year: that summer, it involves the creation of a sort of plant stage-set with every possible shade of blue. Although inspired by the color of flowers, its link to the natural elements is only futile and superficial, inasmuch as it is manipulated to reflect and mirror "all shades of blue" of the women's gowns, in contrast to Indigo, who immediately identifies blue as the color of rain clouds. Thus the ball effectively has a twofold mask: that of the ostentation of wealth in a gilded indolence, but concealed by charitable intentions, endorsed by the condescending and towering presence of the bishop during the preparations.

Every scene is dominated by spaces constructed with implacable geometric predictability — which is only an artifice and denies all intimate contact with that which it aims to create. It is not a space modeled by nature, and it is animated by no vital life force: rather, it is a celebration of precariousness, just as it is inspired by a precise assemblage of colors, as precise as it is restrictive.

Cages, greenhouses, glass houses, walls create a continuous sense of separateness; plants, forcibly made to emigrate from their natural habitat, are turned under duress into poor erratic valuable display items, exhibited as focal points of a new garden which is in turn alien to that landscape, disoriented plants at a loss in a hostile context.[7]

In a cultural memory loss, nature has become a product of fashion. In these days of tumultuous excitement at Oyster Bay, Indigo, on the other hand, shapes her time in quiet observation of what is moving around her, but the surprise she feels by no means stems from the splendor—a man-made artifice—that surrounds her. Rather, it arises from the absence, or insignificant presence of familiar things or plants which for her represent the sole source of food and survival, or from the sight of animals which, with the exception of Mr. Abbott's goats, are viewed as mere objects to adorn the scene, like the fish in the pond or the parrot Rainbow that is given to her to buy her silence after she has caught a glimpse of the gardener and Edward's sister making love naked in a hidden corner of the garden.

Erecting a sort of filter between herself and the garrulous babble of voices from the ball, "Indigo imagined the loud buzz was bees, not human beings" (198), and on seeing the glowing reflection of the flowers "Indigo was reminded of the Messiah and his family and all the dancers in their white blankets all shimmering in the light reflected off the snow" (198). The same image that floats from earth to the waves of the ocean and continues to dominate her thoughts when she is with Hattie and Edward on board the ship that sets sail for Europe, "crossing the same water that the Messiah crossed long ago on his way to Jerusalem . . . She took heart because the Messiah and his followers visited the east and returned; she would too" (199). The Masque of the Blue Garden, with a themed title that has something Poesque about it, sinisterly evocative of a deathly color, lives in Indigo's memory through a transformative power that speaks to her of other places, other lights, other voices, awakening in her a powerful feeling that she can one day return.

Only five days after the ball, a transition to a different place does indeed take place, with the Palmers' departure on the steamship bound for Europe. In England they make the acquaintance of Aunt Bronwyn, an aunt on Mr. Abbott's side, English by descent and American by birth, who has the Palmers and Indigo to stay for a few days in her home, a Norman abbey in Bath, of which only the cloister and the garden remain. As a member of the Antique Rescue Committee, and as one "who abruptly left the church after her husband died and moved to Bath to live in seclusion and study the prehistoric archeology of the British Isles and Old Europe" (167), Aunt Bronwyn wages a vigorous struggle in favor of the defense of ancient oaks and stones.

In the description of the English landscape, from the city to the countryside, emphasis is placed on forms of oppression in a past whose architectural and natural vestiges are on the verge of disappearing completely. The fierceness of campaigns against the ancient religions is cited as one of the main causes of this ruin and destruction: "[Silko] links the suppression of the Ghost Dance religion with earlier persecutions of non-Christians. For Silko England is a 'contact zone' in which opposing religions fought for supremacy" (Ruoff 186). In this thematic context the distinctiveness of Aunt Bronwyn and Hattie increasingly comes to the fore—Aunt Bronwyn with her forsaking of religious orthodoxy and Hattie with her thesis on the Gnostic Gospels, rejected by Harvard, on the subject of which, however, she happens to hear from Aunt Bronwyn herself that "certain Coptic scrolls obtained years before by the British Museum had just been authenticated" (268). More and more, Aunt Bronwyn's life, activities and beliefs seem to awaken in Hattie the awareness of a model to be followed and a world she could belong to.

Unlike the New England garden, one quadrant of the old medieval kitchen garden still retains its old function, albeit with a design and shape that favors spontaneous growth wherever possible, in contrast to the original cloister garden which Aunt Bronwyn found depicted in old church maps and diagrams, with "its severe plain lines and sparse plantings designed to mortify the soul" (242).

The vitality of this kitchen garden is manifested in the extreme variety of the vegetation, from fruits of the land to flowers, carefully arranged in separate quadrants:

> The kitchen garden was the modern garden as well, she explained. Plants from all over the world—from the Americas, tomatoes, potatoes, pumpkins, squash, and the sweet corn; and garlic, onions, broad beans, asparagus, and chickpeas from Italy—grew with peppers from Asia and Africa.   (242)

This geographic division seems to imply respect and, as it were, a sense of duty to acknowledge the provenance of the plants as a gift from other parts, a mark of recognition of closeness to other lands, which has been assiduously and patiently sought because Aunt Bronwyn is a follower of the theories of Gustav Fechner "who believed plants have souls" (242), "then Aunt Bronwyn decided to acquaint herself with as many different beings as possible" (244). Just as in the Sand Lizards' gardens, here too there seems to be no discontinuity with the past, which lives on in the various and often winding paths:

> In the north quadrant, Aunt Bronwyn planted the old raised beds with indigenous English plants—kales, hellebores, dandelions, pinks, periwinkles, daisies. Little white flowering violets cascaded over the edges of the raised beds. The east side of the garden was planted with all the plants the Romans and the Normans introduced: grapevines nearly obscured the weathered wooden pergola that slouched down the path between the raised beds planted with cabbages, eggplants,

chickpeas, and cucumbers. Hattie was surprised at how few food crops and flowers were indigenous to England; the climate here did not seem unfriendly in the least compared to the dry heat of Riverside.

The south garden and the west garden were planted with plants from the Americas, Africa and Asia.   (245)

Many of these plants come from exotic places, seized from faraway populations with the violence of a conquering colonial policy. This division into small plots of land does not mean scientific separateness or the contribution of botany to an emergent global capitalism, as in Edward's intentions, but rather awareness and acceptance of diversity. The kaleidoscope of colors thus leads to the metaphoric creation of a palette — not, of course, in the simplistic romanticized approach — with reciprocal enhancement of a dazzling chromatic variety which heightens knowledge and awareness of otherness.

In this garden, Indigo undergoes a change from the detached and almost imposed observation of Oyster Bay to an increasingly frequent, instinctive participation, springing from the memories Aunt Bronwyn and her world awaken in her, like the sight of plants of vital importance and very familiar to her — corn and pumpkins — which she runs towards with enthusiasm and nostalgia — or datura, "sacred plant of the Pueblo priests, mighty hallucinogen and deadly poison" which has the power to purify contaminated water because "for datura, all water is sacred" (Silko, *Sacred Water* 75). Even toads become part of this shared memory, protected as they are by the Rescue Committee members during their migrations, for toads are well represented in the pueblo world because they are regarded as "beloved children of the rain clouds" (Silko, *Sacred Water* 6), a conception that has a parallel in their special veneration by the old Europeans as "incarnations of the Primordial Mother" (243).

The strange excitement Indigo feels at the sight of the gladioli — which unconsciously forge a link to the metaphorical journey from their place of origin — is suggestive, at the end of the novel, of the genuine possibility of an exchange, with the creation of a new garden. For in this framework of the iteration of the image of gladioli, present in Italy as well in Laura's garden, it is hardly unbefitting to note their African origin, introduced as they were in Europe and the Americas during the most intense years of the slave trade. The "golden triangle of world trade" (Bristol/West Africa/America/Bristol) is significantly mentioned by Aunt Bronwyn to her guests as she shows them the site of the old slave market, a sight that arouses Indigo's interest because Grandma Fleet told her stories about such places, but even more importantly, she always taught Indigo how to hide from the slave hunters, while "Off in the distance we saw the children tied together in a line" (233). No longer a piece of history consigned to the past, slavery bursts into the contemporary era in the face of the disbelief of Hattie and Edward, but not of Aunt Bronwyn.[8]

The affinity that becomes established, from this very first meeting on, between the eccentric old lady and Indigo receives further confirmation in Aunt Bronwyn's insightfulness as a storyteller when she recounts to the young girl the legend of the Knights of the Round Table, or when, almost as if she were intoning a song, she called the cattle: "The calls were lovely and made Indigo think of the old gardens and Grandma Fleet and Mama and Sister Salt" (240). Once again, for Indigo, places and episodes of continuity in memory, continually inlaid with deep energies that well up from her own land.

The excavations of the baths under the modern and cosmopolitan Pump House Hotel reveal a sort of underground garden: not plants but instead, stones, which like the immemorial oaks from the Celtic era protected by Aunt Bronwyn, chart the history of those peoples, testimony of occupations and devastations, but even more essentially, stones and artifacts that are imbued with life and tell of the old land. On the lowest level there are remains from the Roman invasion, and the steps leading down exhale "a damp odor of clay and decaying organic material" (257), the same smell that reminds Indigo of what she and Sister Salt tried to avoid at the edge of the river, a place of other conquests. The temple built by the Romans on a site sacred to the ancient Celtic god Sulis was a first act of deliberate and ruinous conquest; only later was there an attempt to make up for this devastation, when the Romans, "always wary of offending powerful local deities, prudently named their town Aquae Sulis. But the Romans could not permit Sulis to rule supreme any longer, so they built a temple with a great pool over the springs, dedicated to Sulis and Minerva as well" (236). As LaVonne Ruoff maintains, "Excavations in and around Bath reveal the periods of occupation by the Celts, Romans, Normans, Tudors and Elizabethans. Bath is now the refuge of 'business tycoons from London and Bristol' who cut down ancient oaks on the hills to make way for gigantic mansions . . . This history underscores Silko's theme of the drive of human kind to destroy the remnants of earlier civilizations in order to reshape the land according to its own vision or greed" (185–86).

In the dark damp excavated area all the characters have a feeling of obscure fear, a sense of loss, curiosity, sense of belonging. What they experience not only represents a light authorial touch that heightens their respective role in the unfolding story, but in fact the characters' very disposition and individual history seems to be already sedimented among those stones. Hattie appears at times to distance herself from that strange magnetic atmosphere that pervades the excavations, but the reassuring and aseptic routine of Riverside is now progressively giving way to emotive states of uneasiness or heady restlessness as in her sleep-walking episode. Thus she has the impression that the flat rock she sees herself sitting on in a graveyard during the dream she had at Oyster Bay is almost identical to the altar platform she sees in the underground passage, "which left her feeling a bit light-headed, but not unwell" (258). The Celtic tin mask Edward dons more or less as a joke materially signals the distance that is gradually moving him further and further away from the others, but it is also the mask that conceals the money-oriented and practical observer behind the aesthete, the exotic artifact trafficker behind the scientist. Indigo is attracted by the boxes that store the artifacts, "good boxes for storing seeds" (259), unconsciously forging a perfect synthesis of the "seeds" found in the earth of an ancient culture with those that the earth itself causes to sprout anew in every place. Those stones still speak to Aunt Bronwyn, who senses they are throbbing with life and realizes the cruelty and pointlessness of having closed them up "into little coffins" (259), some of which, carved like "a cloud chalcedony," represent "three cattle under an oak tree" (259) and look just like the white cattle Aunt Bronwyn keeps in her meadows around the abbey.[9]

The worship of stones, which are the repository of myths and cultural attributes, points to a progressive *rapprochement* of Hattie towards Aunt Bronwyn's pre-Christian European beliefs. It is no coincidence that Aunt Bronwyn is present in Hattie's above-mentioned dream at Oyster Bay: as she is sitting on that strange flat stone, Hattie realizes that Aunt Bronwyn is by her side, "urging her to slide her seat along on the stone. Hattie tried to scoot herself the length of the stone, but the cloth of her dress snagged on the corner of the stone. In her dream Hattie tugged at the cloth so hard she woke herself with the bedcovers in her hands" (165). This suggestion can be seen as a appeal by the old lady for Hattie to share a cultural and existential space with her, even though Hattie is at that moment still "snagged" in some obstacle she is trying hard to get away from.

It is the same stone Hattie finds herself lying on, even more concretely, after her sleepwalking episode in the garden in Bath, where, amid corn and sunflower leaves, she sees a glowing light that fills her with profound joy, after a first moment of fear and consternation. It is an epiphanic moment experienced in no less than the very place where she is destined to return, perhaps for ever, and whose memory permeates her like a wind that carries all away before it. "Words from her thesis notes cascaded before her mind's eyes, then suddenly scattered as if suddenly the words were dry leaves blowing away in the wind: poor judgement, bad timing, late marriage, premature marriage, dread of childbirth, sexual dysfunction" (251).

The realization of having the power to regain her own life culminates in her discovery that "she belongs to Europe," a place she feels to be "the place of her origins," in contrast to the Riverside house that "would not let her be" (251). This discovery is immediately followed by thoughts about those who undergo the violence of a forced removal, which links her to Indigo: "Suddenly she realized they must help the Indian child return to her sister and mother!" (251). Detached from the notes of her manuscript on Gnostic gospels notwithstanding her defiance of the thesis committee, she feels only that she is drawing closer to the real, ancient "family spirit," as also underlined by Aunt Bronwyn herself. However, the process is still destined to be long-drawn-out, as testified by the complex relationship she has with Indigo despite the intention of restoring the child to her own community. It is a relationship which, as we see at the end, does not include that physical presence which Hattie would like. It implies neither Indigo's removal towards western civilization nor that of Hattie to an Indian land to which she does not belong and where she is actually the victim of almost fatal violence—perpetrated by a white man. Yet at this point the theme of a return to the respective lands is already delineated, a return to the land where one belongs, but carrying a few "seeds" that grew in the past on a common land and which now can offer the hope of a new hybridization. It is the same seeds that Aunt Bronwyn gives to Indigo at the moment of goodbye, together with a notebook of immaculate white pages on which to record a cultural history that has yet to be written.

While the journey continues towards the Mediterranean, with Corsica as the final destination where Edward plans to get hold of cuttings of the precious citrons, the "seed" of change begins to touch even more intimate spheres. The image of Italy, and in particular the stay in Lucca, abounds in a sense of freedom and a progressive, albeit almost subterranean erosion of environmental-cultural or religious restrictions.

At Laura's—where Aunt Bronwyn, a friend of Laura's, has arranged for them to stay—the garden embodies a life of open spaces, of land and vegetation shaped according to natural patterns and thus protected, with corners of forest (and not flowerbeds) bestrewn with flowers that reveal themselves almost unexpectedly beyond tall trees. Earth slides, debris, deadwood are part of this garden that thus retains life and decadence in the implacable but at the same time serene passage of time. Hattie and Indigo seem to immerse themselves in this brilliantly colored landscape, mottled with every shade of green, with red and black spreading upwards from the soil, the blue of the decoration of the fountain, the intensity of sunlight shimmering in the air. Laura seems to hand over these colors to Indigo when she gives her the box of color pencils, a gift that enables the young girl to make a colored drawing for the first time. But stirred by the constant memory she carries within her and the independence that is her distinctive feature, the pencils "transfer" the colors onto Indian plants she immediately draws. Hybridization acts only on that which can be inserted in another culture and is almost "bent" to illustrate other elements, but without overlaying or erasing founding parts that are constitutive of personal and cultural identities. The mirror where Indigo catches sight of herself by chance when she is alone in the bedroom transmits to her a dark face she'd almost forgotten, long surrounded as she has been by lighter faces, but the smile with which she greets this image is one of amused awareness with regard to a belonging that cannot be altered or replaced.

The outdoor exhibition of precious artifacts does not correspond to a mere decorative arrangement, but rather reflects an intimate blend of art and nature, where each finds its raison d'être in the other: human essence that issues forth from the earth and artistic reproducibility in a constant dialogue of cultural elaboration. Edward's scorn of this careless attitude towards the artifacts, which he sees as being left at the mercy of the elements, once again consigns him to a paralyzing classificatory erudition as well as an exclusive—and limiting—appreciation of the work of art within the confines of a museum.

The statues seem to spring from the earth and even the damaged ones must not, in Laura's vision of her garden, be replaced by copies. In this atmosphere of authenticity, they are an imposing sight, arising before one's eyes with great expressiveness: from beings that are almost always half human and half animal—centaurs, minotaurs, medusas, snakes with arms, or a mother bear and a human vulva—there emerges an intense sexuality, revealing itself as unaffectedly as the garden offered itself before the eyes of the guests, an intricate and equally sensual pattern of colors, shapes, and scents.

These are creatures that draw from their dual nature a vibrant and by no means wild force, with a reiterated symbology alluding to fertility and motherhood: bodies that do not deny each other but rather bestow life, with the bellies, breasts, genitals offered unashamedly in a vitalistic physicalness. Rain, the greatest good for the Sand Lizard, has an even more life-giving parallel in the rain garden, since—as Laura explains—Old Europeans made a link between rain drops and drops of breast milk.

"The fertility figure," as Edward calls the human vulva, out of his prudery, prompts the Palmers to move Indigo away from those images and above all from a strange stone figure with a large phallus. Indigo, though, with a closeness to nudity acquired from her own culture, experiences it with her customary naturalness. But the song she eventually makes up, ironically contesting Edward, "See you can't see what you see. See you can't see what you see. See, see, see!" (304), is an open and astute challenge to the man's attitude and everything connected with it: his sense of sin linked to sexual images, his repugnance at the concept of a fusion between libido and art, and thus his distaste for an artistic culture and a manner of experiencing sexuality that are unfamiliar, with the ensuing revulsion against this difference.

But if at first Hattie is seized by the same fears, these images in Laura's Italian garden awaken in her disturbing pulsions and feelings, prompting a sort of erotic and maternal identification, but they continue to remain unsatisfied when that evening, in their bedroom, Edward rebuffs Hattie's move towards complete intimacy. He allows his thoughts to wander instead towards talk of death to commemorate his father, the anniversary of whose death falls precisely on that day. But he also continues to move ever closer towards the sterility of his own death and to close himself in a blindness that fails to see a past of shared beliefs and myths from whence many civilizations such as those exemplified in Aunt Bronwyn's English garden have blossomed, or the constant pulsing of life in all its aspects in Laura's Italian garden.

Two dominant images are present in this Italian garden, drawn from the animal and plant world: that of the snake and that of the black gladioli. The snake appears in almost all the statues, not as a decoration but intrinsic to those shapes of bodies, often holding, cradling a baby snake, present in a spiral design on the belly or attached to human breasts. As Laura explains, there still exists "a snake devotion in rural villages of the Black and Adriatic seas" because they are "guardian spirits who protected their cattle and their homes" (300). This charts an obvious line of continuity with the culture from which Indigo comes—a parallelism denied by Edward in order to avoid giving the young girl the impression that "Old Europeans were no better than red Indians or black Africans who prayed to snakes" (300). But it is also true that this insistent image overturns that of the snake as symbol of evil and sin in the biblical garden and above all in the cradle of Catholicism that is Italy,[10] where it has always been represented iconographically as defeated beneath the feet of the Virgin. This image is evoked again by Hattie herself in the dream she has before leaving Lucca, but it is overlaid by that of a woman and a snake with a detectable sexual symbolism that must have been built, as Hattie says to herself, "on a figure from earlier times" (306).

During the same night the snake also penetrates into Edward's dreams and Indigo's as well. Terrified, Edward perceives the presence of a giant African snake in his bed and, upon awakening, he explains it to himself as Hattie's arm shaking him to free him from the nightmare. An evident oneiric interpretation seems to reveal that the physical maiming he suffered during the South American expedition may not be the true cause of his impotence, which is attributable instead to far deeper causes.

In her dream, Indigo once more transfers the Italian colors to a canyon of her old gardens, where she is together with Linnaeus and Rainbow, but where instead of sunflowers, corn plants and squash there are gladioli of various species growing, and where, by a spring, she meets the big rattlesnake who asks her "Where's my corn pollen?" (306): a new wealth of flowers, which, however, must not erase another heritage, equally rich, that Indigo always carries with her.[11]

The stand of black gladioli expands the geographic and cultural horizon. As already mentioned, gladioli are hybrids that came from Africa during one of the periods of intense slave trade from Africa. The association seems evident, not only for mixed bloods like little grandfather (Sister Salt's baby by an AfroAmerican) and all the others who live in the Colorado desert.[12] In fact black is not the color of night and death that is Edward's legacy from Western civilization, but rather, as Laura states, for the Old Europeans it is the color of fertility and birth, that of the Great Mother (298). And also that of the first man, Silko seems to tell us, who was born not in the Garden of Eden but in an African "garden." For "Mediterranean" does not mean only Europe, but also Africa and Asia, criss-crossed as they are by a dense network of communications, with vitalizing transition zones, in a more ancient and vaster European horizon. In this evolutionary framework that stretches across the millennia the individual European cultural identities have been shaped through processes of osmosis and exchange. The Great Mother, the female guiding spirit, preserves this memory, transmits it, renews and diffuses it.[13]

The journey to Corsica progressively leads Hattie to a heightened and different awareness of the sterility of her marriage, prompting a search for a definitive path to self-determination. In a novel that overturns commonplace beliefs, Indigo—at first a poor Indian child to be instructed so she will learn to behave properly in Western civilization—becomes instead a sort of guide who, with her independence and visionary power, helps Hattie to reshape her life, establishing new priorities, in order to secure a firm knowledge of who she is.

The "glowing light" that appears to Hattie in various ways at every stage of her journey, the symbolic sign of a cognitive process that "illuminates" its surrounding context, assumes more precise and in certain respects unifying connotations of some of the novel's themes. The light that appears on the wall of the schoolhouse in the village in Corsica—which the Palmers are taken to see by the family that has offered them hospitality and has shared a meal with them—seems for the first time to acquire a more clearly defined shape, above all for the poor townsfolk who watch and wait in fervent expectation of that apparition at dawn and sunset. Their sincere devotion, their confidence that they are witnesses of a miracle granted to their poverty-stricken lives, is in no way impaired by doubts concerning possible strange reflections of light off metal or glass, as Hattie seems to wonder at a certain point, even though she herself is also mesmerized by the same intense participation. And although this vision is, effectively, "transmitted" to her—rather than genuinely experienced, since Hattie "sees" it with the eyes of the others—it is also true that this scene strongly reasserts the spirituality of a female guiding principle. The presence of the monks who appear with a threatening mien to chase away what they interpret as the work of the devil is in actual fact an attempt to turn the faithful and tourists back to veneration of a traditional Madonna covered with gold and silver, kept in the nearby abbey and, above all, the source of rich offerings. The orthodoxy of the patriarchal church is again waging war on popular religious beliefs out of love for power and wealth:

> From an orthodox point of view, the monks and the abbot have every reason to be disturbed. The villagers are already receiving religious instruction at the schoolhouse, rather than at the abbey. Now, without knowing it, the excommunicated Corsican villagers have established communion with a foreign visitor, Hattie, the 'heretic of Oyster Bay' and a 'pagan' Sand Lizard, with whom they have broken bread and to whom they are telling stories of the disputed miracle. (Fitz 223)

Indigo, for her part, see the apparition on the wall once again with the eyes of memory, associating it with the Ghost Dance she witnessed with Sister Salt, Mama and Grandma. In the background stand the citron groves, from where Edward sees the whole scene, pretending to be interested only in taking photographic exposures with his powerful viewfinder. But his real purpose is to get hold of dozens of twig cuttings, which he then intends to grow and develop as a commercial enterprise, and also to use as future capital to invest in the joint venture with Dr. Gates (a somewhat shady character Edward met on the ship on the way to Corsica), namely, shares in the citron stock in exchange for shares in the meteor mine in Arizona: yet another case of violence against the earth, the latter being reduce to a mere exchange commodity. In effect, by chopping off luxuriant citron cuttings, he is cutting himself away from his own life and from that of others, not only because he is physically and emotively distant from that wall which unites them all, but also because this leads up to Hattie's definitive turning away from him in Livorno when she discovers he has been arrested precisely for smuggling the twigs, and realizes that her presence and Indigo's as well were none other than a sort of decoy to cover the real reason for their European journey, to give the impression of a quiet family tour to see some of the famous places.[14]

The America we find in the last part of the novel is the area between the Southwest and California which in various ways accompanies the characters towards the inevitability of a destiny of which they themselves are the major creators. The chaotic and frenetic community that gravitates around the dam construction site, which features fearsomely tough working conditions, gambling, prostitution, drinking and the money cunningly accumulated from these activities, is the place where Sister Salt ends up living for a fairly prolonged period of time, and forms a relationship with the Big Candy, a black who, together with his boss, manages these lucrative goings-on with the aim of achieving a better life at a later date.

The "garden" amid the sandy hills where Sister Salt wanders to at a certain point, almost as if to flee from the devastating "sinister hump" formed by the earth removed to build the dam, remains with her, alert and protective, in the moments leading up to the birth of the baby she is expecting from Big Candy. The fruits she finds along the way—the same ones as in the old gardens—seem to become life-giving nourishment that miraculously enables her to give birth, all on her own, to the baby Sand Lizard. The newborn is gathered up by an earth that becomes steeped with blood almost as if to forge a single entity, like in the poem by Joy Harjo "as she squatted down against the earth to give birth" (Harjo 18), where earth and woman's body fuse and become confused in the act of giving birth and in the very same moment woman/earth gives shape and substance to life: "My Sand Lizard grandfather has come to take me home" (343).

Big Candy turns his back on any bond with Sister Salt and the baby boy, convinced, with guilty obstinacy, that the baby is soon going to die, and he then throws himself into a paroxysmal and utterly useless pursuit of Delena, the woman of the fake "Dog Circus" who, by digging up the safe from that same violated earth, has sneakily made off with the money accumulated by all of them in the gambling and catering they laid on for the workmen occupied on the construction site. Thus the earth itself seems to strike back at its assailants: for that money will be used to finance the guerilla war in Mexico. Big Candy himself actually becomes an unwitting accomplice in this war when he is hired to transport a "special load," after finally reaching Tucson following a hair-raising trip during which he has a close shave with death in his blind pursuit of the woman. Thus money, gold and silver, thirst for power and conquest constitute, right up to the very end, an adverse force standing in opposition to those gardens which, instead, preserve connections, traditions, spiritual wealth that have always been present on either side of the ocean. Overall, what is delineated is an itinerary that charts not only a crossing of geographic and cultural boundaries, but also species boundaries, as becomes apparent from Indigo's close relationship with her travel companions—the monkey Linnaeus and the parrot Rainbow, or the veneration of plants and stones. Moreover, these borders are also crossed by a constant reference to the spiritual element, most importantly the Messiah, whose presence Indigo has in mind even in England, Italy and Corsica.

Whatever energy Edward has seems to be sucked up by that meteor crater whose rocks, apparently rich in iron and precious metals, he wants to use as the basis for setting up a commercial concern, with—duped by—the shifty Dr. Gates, who is the source of this idea and Edward's partner in this last enterprise. This project is connected, as usual, with an unlawful expropriation whose intimate meaning is none other than a "conquest of the other." Edward's bungled faith in science in the end leads him to death, partly on account of the experimental treatment he submits himself to as a supposed cure for the illness he contracted at the meteor crater, a treatment ordered, possibly with evil ulterior purposes, by the very same Dr. Gates himself.

The fire Hattie accidentally sets in her frenzied flight as she tries to avoid being taken back by her father to the stagnant atmosphere of Oyster Bay bursts into a blaze that almost destroys the city of Needles: an emblematic redress for the wrongs and violence she has suffered after having been instrumental in helping Indigo to find her sister, and perhaps a subconscious attempt at purification of a whole world around her. But also, flames that burn the entire life Hattie has so far lived through amid Victorian conformism and touches of unfruitful rebellion. Her journeys have not been itineraries on a quest to discover new lands, but a new way of entering into life and, at the same time, the capacity to move beyond herself, that self she has been so far, increasingly interpreted and filtered by the closeness of Indigo. From a self reduced to separateness—in the first place from Edward and from an existence charted out by that marriage—she gradually sets out on another path, the final arrival point of which is the return to England. This return becomes a union towards the garden of her memory, towards a newly rediscovered identity in a place that has recognizable moulds and footprints: a cultural framework that reveals the female spiritual principle dating back to pre-Christian religions of Old Europe—much like Indigo's beliefs as well as an understanding of the power of the land and its vital connection to human beings.

The old gardens where Indigo and Sister Salt return after the police has, on the penultimate day, interrupted the ritual dances on the river designed to propitiate the arrival of the Messiah, have been trampled and laid waste by the passage of outsiders, but within the space of a winter the signs of an obstinate rebirth make their appearance. Leafy shoots grow at the base of one apricot stump, the rows of gladioli planted by Indigo (significantly to resemble corn kernels and together with datura), whose spuds she herself puts in the stew where there is "a little of everything" (476), not only appear as chromatic harmony which anthropologically overcomes any "color line," but also become food that sustains an arduous survival. It is unity of matter and spirit, of aesthetic beauty and use of everyday things, the natural element entering into human life, where all is an intermediation with earth: it is the meeting with nature, with its evolutionary cycle, its multiplicity of living forms and of life-death that takes place in that space of the garden, a limited space yet also open to the world, to the entire universe.[15]

In the complexity of this narration, dense with events in diverse worlds, even the beginning and end seem to join up in a circular motion. All the "gardens" visited lead back to those gardens in the dunes, and like the latter, all the gardens in the various places are in various ways infused with matriarchal spirituality. If Hattie and Indigo meet initially in a Californian garden where Hattie is jotting down the measurements of the grounds on note cards she used to keep for scholarly bibliographic references, it is in the garden of the Southwest that their reciprocal acquaintance takes shape more solidly—within their respective differences—with Hattie once again writing, not about calculations and geometric arrangements, but words in a letter to Indigo from England, with those old/new words she has perhaps found in the land where she belongs.

The devastation and ruin of ancient civilization in the New World at the beginning of the novel—the rape of America—has a parallel testimony in that rape of Europe Hattie finally writes about, that Europe whose vestiges Hattie proposes to safeguard following Aunt Bronwyn's example.

The big old rattlesnake who watched over the peaceful life among the dunes and was subsequently slaughtered by the invaders lives again together with the thousand statues in old snake's beautiful daughter who gracefully appears at the old spring.

Memory, for Indigo and for whoever stops to listen to her, is a "delta in the skin" (Harjo 42): not a subtle and evanescent element, but a corporeal element, concrete testimony over time. And in the interiority of memory, time neither proceeds nor recedes, but *is* in its circularity, in its motion along itself, in its copresence. Building with memory is also building with nature that preserves everything, first and foremost an individual and collective legacy by virtue of which "all who are lost will be found" (322).

NOTES

1. Leslie Marmon Silko, *Gardens in the Dunes*. New York: Simon & Schuster, 1999. (Subsequent references to this edition are given parenthetically in the text).

2. In this regard Silko cites "Elaine Pagel's wonderful book, *The Gnostic Gospels*. She was in the first group of MacArthur fellows with me, and they called us back to Chicago in 1982 for a reunion. Later she had her publisher send me a copy of her book, *The Gnostic Gospels*. Well, I was deep in the middle of writing *Almanac of the Dead*, and that book sat on my shelf for years. So recently I wrote her a letter and thanked her for it, and I said, oh, by the way, I wrote a whole novel partly because of your book. I started to realize that there are lots of different Jesus Christs, and the Jesus or the Messiah of the Ghost Dance and some of the other sightings of the Holy Family in the Americas were just as valid and powerful as other sighting and versions of Jesus. And I didn't realize until just recently that there are all kinds of Celtic traditions of Saint Joseph and Mary being in England and Ireland. There's always been the Messiah and the Holy Family that belong to the people. And so that got mixed in too" (Arnold 164).

3. In a stimulating and well thought out comparison, Brewster E. Fitz examines the presence in the novel of the various alternatives and affinities to orthodox western religion and thought with reference to the Ghost Dance and the scene of the apparition of the Holy Mother on the schoolhouse wall in Corsica, supplying in particular an extensive discussion on the problems raised by the phenomenon of the "gift of tongues" when the Holy Ghost descended upon the apostles at Pentecost (Act. 2). He cites in this regard the argument by Umberto Eco in *The Search for the Perfect Language* in which Eco attempts to distinguish "glossolalia" from a related phenomenon, "xenoglossia." Fitz also identifies a correspondence, revisited by Silko, between "a passage from the Acts of John, a Gnostic text quoted by Pagels in her discussion of Christ as a spiritual rather than a material being (that) depicts Jesus teaching his friends to dance in a circle around him as he chants in the Garden of Gethsemane . . . Just as the Roman soldiers arrive to arrest Christ and saw confusion among his dancing disciples in the Garden of Gethsemane, so the U.S. soldiers and Indian police arrive to arrest and disperse the Ghost Dancers in *Gardens in the Dunes*. The Ghost Dance, as conceived by Wovoka, stirs together Christian myths and Native American culture. Silko subtly adds readings in Gnosticism to this swirl. The goal of the Ghost Dance, as it is described by Silko, is not only to restore the land to what it was before the arrival of the European settlers, but also to heal the wounds inflicted on tribal cultures by the totalitarian, urbanizing, analytic, and linear narrative of Western culture" (203–04). Silko states that, as reported by Mooney, in 1893 there was a Ghost Dance held in Kingman, Arizona, which, by "poetic license," she has moved to Needles, California. She subsequently discovered that in the same period the dam was put on the Colorado River to build the acqueduct to Los Angeles. On the subject of the Messiah, she states in the same interview: "When you really look at things, even in the early church, there are these different versions or different visions of Jesus. So I want to add the different Native American [versions], to show that in the Americas too there is a Jesus" (Perkins' interview 120).

4. Cf. in this regard the essay by Karen E. Waldron, "The Land as Consciousness." The author cites the well known arguments by Leo Marx in *The Machine in the Garden*, and those by Annette Kolodny in *The Lay of the Land* and *The Land Before Her*.

5. The name derives from Carolus Linnaeus (Carl von Linné, 1707–78), the Swedish botanist to whom the modern classification of plants with the Latin scientific name is owed. Significantly, the animal was captured by Edward in one of his exotic journeys and it was Edward himself who gave the monkey its erudite name, to flaunt his educational background and scientific knowledge, which. however, Silko ironically overturns by attributing to Linnaeus human gifts superior to those of his master.

6. See also "Interior and Exterior Landscapes: The Pueblo Migration Stories" and other essays in Silko's *Yellow Woman*.

7. The same can also be said for the artifacts from various parts of the world that contribute to the décor of Edward's study at Riverside. These have been removed from the place where they originally belonged through an act of mere appropriation, and stand in strange contrast to the scientific instruments of the botanist, which are also in full view in the room, almost as if to indicate a cultural superiority.

8. Fitz helpfully traces the genesis of the name "gladiolus:" "The Latin word *gladius*, sword, from which the diminutive is formed, is of Celtic derivation. From *gladius* is derived *gladiator*, the captive or slave trained to fight professionally to entertain the Romans in the arena" (230).

9. "She (Aunt Bronwyn) was inspired by my friend in Tucson, Sheila Ward, who has ancestors from England, and Spain, as well. Sheila used to keep about fifteen or twenty Hereford cattle at her place on the east side of Tucson, and she would never sell them, never slaughter them. When I'd go to visit Sheila, the bulls, these huge bulls, would block the driveway. So I took some of those elements from my friend, who's eighty-four now, and put them into Aunt Bronwyn" (Perkins' interview 116).

10. It should be noted that in this sort of Grand Tour at the turn of the nineteenth century, a stage in Rome is completely ignored. "This is the crisis point where Indigo's narrative of her travel into Europe reveals connection to tribal meanings, an original hybridity that positions the human form not in binary separation from the animal world, but which integrates female and snake forms, human and animal relations, just as such systems and ways of being were presented as integrated in Indigo's early life experiences in the gardens in the dunes with her grandmother" (Regier 148–49).

11. The frequent use of dreams is explained by the author as follows: "First of all, in terms of mechanics, as a device, the dreaming was a way I could keep the sisters united. And it was also realistic in the sense that it was Indigo's way of not dying of sorrow or dying of being cut off" (Perkins' interview 122).

12. ". . . Sister Salt perceives her child, resulting from intercultural contact at the river project, as a returning ancestor rather than a bicultural child diluting the blood line" (Regier 147).

13. "There's just this wonderful fluid cooperation that you find between little small communities and within tribal groups and it existed in England and Europe. They had the tribal commons. It's capitalism and industrialism that destroy the harmonious fabric of European patters which were much closer. It happened longer ago, but it's quite similar to what was done with other aboriginal people" (Perkins' interview 99).

14. Fitz insightfully comments that at this point Edward assumes a primary role of a heretical version on the story of the Fall: "The narrative in Silko's text obliquely glosses the stories from Genesis, undoing the misogynic patristic interpretation and reattributing and redefining the culpa as infelicitous male blindness. In this Corsican orchard, at the moment that the townspeople, Indigo and Hattie are awaiting the reappearance of the Blessed Mother on the schoolhouse wall, it is not the woman but the man who is responsible for the theft in the garden. Furthermore, Edward is not seduced by the Serpent, who offered knowledge to Eve, but by his blinding desire for wealth, a desire mediated by his modern Western worldview, which is capitalist, scientific, and scholarly" (218–19).

15. On the question of the gladioli and other initial images of the novel, Silko comments: "As far as the beginning of this novel, I had years ago wanted to write a short story about a male character, an Indian man, who goes to Sherman Institute and a teacher there teaches him about gladioli and then he comes home. I never got round to writing that short story . . . I guess the image that stayed with me even from the time I wanted to do that short story was the incongruity of a gladiolus plant growing in

New Mexico or Arizona . . . When I started, the strong impulse was the image of the gladiolus in the desert. The next impulse was I wanted to write about sisters. I was also thinking about those poor tribes along the Colorado River that were completely decimated; they're completely gone now. They were just little desert bands. So that's what gave me the idea to make up the Sand Lizard people that are almost extinct and the two sisters" (Perkins' interview 108–09).

WORKS CITED

Arnold, Ellen L, ed. *Conversations with Leslie Marmon Silko*. Jackson: U of Mississipi P, 2000.

Cohen, Robin. "Of Apricots, Orchids, and Wovoka: An Interview with Leslie Marmon Silko." *Southwestern American Literature* 24.2 (1999): 55–71.

Eco, Umberto. *The Search for the Perfect Language*. Oxford: Blackwell, 1995.

Fitz, Brewster E. *Silko. Writing Storyteller and Medicine Woman*. Norman: U of Oklahoma P, 2004.

Mooney, James. *The Ghost-Dance Religion and the Sioux Outbreak of 1890*. 1892–93. Lincoln: U of Nebraska P, 1991.

Pagel, Elaine. *The Gnostic Gospels*. New York: Vintage, 1979.

Perkins, Owen. "An Interview with Leslie Marmon Silko." *Plains Literary Review* 15 (2005): 81–124.

Regier, Ami M. "Revolutionary Enunciatory Spaces: Ghost Dancing, Transatlantic Travel, and Modernist Arson in *Gardens in the Dunes*." *Modern Fiction Studies* 51.1 (2005): 134–57.

Ruoff Brown, A. La Vonne. "Images of Europe in Leslie Marmon Silko's *Gardens in the Dunes* and James Welch's *The Heartsong of Charging Elk*." *Sites of Ethnicity. Europe and America*. Ed. William Boelhower, Rocio G. Davis, and Carmen Birkle. Heidelberg: Universitatsverlag, 2004. 179–98.

Silko, Leslie Marmon. *Gardens in the Dunes*. New York: Simon & Schuster, 1999.

———. "Landscape, History and the Pueblo Imagination." *Antaeus* 51 (Autumn 1986): 83–94.

———. *Yellow Woman and a Beauty of the Spirit. Essays on Native American Life Today*. New York: Simon & Schuster, 1996.

———. *Sacred Water*. Tucson: Flood Plain P, 1993.

Waldron, Karen E. "The Land as Consciousness." *Such News of the Land*. Ed. Thomas S. Edwards and Elizabeth A. De Wolfe. Hannover: UP of New England, 2001.

FLASHBACKS AND FREE INDIRECT DISCOURSE IN *GARDENS IN THE DUNES*: A LINGUISTIC ANALYSIS OF NON-CHRONOLOGICAL NARRATION

Rachel Barritt Costa

One of the widely debated issues at the intersection of linguistics and literary semantics is the portrayal of time, with the related issue of time as perceived by a character in a novel, and time as communicated by the narrator. Attention has often centered on the way expressions of time in language, including the verbal tense system and deictic phenomena involving "here and now" concepts anchored to the various temporal profiles, can be exploited to convey subtle variations in subjectivity and point of view, as well as greater or lesser mediation by the narrator.

Furthermore, it has been noted that the portrayal of time tends to intermesh with another widely discussed literary device that facilitates representation of reflections from a character's "point of view," namely free indirect speech or thought (henceforth FI).[1] This linguistic form, a hybrid between direct and indirect speech, is generally described as involving an understood verb of reporting—or of thinking—yet what is communicated to the reader is not an externally or heterodiegetic narrator-derived "X said/thought that Z" but, in a sense, the actual contents of the thought or speech act, filtered or "focalized" through the character.[2] Consequently, as compared to a pure narrative sequence with an "omniscient" narrator, FI is claimed to enable the writer to move seamlessly back and forth between interior and the exterior perspectives, thereby allowing more immediate access to the character's mental processes. Thus it is often described as a means of breaking down the barrier represented by the narrator which intervenes—mediates—between the reader and the character; this barrier is at times further overcome by the incorporation of expressive elements typical of direct speech—i.e. of subjectivity—such as question constructions or exclamations, together with lexical features characteristic of orality, which help to convey the impression of communicative immediacy on the part of the character.[3] To account for these curious Janus-like forms, the concept of "dual voice" has sometimes been invoked, with the implication that it allows both the voice of the narrator and that of the character to be heard.[4]

Such forms are well illustrated in *Gardens in the Dunes* (henceforth: *Gardens*) by Leslie Marmon Silko.[5] A classic example of FI featuring a question is seen in a fragment appearing partly in quoted direct speech and partly in FI with an implicit verb of musing, in which Edward wonders whether the mysterious Maya Negress has mistaken his intentions: "'Go away! You cannot buy them but you will pay!' Had she misunderstood him?" (88).[6] An interesting FI example from *Gardens* containing an exclamation is found in a fragment where Sister Salt, having given birth to her baby in the sandy desert environment, begins to wonder how she will survive without water and manage to get back to the camp. "She was so thirsty. She'd never go for a walk without a canteen again—not even in cool weather! Good thing she was only a few miles from the river" (343). Naturally, the exclamation is not a cry of surprise by the narrator but rather is understood to reflect Sister Salt's interior state of mind, as further confirmed by the typically oral phrase of the immediately following sentence, "Good thing. . .," i.e. the kind of vocabulary and grammatical construction she could have used had she expressed her thoughts in direct speech.[7]

That FI intermeshes in particular with the temporal dimension emerges from the well-known fact that its verbs are almost always "back-shifted:" that is to say, they appear in a tensed form which is one degree further in the past than would be expected in the direct speech equivalent.[8] One of the most familiar manifestations of back-shifting, which will form the major focus of attention in this paper, is the pluperfect.[9] The pluperfect is well-known in true indirect discourse, where the verb of reporting can be an actual communication verb, as in the following examples from *Gardens* (pluperfect forms underlined, reporting verbs in cursive script): "Aunt Bronwyn *explained* at one time the entire area <u>had been devoted</u> to vegetables to feed the Norman nuns" (239), "Hattie discussed the child's fears with Edward, who *admitted* that he <u>had been taken</u> aback by the ill temper displayed by the cook towards the child" (113), "Hattie *asked* Edward how he <u>had arranged</u> for the Indian boys to work for him" (110). At times, the reporting verb may be postposed in the manner of a parenthetical, as in "His friends <u>had departed</u> that very morning at daybreak on the Louis XV downriver to Pará, the mestizo brothers *told* him" (146), and on occasion it may be a verb of mental attitude, for instance: "She still *regretted* she <u>had not asked</u> her aunt more about the story of the luminous glow seen in the King's bath" (300).

By manifesting the reporting verb, such true indirect discourse constructions allow the overarching temporal profile to be anchored to the story-line which is presented—in the conventional narrative past tense—by the heterodiegetic narrator of the story, through whom the events affecting the characters are mediated; the pluperfect then acts as a relative tense (Michaelis 8), fulfilling the function of situating the reported event at an earlier time with respect to that of the reporting verb in the unfolding story. But in FI, where the verb of reporting or thinking remains implicit, the appearance of the back-shifted pluperfect form often seems to play a more significant role; it alerts the reader to the possibility that a given content embodies a penetration into the mind of the character. It thus seems to convey a recollection of prior situations filtered through the character's perception rather than a mere continuation of the narrator-based narration. For precisely this reason, the FI pluperfect can play a crucial role in shifting the perspective away from a purely narrator-mediated report and foregrounding a different vision of the situation, as hinted in the following example from *Gardens*:[10] "Laura put her arm around Hattie's shoulders and told her not to worry; she had posted the bond for Edward's release and he would be along in an hour or two" (325). Here the unfolding story concerns the events taking place after Hattie and Edward are detained by the customs authorities upon their return from Corsica, and ostensibly focuses on Laura's friendly gesture together with her verbal act of telling, whereby the posting of the bond is understood by the reader as having taken place earlier, on account of the pluperfect "had posted." However, since the reporting verb "told" remains implicit in the second part of the sentence, the situation, although still focalized through Laura and suggesting her concern for her friend, is not one of merely stating what Laura said and had done: it seems to evoke an added and yet intangible layer of complexity, a communicative situation where some train of thought, perhaps some reflection on the impact of Laura's action, remains implicit yet contributes significantly to the tone of the events reported.

A related example is given by Lawn, building on Banfield's (209) contrast between reflective and non-reflective consciousness. In her study of Lowry's *Under the Volcano* Lawn suggests that the sentence "Unconsciously, he [Hugh] had been watching her, her bare brown neck and arms. . ." (24) could represent Hugh's recall of the flow of his thoughts, his realization that he had been watching her unconsciously, i.e. it could be taken as the reflective recall of prior non-reflective consciousness, and could thus be read as free indirect thought, whereas the unshifted past "he was watching her" would have induced no such implication.

Lawn's observation provides a useful starting point for an analysis of some examples taken from *Gardens*. Consider for instance a sentence that displays a striking structural similarity with the case cited by Lawn: "As Hattie listened a sinking feeling began to overtake her; he had been following a clandestine plan all along" (329). The pluperfect "had been following" not only embodies an indication of prior time as compared to the time of the simple past tense "listened," but it also suggests a realization on Hattie's part; that is to say, it seems to involve a reflective recall and mental re-elaboration of a previous state of affairs, as indeed is implied by the first part of the sentence, where Hattie's "listening" prompts the onset of mental processes, a "feeling."

Consider also the following passage from *Gardens*: "The Bible was the only book Vedna could find to practice her reading. They had gone to school and learned to read when they lived in Winslow with their father. Their Chemehuevi clanspeople were troubled because their father wasn't Chemehuevi: he had been from Laguna Pueblo, working on the railroad" (334). Although opening with a reference to the Bible as reading material, what is conveyed in the passage, by virtue of the FI pluperfect, is Vedna's train of reflections on an earlier stage of her life, sparked by the mental association of reading with her schooling back in her childhood; this recollection then expands into a revisitation of her life in the past, her origins and her various experiences during childhood and adolescence.

Another striking case, exemplifying both the "reflective recall" aspect of the pluperfect as well as the strongly expressive potential of the FI form, is the following example: "Hattie asked if these were the old families of Bath, and Aunt Bronwyn laughed merrily. Fled long ago, they had, to escape the milling flocks of tourists and vacationers and the traffic jams like this one forcing their coach to inch past the hotels and shops" (264). Here, Hattie's questions addressed to Aunt Bronwyn and the Aunt's replies are both understood to take place at the corresponding stage of the unfolding story, i.e. during the visit itself, but the disappearance of the old families is understood to have occurred much earlier, by virtue of the pluperfect with "had." Furthermore, their disappearance is clearly reported in such a way as to reflect an attitudinal reflective recall by the implicit subject of the reporting, i.e. Aunt Bronwyn.[11] The reader is thus granted a glimpse into Aunt Bronwyn's feelings towards the impact of mass tourism on local families that would not emerge so clearly from normal indirect speech. That is to say, had the sentence simply been "Aunt Bronwyn said that they had fled years before," the report would have been mediated through the external point of view of the narrator to whom the narrative simple past tense of "said" would be attributed. Moreover, the sentence would have been far less likely to contain the deictic adverb "ago" that signals a deictic anchoring to an actualization of the character's "now."[12]

The above observations provide an interesting interpretive key for an analysis of *Gardens*, which, as insightfully pointed out by Fitz (207), makes very extensive use of the free indirect speech technique. Yet it soon becomes clear that the picture sketched above is oversimplified, for in significant cases the FI verbal form fails to show the expected back-shifting to the pluperfect. Consider the following example:

> Hattie was quite fond of her father and mother, but she was not eager to return so soon to Oyster Bay and the whirl of teas and dinner parties her mother and Edward's sister would organize to honor their visit. During the dinners and festivities that had celebrated their engagement she had commented that she felt she was on display, and Edward reminded her that he himself was a subject of curiosity because of his expeditions abroad.
> Hattie felt tears spring into her eyes when she saw the child and the monkey cling to each other as the watched the luggage and trunks carried outside to the coach. (113)

Here the pluperfect forms "had celebrated" and "had commented" appear to be instances of 'reflective recall'; but these forms then give way to the simple past ("reminded"), a tense form which would normally be expected to resume the overall story-line. However, it appears from the context that there is no interruption of the reminiscence until the next paragraph, which concerns their planned journey to New York with Indigo rather than Edward's ill-fated and eyebrow-raising expeditions. Consequently, Edward's act of reminding is felt to belong to the reminiscence even without the grammatical cue of back-shifting.

Numerous other examples can be cited, some with quite complex temporal threads. Consider for instance the following reflections by Hattie during her visit to Laura's home, in which she silently recalls her experiences at Aunt Bronwyn's: "Hattie wanted to ask Laura about the luminous glow in the story—so similar to the glowing light she saw that night in Aunt Bronwyn's garden. She still regretted she had not asked her aunt more about the story of the luminous glow seen in the King's Bath" (300). The reader knows by this time that the visit to Aunt Bronwyn occurred prior to the visit to Laura: this discourse knowledge will prompt the reader towards a back-shifted interpretation of "she saw," despite the lack of overt pluperfect tense. Such an interpretation is then confirmed by the canonical back-shifted pluperfect of "had not asked," so that the reference time of the latter form is roughly the same as that of "she saw" despite the grammatical difference.

Or consider: "The dressing of the table must have required as much time as the preparation of the courses of vegetables and pasta. The *professoressa* was happy to hear about their visit to the excavations in Bath. She began her studies with Roman antiquities, but the earlier cultures won her over. Hattie described the tin mask, pre-Roman, crude, but quite powerful, which interested the *professoressa* a great deal because a number of pieces in her collection were figures in masks" (284). Should one regard "She began" as having the same time reference as "Hattie described," namely the time of the narration, i.e. the narrator's conventional past tense? Naturally, this would be preposterous, as it would suggest a sudden intrusion of an event of studying antiquities taking place in the time-compressed interval between the *professoressa* hearing about the visit to Bath and Hattie's description of the tin-mask. Rather, the reader integrates an anteriority meaning, mentally expanding the passage to include something like "The *professoressa* explained that she too was interested in excavations, as she had begun. . .," thus supplying back-shifted form even though it is missing in the text.

Another interesting and highly complex example is found in the following passage, where Hattie, Edward and Indigo are on board the ship on their way to Europe, after Hattie has just read Indigo a bed-time story.

> 'Tomorrow', Hattie said, firmly closing the book. 'Good night and sweet dreams'. 'Sweet dreams', Indigo replied. She [Hattie] tucked the covers around Indigo and kissed her forehead. The parrot's head was tucked under its wing but a glittering eye watched as she put out the light. It was after nine so she did not disturb Edward in the adjoining cabin, but she did not feel like going to bed quite yet.   (227)

Here the fragment opens with a series of past tense verbs that plausibly represent actions taking place chronologically on the boat at that particular point of the story (said, tucked, kissed, put out), and they follow on naturally from the prior context of saying goodnight (the verbs describing states, "was," "watched," "did not," do not actively participate in the chronology but neither do they contradict it).[13] On the other hand, the same cannot be said for the immediately following sentence:

> During the afternoon she felt an odd lethargy that slowed her motions and demanded her conscious effort to climb the steps to the ship's dining room. She recognized the feeling at once: it was that old companion of melancholy, inertia, which the doctors blamed on her reading and writing and lack of exercise.
> When she was first stricken, the doctors mistook her lethargy for a more serious illness; fortunately her introduction to Edward at the ball banished the symptoms. Surely the melancholy had not returned!   (227)

On the assumption that the storyline is continuing, should the reader believe that the time frame of "during the afternoon" has shifted to the following day—given that the previous actions were situated at night-time, before going to bed and therefore presumably not in the afternoon? But in the absence of contextual confirmation of a forwards shift in time, the reader may not rule out the possibility of a reminiscence, which is then corroborated by a mention of events the reader knows to have occurred in prior time, namely the time when, after rejection of her thesis, she was first stricken with her malaise, and then her subsequent first meeting with Edward at the ball. Yet it is only this interpretive integration that allows the verbs "mistook" and "banished" to be understood as referring to anterior time despite the absence of back-shifting that would have resulted from a genuine form of FI approximating "she recalled that during the afternoon she had felt. . .," or "she reflected that her introduction to Edward at the ball had banished . . . ." That such an integration is warranted is confirmed by the next sentence, "Surely the melancholy had not returned!," partly on account of the pluperfect "had returned,"[14] but above all on account of the characteristically expressive exclamatory form, suggestive of FI.

The same interpretation continues into the subsequent sentence: "How ironic if the malaise were to return during their visit with Aunt Bronwyn" (228), which is likewise couched in an expressive quasi-oral mode.[15] This is followed by the fleeting appearance of an actual pluperfect, 'had meant': "In the months she suffered most from melancholy, the letters from her grandaunt had meant a great deal to Hattie. Aunt Bronwyn followed the latest theories of the mind and emotions, and it was her observation Hattie's illness could be cured if she completed her thesis" (228). Admittedly, the mention of Hattie by name (characteristic of an external perspective) rather than the pronominal form could be taken as pointing to a sudden narratorial incursion designed to specify anterior time, yet there is evidence elsewhere in *Gardens* that the mention of a full name does not necessarily contradict FI but can instead invoke a dual-voice phenomenon.[16] That the FI reading, approximately equivalent to "Hattie realized that in the months when she had suffered most from melancholy, the letters from her grandaunt had meant a great deal to her" is the most likely is further suggested by the line of reasoning arising from the immediately following sentence, although simple past forms take over once more: "After the announcement of their engagement, Hattie's melancholy lifted and she was reluctant to return to the notes and manuscript for fear the anxiety and hopelessness might reoccur. Once or twice during Edward's absence a fatigue tried to take root, but Hattie warded it off with cool baths and green tea" (228). Namely, since the reader knows at this point that Hattie and Edward are together on the ship, and therefore Edward is not absent at this moment, it is evident that the simple past forms in the above passage, "lifted," "tried," "warded," cannot be part of the storyline and must instead be instances of the FI recollectional mode.

But if these forms belong to the recollectional mode, the reader is quite justified in expecting the recollection to continue into the following sentence and into next paragraph:

> Since Indigo's arrival, Hattie felt so fit and was in such good spirits she assumed herself cured. After travel and a visit with one's family, fatigue was not unusual, but Hattie also felt a vague discouragement that she could not articulate, a feeling similar to the one that preceded her illness before.
> She summoned all her energy to break free of the heaviness in her limbs to pick up the portfolio. She did not open it at once; the very sensation of its weight in her hands brought back vivid memories. So much had seemed possible in the beginning; Hattie took pages and pages of notes—copying entire sections of Dr. Rhinehart's translations.   (228)

However, a more careful inspection of the text may pick up on the reference to travel, which could be indicative of a return to the main storyline, namely to the sea voyage; furthermore, the mention of "the heaviness in her limbs" suggests a link-up to the earlier statement of "an odd lethargy that slowed her motions," which, as described above, can be traced to dinner time on board ship when she had to make a "conscious effort to climb the steps to the ship's dining-room," i.e. to the evening and to the actual time in the unfolding story when Hattie kisses Indigo goodnight. It therefore embodies a return to the main story line. In other words, despite a contextual signal of "memories"—which seems to warrant the expectation that it is indeed the world of memories that is being invoked—there is reason here to believe that the simple past verbal forms "She summoned all her energy . . ." and "She did not open it at once" are bona fide narrator-originated past tenses.

Yet even this resumption of the chronology is immediately abandoned once again with the occurrence of another back-shifted FI pluperfect, "So much had seemed possible," as if to suggest "Hattie mused that some much had seemed possible." This in turn provides the cue for a new return to non-shifted FI, allowing "Hattie took pages and pages of notes" to be understood as describing an anterior event despite the lack of overt back-shifted pluperfect. Of course, this is consistent with the reader's understanding of the logic of the events portrayed, for the reader is by now well aware that Hattie's note-taking took place during her university days and that Hattie frequently indulges in recollections of the various events that befell her. Hence the reader is unlikely to be misled into believing that Hattie took notes on the boat on her way to Europe.

By contrast, the situation is less clear with regard to the immediately following sequence: "She shuffled through the pages of notes until she found the quotations from the Coptic manuscripts she intended to use to illustrate her thesis. Here it was! the passage that had excited her so much, and inspired her thesis—the same passage that caused such consternation on the thesis committee" (228). If, as argued above, the opening of the portfolio forms part of the narrator-mediated storyline, then in all probability so does the shuffling through the pages. But once more the point of view then immediately focuses again on Hattie's interior attitude, with another exclamatory form: "Here it was!" in which the indexical 'here' signals an anchor to the character's deictic center—and hence to FI. This leads in to the immediately following back-shifted pluperfect "the passage that had excited her," which, in addition to corroborating reflective recall by Hattie, could be said to function as a form of anterior time route indicator or flag to orient the reader in unraveling the temporal perspectives.

This intricate weaving in and out of temporal perspectives abounds throughout the novel. There are multiple transitions from the narratorial storyline to FI to genuine reported speech mediated by the narratorial temporal reference (the narrator's past), and as illustrated in these passages the transitions may occur abruptly, leaving the reader's mind in a whirl in the attempt to disentangle the layering of events.

A particularly significant illustration of this type of dizzying situation is found in the scenes in the early part of the novel in which Hattie has her first encounter with Indigo, where the events shift from one perspective to another through free association of ideas within the character's mind. For example, shortly after Hattie takes one of her customary strolls around the garden of the Riverside house, absorbed in "renovation plans for the arcade," she "became so engrossed . . . the child under the lilac bushes slipped her mind" (73). The child having momentarily faded out of her consciousness, Hattie's inner reflections are free to dwell on the garden-related subject of Edward's house and grounds, her marriage to Edward and her life before marriage, whereby the reader learns that she "wanted to reassure Edward that she was not at all bothered that the [Bahamas-Key West] expedition had come so soon after their wedding" (73). This could be taken as a narratorial description of Hattie's state of mind, but it could be a mental attitude focalized through Hattie. Certainly, the reflective recall of an expedition, as signaled by the back-shifted FI pluperfect, "had come," seems to set the scene for a reminiscence concerning some aspects of the expedition which are likely to have been of particular significance for Hattie, consisting in this case not of Edward's own activities during the actual expedition, but of the activities Hattie engaged in to occupy her time during his absence. The reader is thus prepared for Hattie's musing that "the expedition had been planned well in advance of their engagement; Edward always kept a busy schedule" (73).

This is followed by a description of Hattie's state of mind, again in FI mode as shown by the expressive term "Actually," in "Actually, she looked forward to this time by herself to get accustomed to her new home and new life" (73). Here the non-eventive verbal phrase "looked forward to" portrays a durative setting, and the reader is thus likely to be all the more surprised to find that "The day after his departure, she rose at dawn and gathered pink rose petals from the old climbing rosebush . . . While the petals dried, she sewed sachets from white satin remnants of her wedding gown" (73). For it seems undeniable that the verbs 'rose', 'gathered', 'said', and 'walked' here refer to non-durative single individual past actions that occurred at a specific moment in the past, namely the day after his departure: does this signal that the perspective has shifted away from the previously introduced reminiscences (which were presented from Hattie's point of view) and has moved back, as it were, into straightforward past time narration, i.e. the time mediated by the heterodiegetic narrator? And if so, what is the past time to which the events are anchored in sequence here? Could it be a past time set in chronological sequence posterior to Hattie's discovery of Indigo? In other words, is the reader justified in building a scenario as follows: Hattie finds Indigo ⇨ Edward departs ⇨ Hattie rises at dawn?

If this were so, then one would be led to interpret the simple past verbs that follow shortly thereafter as continuing in the same sequence: for instance "walked" in "The first week Edward was away, she walked from room to room; from the polished oak floors to the oak paneling and high ceilings, she could find nothing out of place. Edward's mother died ten years before they met, but her presence still was there" (73). Yet such an interpretation is then contradicted by the reference to an event which necessarily happened at a prior time, namely Edward's mother's death, stated to have occurred before Hattie ever met Edward. Moreover, the reference to "walked from room to room" is soon followed by references to even earlier events from Hattie's childhood, again recounted with simple past verbs which cannot possibly stand in consecutive sequence with "walked:" "She discovered books when she was four years old . . .," "Hattie rapidly lost interest in the dolls dressed in elegant gown and the tiny china teacups and plates she was given on her last birthday" (74).

The point is that in order to understand the flow of events in Hattie's reminiscences, and discriminate them from the conventional past time of the heterodiegetic narration, i.e. from unfolding events in the main story, it is necessary to interpret the stream of associations in Hattie's mind rather than following the apparent chronology of a sequence of linearly narrated past events. This same power of association then jolts the reader's mind, just as it does Hattie's when, in the opening sentence of the immediately following paragraph, there is a sudden return to the concept of 'measurements', from which this particular series of recollections had started out, triggered by the physical presence of a card that mentally transports Hattie back to an earlier period of her life and other people's lives. Thus the recollection, which began a little earlier, as she "paced off the width of the grassy area and noted the *measurements* on one of the note cards she carried in her pocket, a habit left over from her days of scholarly research into early church history" (73), and which sprang from the realization that this grassy garden was part of Edward's life, ends at the moment when, "[a]s Hattie finished noting the *measurements*, she glanced down and saw the bread and jam were gone from the tray" (emphasis added, 74). Here the reader is indeed restored to the time of the narration by implicitly reconnecting with the flow of events that surrounded Hattie's discovery of Indigo—namely her concern for the small runaway, for whom she had "carried the bread and jam and a cup of water on a tray" (72). But it is only this interpretive line of reasoning that enables the reader to correctly understand the time profiles involved, since, as illustrated, many of the reflective recall phrases are not marked by the pluperfect and are thus grammatically indistinguishable from bona fide narratorial past tenses.

Now, when these phenomena are considered within the overall perspective of this novel, one of the fundamental queries must be whether the sudden temporal swings and the resulting potential confusion is actually a non-issue, to be explained simply by assuming that the variation between FI with overt pluperfect and FI lacking pluperfect is purely random, due to the intrinsic convolutions of such a dense novel, or serves to alleviate the "cumbersome" nature of the pluperfect.[17] One might also be tempted to suggest that it is perhaps merely based on a language variety (informal American English) that makes little use of the pluperfect, or possibly that it is related to the use of irony, which has been argued by Fitz (207) to constitute one of the characterizing aspects of FI. I will try to counter these hypotheses, and seek to put forward an alternative explanation.

First, as far as irony is concerned, I would agree with Vandelanotte (568) that one may raise doubts at to whether it arises specifically from FI itself: rather, it could arise more as an outcome of the tension between the communicated content of the story and the represented interaction among the characters. Thus in cases where a character's inner thoughts conveyed by FI appear to contrast with presumably objective information the reader has acquired through the narrator's mediation, the character's attitude may seem to be ironically misguided. But this implies, as Jahn points out ("Contextualizing" 356), that narratorial FI irony can plausibly arise in the same fashion as with any other mentioning technique such as direct speech or direct thought.[18]

Although clearly a fascinating topic of investigation within the field of narratology, I believe it would go beyond the scope of this linguistically-based paper, which seeks to shed light above all on the implications of the interaction between FI and the presence or absence of the pluperfect. Furthermore, since the FI nature of the unshifted simple past forms analyzed here is not in doubt, whatever irony attaches to the pluperfect forms would also attach to the corresponding simple past forms, and would not act as a discriminating feature. Attention here will therefore center on alternative hypotheses.

Let us now examine the question of the language variety. It may be relevant to note that there is an on-going debate among linguists, and in particular among English as a Foreign Language teachers, concerning the alleged obsolescence of the Pluperfect, especially in American English, in cases where the surrounding discourse context already makes the temporal anteriority clear.[19]. However, evidence against the interpretation of such a phenomenon as a new American trend comes from a concordance search on a corpus of British English (McGill 25) which showed—though no explanation was offered—that in very many British English cases anterior time forms are in fact reported in the past tense instead of the pluperfect, citing an example from as far back as 1961.[20] Thus if the pluperfect is falling out of use, it is not a purely American phenomenon, neither is it a recent innovation.

Additional evidence against the suggestion that the pluperfect is obsolescent in modern American English comes from what has been described by Celce-Murcia (6) as a discourse strategy exploiting this tense as a closure frame, above all in written narratives where it serves to signal the writer's purpose for relating the narrative—often in the form of a recapitulating "had begun" or "had commenced."[21] An interesting example of this type can be found in *Gardens*:

> Laura glanced around at the old forest and smiled, then in a soft voice she told Hattie: On the eve of the battle, her husband deserted his army command in Eritrea. The following day, Italian forces suffered terrible losses against the rebels; at first he was feared lost or taken prisoner. It was this confusion that brought such embarrassment later—early newspaper reports called him a "fallen hero," but weeks later army intelligence learned the colonel had fled to Cairo.
> They were both silent for a moment; Hattie kept her eyes to the ground, but Laura patted her arm cheerfully and smiled; it was for the best, she said.   (289)

Note, firstly, that the fragment offers a striking illustration of FI, cued in this case by the literal introduction of the verb of reporting, "told," which, however, is here shorn of the expected subordinate clause of indirect speech and continues as if recounted directly despite retaining the 3rd-person pronominal form ("her husband") of indirect speech. This disconnected effect is rendered graphically in the form of the colon followed by the capital letter without inverted commas, thereby alerting the reader to the change in tone.[22] The fragment also embodies another striking illustration of the phenomenon of absence of back-shifting, in particular with the verbs *deserted, suffered, brought, called, learned*, all appearing in the simple past tense, just as is—in appearance—the case for the verbs of the subsequent paragraph, e.g. *kept, patted, smiled, said*. The crucial signal that marks a distinction between the implicit anterior time of the former group—past with respect to the character's "now"—and the narrator's past of the latter group is precisely the significant intervention of a recapitulating pluperfect, *had fled*, which brings the reported event to its climax and conclusion. This reorientation is then made clear by the return to the unfolding story-line in which the two women are involved together, where they become the grammatical subject of the sentence: "They were both silent for a moment."

Overall, then, on the evidence of *Gardens*, in the immediately preceding example and also in the numerous examples cited earlier where the pluperfect does appear, it hardly seems warranted to invoke the wholesale obsolescence of the pluperfect: rather, it is simply its periodic elision that remains mysterious.

It would therefore seem plausible to suggest that if discourse strategies are involved in the above cited "conclusive" use of the pluperfect, then it is rational to assume one may find some type of discourse-governed account of other linguistic issues involving this verbal form, in particular its elimination in certain free indirect speech contexts in *Gardens*, rather than suggesting a purely random distribution of pluperfects and simple pasts. I will propose an explanation that appeals to the concept of flashbacks, suggesting that some of the characteristics of flashbacks are exploited by Silko in a rather special way.

We have observed so far that one of the curious features of *Gardens* is its kaleidoscopic darting to and fro between temporal perspectives, interweaving the past with the forward-moving elements of the unfolding story. Abrupt transitions abound: some are fleeting, more in the nature of a sudden flash, while others may extend over a considerable stretch of narrative. Extended flashbacks play a particularly significant role in the early part of the novel, when the reader first makes the acquaintance of Hattie and Edward. Indeed, this early part is almost entirely built around flashbacks providing background information and descriptions of prior events and aspects of the characters' lives, for instance Hattie's experiences at university and her fascination with paleo-Christian manuscripts, or Edward's expeditions to Central and South America where he hopes to get his hands on botanical species that offer the potential for commercial exploitation.

Now, it seems logical that in an analeptic construction like a flashback, some indication of prior time would be a fundamental component, not only in terms of the logical representation of the temporal profile but also as a "navigation" signal to the reader who seeks to recompose mentally the fragmented aspects surfacing in the characters' consciousness. And in fact this is indeed frequently the case in *Gardens*, in that the flashbacks quite often—although by no means systematically—begin with, or place fairly near the beginning, a putatively back-shifted pluperfect, which in this case can be seen as a grammatical frame of anteriority that cues the initiation of a flashback; the pluperfect then gives way to simple pasts which, in context, still continue the flashback. Several examples from *Gardens* are given below, but numerous cases can be found throughout the novel:[23]

> The voyage from the Keys across the lower Gulf <u>had taken</u> a week longer than scheduled as the ship was forced to take refuge in protected coves . . . When they departed Veracruz the skies were blue and the wind calm, but as they began to cross the Bay of Campeche, the wind speed intensified . . .   (86)

> Hattie woke from a dream about England. She <u>had been</u> in an old churchyard . . . . She did not recognize the old stone church . . . Hattie tried to scoot herself the length of the stone, but the cloth of her dress snagged . . .   (163)

> An early hurricane season in the Caribbean Sea <u>had forced</u> them to cut short their expedition. One after the other, the tropical storms lashed the Bahamas and the Keys. they attempted to wait out the first storm in St. Augustine, but a great gust of wind and ocean surge flung the small boat containing all their supplies against the crushed pier . . . Edward tried to send a telegram . . . but the high winds from the approaching storm knocked out telegraph communications as far north as Atlanta. Weeks later the downed lines were still not repaired, which was the reason his telegram to Hattie <u>had arrived</u> only hours before Edward.   (84–85)

The function of the pluperfect as an opening frame emerges particularly clearly in the example recounting the Bahama-Keys expedition, where Edward's reflective recollection begins with 'had forced', as if hinting at a parallel with a mental process of remembering or telling which, had it been rendered explicit by the narrator, would have approximated "Edward recollected / related to Hattie that an early hurricane season . . . had forced them . . . ." But the narration then continues with the simple past tense (*lashed, attempted, flung, tried, knocked*), as if the reported events were simply a past tense narration, focalized through Edward and presenting his reasons for the expedition's failure, until this is interrupted by another pluperfect (*had arrived*) which once again breaks up the temporal flow. This second insertion of the pluperfect conveys the impression of an intervening—but suppressed—reporting verb: "and he explained this was the reason why the telegram to Hattie had arrived only hours before."[24] If this suggestion is combined with Lawn's observation, mentioned earlier, that the use of the pluperfect can serve to signal reflective recall and with Celce-Murcia's conclusive pluperfect, then it can be argued that the pluperfect to some extent plays a discourse role as a frame signaling openings and closures of flashbacks in which a character relives a previous experience.

On the other hand, as has been illustrated in this paper, the back-shifted forms are not applied systematically, and while I believe that the framing concept has some validity, it does not in itself provide all the answers. For as we have seen, the fact that the back-shifted pluperfects frequently give way to an unshifted simple past form generates one of the curious features of *Gardens*, namely the sense of an overlapping of the time of the flashback with the time of the narration. That is to say, one has the impression that once the frame of the flashback is established via the pluperfect of anterior time, the events recounted in the flashback lose their anteriority and emanate from the same time as the basic narration, so that the temporal reference point of the past tense narration seems to merge with the temporal dimension imposed by the character's perspective and what is foregrounded is the character's direct experience of the events.

But why should *Gardens* be structured in this way? Why make such extensive use of flashbacks, only to erase or fade out the overt indication of the flashback? And is *Gardens* an isolated example of the use of such a technique, or are similar phenomena known from other literary texts or forms of written discourse?

That this is indeed a recurrent phenomenon in other works as well is noted by a number of critics addressing the interaction between linguistics and literary analysis, who have observed that the distinction between free indirect forms and explicit direct or indirect reporting is by no means clear-cut. Rather, one is far more likely to encounter fuzzy borders, suggestive of a cline of subjectivity, where it cannot be ruled out that the distinction between FI and non FI forms may be contextually determined. For instance, in the pioneering work by Leech and Short (181; 330–31; 339–40), it is noted that in cases where no reporting clauses are present, there is evidence of considerable ambiguity between narration forms and Free Indirect forms, particularly with respect to thought presentation; the authors thus posit a "cline of narratorial interference," with free indirect forms offering a more mimetic rendering, although the authors do not specifically address the distinction between pluperfect and simple past. Building on this approach, though considering a wider range of forms than merely free indirect constructions, Semino, Short and Culpeper (34) point out that a cooperative strategy by a discourse-sensitive reader is often required in order to restore an understood verb of reporting and thus to correctly interpret certain sequences, as in cases where one sentence acts pragmatically like a reporting clause for the second.[25] Wiebe, in an interesting investigation on "Tracking Point of View in Narrative" concerning an algorithm for devices that enable readers to find their way among complex changes in point of view and expressions of subjectivity, mentions in passing that the pluperfect is potentially subjective because a character can reflect on what occurred or might have occurred in the past, but — significantly — it may be expressed by the simple past tense in the midst of a subjective context (258). Examining this issue more specifically, Ikeo (39) notes that a sentence which would not be regarded as a free indirect form if considered in isolation can acquire such an interpretation in the appropriate textual context, for instance if it appears in the middle of a text as part of a character's memory.[26] Ehrlich, who also considers sentences that do not display the characteristic free indirect markers such as direct speech syntax, exclamations or subjective expressions and which may therefore not immediately be recognizable as free indirect discourse, notes that a wide variety of sentences can, given the right context, become amenable to a free indirect reading if a sentence contains character oriented subjective expressions or is accompanied by a parenthetical indicating a reflector (40ff).[27]

Yet in spite of this awareness of the interplay between character subjectivity and narratorial presence, and the emphasis on the need for tracking devices to assist the reader, relatively little attention seems to be paid to the search for an explanation of the tense alternation phenomenon. But interesting observations are put forward by Emmott (*I*), adopting a text-oriented and cognitive-functional approach to discourse analysis that seeks to identify cognitive reasons for the use of a particular grammatical form at a specific point in a text. She notes, as I also showed earlier for *Gardens*, that in flashbacks many of the pluperfects are found predominantly at the beginning, to establish the anteriority of the ensuing sequence of events, and at the end, to reaffirm the anteriority of the flashback time frame, while during much of a flashback the simple past may be used, because the reader's assumption of the continuity of events within the "past in the past" time band would make repeated grammatical signaling unnecessary.[28] Emmott suggests two possible advantages of this technique: the simple past may be easier to sustain over long stretches of text since it has what she describes as a "less cumbersome" structure than the past perfect, and a lack of repeated signaling would allow greater involvement in the action, making the events "come to life" for the reader. While I believe that the first explanation is simplistic,[29] the second can help to illuminate significant aspects of the complexities of *Gardens*.

More specifically, I would argue that the sense of "involvement" can be associated with the sense of vividness (a term also used by Emmott, albeit somewhat generically) conveyed by the unshifted simple past forms: for one cannot escape the intuitive impression that the simple past forms narrate with greater immediacy, thereby discarding the atmosphere of "reflective consciousness" in favor of something approaching a more direct narration. In this interpretation, while the unshifted forms retain one of the major hallmarks of indirect discourse—third-person pronouns—they serve a precise purpose: that of communicating to the reader that the mode of discourse involved has the immediacy of story-telling.

That is to say, through the way the characters' recollections are presented, the "reflective recall" mode fades and, crucial though it is to the FI technique, it is no longer awarded priority, so that the simple past seems to become a more immediate form, in some sense approximating the more mimetic form of direct speech.[30] One can therefore advance the hypothesis that this curious feature of *Gardens* represents a story-telling technique utilized by Silko to recreate something approaching the atmosphere that belonged to the oral tradition, in which events were related directly without narratorial mediation. At the same time, however, Silko's world is obviously no longer that of the oral tradition, and the latter can only be hinted at indirectly by intensive exploitation of literary and linguistic means, one of which is precisely the subversion of the carefully constructed edifice of western literary story-telling techniques.

The FI forms, both in their back-shifted but particularly in their unshifted forms, also provide the key to understanding another curious feature of *Gardens*. For as Fitz has noted, not only is there a drastic paucity of dialogue in *Gardens*, but there are also numerous cases where the analytically-minded reader might wonder what language certain interactional episodes could have been expressed in: for instance, would the local officials in Corsica (the Mayor etc.) have spoken to Hattie in English? (207–12). But given the above hypothesis of vivid FI, this dilemma does not really arise: by providing a direct line to the ideational processes of the characters involved, the represented thought or speech need not be committed to any specific language: thus the issue of the actual language form is bypassed, and what dialogue there is can be construed as merely symbolic—a sort of reconversion into direct speech of material whose original form need not be specified, and indeed cannot truly be expressed in the inevitably imperfect forms of present-day human language.[31] Furthermore, as originally pointed out by Banfield and taken up again by Jahn ("Contextualizing" 352), the representation of thought inevitably has to contend with the psycholinguistic issue that there is no proven demonstration that thought processes occur in verbal form in the mind: they may well occur "in pictures" or in other associative modes that could not translate straightforwardly into direct speech.[32]

The concept of vividness and the story-telling approach tie in with another feature of the flashbacks, providing a second possible reason why the boundaries between the developing story and the flashbacks tend to be effaced. This feature concerns the position of the flashbacks within the overall structure of the novel. Predominating in the first half of the novel, there are far fewer flashbacks in the later stages; furthermore, they are not equally distributed among the characters, and revolve more intensively around Hattie and Edward than the other protagonists. A trivial explanation might simply claim that in the earlier stages the reader needs to be provided with more background information about the two main characters' prior experiences in order to be able to grasp the story line. However, it is worth noting that Aunt Bronwyn and the *professoressa* also slip into recall of earlier stages and circumstances of their lives—as mentioned earlier in this paper, and even Big Candy has occasional moments when he allows his thoughts to wander over his prior experiences, wherein the same characteristic oscillations between back-shifted FI pluperfects and simple pasts recur as well as traces of narratorial intervention (335–36; 444). A less trivial account might suggest that the interpenetration of the different dimensions given by the flashbacks iconically reflects the fractured minds of the characters, who, assailed by the burden of their memories and the mosaic of their anxieties in the earlier part of the novel, cannot fully untangle the various different and interpenetrating strands of their life experience, and slide from one perspective to another, or from one association of ideas to another, as in stream of consciousness.

This interpretation, which I believe is not to be disregarded, can be integrated by inquiring more generally into the function of flashbacks in *Gardens* as a means of rendering the stratification of memory and time. That is to say, despite the overall developmental structure of the novel, the story also contains within itself aspects of a non-linear non-chronological structuring of time. Indeed, Silko herself, discussing her use of flashbacks in *Almanac* in an interview with Laura Coltelli—but the comments are equally germane to *Gardens*—gives what is perhaps the most eloquent description of the way the flashback technique breaks down the barriers of chronological temporal structure:

> I used flashbacks because I wanted the moments of the past to be as alive as they
> really are; I wanted the reader to be there and to see and feel the aliveness of the
> past. The past does not die. The past is alive, side by side with the present. . . . The
> use of the flashback also prepares the reader for the realization that time is not
> linear, that the past is not left behind and the past is not dead. All the past goes into
> the creation of this present moment.   (71)

But precisely because the past is intermeshed with the present, the various past
episodes appear to radiate outwards from the protagonists without being linked
by overt internal relations of anteriority and priority: they simply emanate from
the protagonist's "now," the latter being deictically re-centered[33] to the character
rather than to the time of narration. This provides a further explanation for the
abandonment of the back-shifted pluperfect forms since, as mentioned earlier,
even in FI the pluperfect necessarily contains a trace of a narrator-mediated past
time—the reference point against which the anterior time is measured—whereas
the unshifted forms simply express a past measured against the character's re-
centered "present." In other words, with the back-shifted forms the reader is made
implicitly aware of a character's consciousness of events which the character,
reflectively, knows to have happened at an earlier time, but with the unshifted
forms one layer of abstraction is cast aside, and the character's thoughts are
communicated by a sort of direct recall, in a form linked more vividly to the events
the character is, in a sense, re-experiencing from a recentered present time point:
not so much the reflective consciousness of "X had happened at that time" but the
direct and vivid recall of "X happened then." And implicitly this enables "the
reader to know the stories of the different characters from the inside, through the
eyes of these characters . . . to feel what the characters felt" (Coltelli 71).

   The above described multiplicity of temporal perspectives within the
flashbacks result in a blurring and multiple layering of the temporal dimensions,
so that the characters appear to slip in and out of different but simultaneously
existing temporal dimensions (reflective recall, direct recall), while the narrative
itself slips in and out of points of view, now of the narrator, now of the character.
This could almost be likened to a cinematographic effect that 'zooms' to parts of
the action which focus more specifically on the circumstances involving a
particular character and/or cuts to different scenes. It is worth pointing out that a
cinematic technique is indeed invoked by Ryan ("Narrative Discourse" 74), who,
in conjunction with her approach based on "story-line windows" that exploits a
metaphor from the world of computers, postulates a "narrative screen" (69) and
suggests that a story-line window is akin to the continuous "take" of an imaginary
camera (62). Although not specifically addressing the issue of flashbacks or FI,
Ryan suggests that windows—which include such concepts as actual and virtual

windows, successor and continuating windows, merging and splitting windows, co-existing windows or overlapping windows—may shift when there is a "referential break" in the text's continuity (63). Referential breaks may occur when, as it were, "the camera goes offline" and shifts to a different location, or the "narrative clock is reset, either forward or backward" (63).

This coexistence of distinct time frames has the effect of mitigating the sequential unfolding of events within the novel, thereby underlining that the temporal horizon of the story is more than a mere linear progression. Construed in the perspective of the computer age, and building on Ryan's concept of "windows," this could almost be likened to the presence of numerous hyperlinks, each of which "clicks" to a different yet co-existing aspect of reality that emanates from a unified central element or, as it were, 'home page', while not being bound to the latter by rigid relations of temporal sequence. In this respect, it is worth noting that an interesting study by Ponzio on hypertext suggests that "the hypertext offers a system or methodics for empowering a non-linear writing-reading process . . . shifting freely, 'surfing' through the net, choosing a trajectory from the multiple alternatives a hypertext offers . . . The hypertext shows that to write and to read is not necessarily to write and to read in sequence, to channel thought into one line after another, and according to a privileged order." That is to say, the hypertext "is a system that can be infinitely decentred and recentred" (5).

Strangely enough, this interpretation of flashbacks as non-chronologically bound hyperlinks may also prove illuminating in seeking to comprehend two aspects of *Gardens* which apparently contravene the by now established flashback pattern. Firstly, a change in pace is felt as the novel moves towards its conclusion, with a decreasing salience of flashbacks after Hattie and Edward's return from Corsica; thereafter, the unfolding developments seem to award greater space to an active dimension of temporal immediacy, culminating in the dramatic events leading up to the sequence in which Hattie is severely beaten up and left for dead. One may perhaps sense that at least as far as the main protagonists are concerned, the chronological realm—with all that it implies in terms of the dominance of Western Culture and the related vision of advancing civilization (epitomized in *Gardens* by the continuing "civilization" of the West and the disruption of the Indians' traditional way of life) as well as the relentless forward motion of time and the sense of failure for what was not achieved in the past, is reasserting itself with a vengeance, thereby signaling a decrease in the power of Hattie's troubled but multidimensional visions. Similarly, Edward can no longer cherish his fantasies of amassing a fortune by exploiting the plant world, and thus what one might term his other lives—those existing in his flashbacks—begin to pale into nonexistence. Thus for both of these protagonists the constellation of flashbacks branching like spokes of a wheel from their consciousness recedes into the background.

This progression differs from the evolutionary parabola of the two main Indian protagonists, Sister Salt and Indigo, who, unlike the other major characters in *Gardens*, are not significantly associated with flashbacks. They do at times indulge in memories, yet they do not appear to be so dramatically engulfed by a recollectional way of thinking. This by no means implies that they are depicted as simplistically frozen in a one-dimensional mindset or in a time warp: indeed, quite the opposite is true, in that both sisters, albeit in different ways, are subjected to quite radical transformations as the world around them changes for ever. Indigo is severed from her original environment by the force of circumstances, and Sister Salt is deprived of the precious continuity of the traditional teachings of Grandma Fleet with her immense store of time-honored wisdom. Yet the sisters do not wallow in reminiscing, and memories of the past appear to merge more concretely with the ability—or rather the need—to cope with new and unfamiliar situations. Sister Salt sets about re-utilizing her awareness of the past—knowledge learnt from her mother about how to take in laundry, knowledge acquired from Grandma Fleet about how to grow plants—in an unflagging determination that focuses on survival in the present and re-creating life; Indigo, despite bouts of homesickness and longing for her sister, and the memory of her former life she constantly bears within her—and the initial disappointment of failing to jump off the train at Needles and get away from Hattie and Edward who are taking her on the long trip east to New York and thence to Europe—seems to adapt to life with Hattie and subsequently re-adapt to life out in the desert with Sister Salt, Vedna and Maytha, accepting both as a form of new present. Thus the two sisters' lives are intensely shaped by chronology, yet in a sense chronology passes them by, as they remain focused on their present, even when their present is in transformation. Therefore no constellation of flashbacks clusters around them.

In effect, it may be suggested that with regard to those who, like Hattie and Edward, have always belonged to the linear dimension of the passage of time, flashbacks convey a departure from this temporally bounded framework, an alternative series of routes that can shape a more all-encompassing representation of man's position in the world. Thus there may be—fleeting or prolonged—moments within a linearly oriented life when a multilayered vision acquires greater prominence and exerts a more significant impact on an individual. With regard to Sister Salt and Indigo, on the other hand, a mechanism embodying an alternative to a chronological way of life would be meaningless, for two reasons. Firstly, far from springing from a background and tradition embedded in awareness of the flow of time, the sisters actually have their shattering first experience of chronological time and their first awareness of "different times" precisely through the dramatic circumstances they undergo; secondly, to the extent to which they become aware of chronology, they stand aside from it because they cling to the belief that the past will merge with and be identical with the future in the full circularity of time: the Messiah will come back, they will find Mama. Thus there is no need for flashbacks that re-actualize the past in a different dimension; rather, the circular motion of the final return to the old gardens shows that the past is transformed into a new present. The potential non-linearity of time that is expressed for the other characters by the presence of flashbacks is incarnated for Sister Salt and Indigo by the circularity of the ending with their return to the old gardens.

NOTES

1. For a general and in-depth examination of the highly complex phenomenon of FI, and the diverse types of terminology used to refer to its manifestations, see Ann Banfield's *Unspeakable Sentences*; Monika Fludernik's *The Fictions of Language and the Languages of Fiction*; Susan Ehrlich's *Point of View*; Geoffrey Leech and Mick Short's *Style in Fiction*; on account of the complex debate on the most suitable nomenclature for this phenomenon, the abbreviated and simplified acronym FI ("free indirect") will be used here as an all-purpose term.

2. Focalization is discussed extensively in Gérard Genette's *Narrative Discourse* and critically re-elaborated in Manfred Jahn's "Windows of Focalization" and "More Aspects of Focalization."

3. Fludernik, studying subjective expressions in a variety of text types, uses the term "enquotation devices," suggesting that they act as a flag to signal that a linguistic form is a representation of a speech or thought act, signaling a transition to the character's code (419).

4. For a general description of the "dual voice," see Pascal.

5. Page numbers cited in parentheses refer to the Scribner Paperback Fiction edition. The extensive use of free indirect discourse in Gardens is noted by Fitz (Ch. 7) in his insightful study of this novel.

6. The question would obviously not appear in exactly this form in normal indirect discourse, for the grammatical construction would not involve Subject-Auxiliary inversion ("Had she. . ."), question punctuation would not be appropriate and the verb of musing would have to be rendered explicit, giving something approximating "Edward wondered whether she had misunderstood him." That FI cannot, however, be conceived as corresponding literally to a direct speech—or genuine indirect speech—equivalent was noted as early as Banfield, who describes it as represented speech or represented thought and suggests that representing means the mirroring of activities of the mind in the medium of language (268; 273). Furthermore, there is no agreement among linguists as to whether thought processes truly mimic the language patterns of real speech, and the interaction between language and thought has long been controversial (not least due to the wrangle over Benjamin Lee Whorf's misguided "linguistic relativity" hypothesis). However, for the purposes of this paper it will be assumed—as is generally done

in studies on FI—that it is possible and useful, at some level, to assume that thought processes can be rendered in terms that would otherwise be used for actual language. Therefore various periphrastic expressions will be used here to convey the approximate thought content and to approximate the verb of thinking. In addition, direct and indirect speech constructions will be cited as rough terms of comparison in discussing FI phenomena, and the concept of orality will be used to refer to the typical speech patterns of spontaneous—and in this case informal, at times colloquial—oral production. However, not all instances of informal speech patterns found in *Gardens* involve FI: a striking case of non-FI colloquial speech (see Labov) is seen in the reported conversation between the sorceress Delena and Sister Salt, when Sister Salt "asked how did the cards know anything" (355): here the non FI indirect question form with subject-auxiliary inversion ("how did. . .") is a characteristically colloquial or so-called nonstandard construction, as discussed in William Labov's pioneering studies on *The Social Stratification of English in New York City*. An example closely paralleling the above mentioned case from Gardens is found in Trotta (69): "She asked me what did he buy in Bolivia" (69), where the nonstandard or colloquial oral effect is likewise mentioned.

7. Note, in this regard, that the kind of grammatical construction characterized by omission of the impersonal subject and the verb be rather than the complete construction 'It was a good thing. . .' is known to be a typical oral feature, as pointed out in Zandvoort (209).

8. This is assumed to be a trace of the application of an implicit "sequence of tenses" phenomenon resulting from a covert main-clause verb of reporting, as would generally be the case in true indirect discourse.

9. A typical example of a back-shifted pluperfect is cited by Quirk and Greenbaum: "The exhibition finished last week," explained Ann ⇨ Ann explained that the exhibition had finished the preceding week (343). However, back-shifting from the simple past to the pluperfect is also affected by considerations of verbal aspect, being less frequent with durative constructions, i.e. with stative verbs or habitual constructions that convey an imperfect meaning. On sequence of tenses phenomena in general, and on the pluperfect in indirect speech, see for ex. Declerck, Kiparsky, Michaelis. But it is worth noting that not all pluperfects are back-shifted from a simple past, as they may represent a back-shifted present perfect (Quirk and Greenbaum 342); furthermore, back-shifting need not necessarily entail a pluperfect in order to be back-shifted, for as observed by many authors back-shifting may involve an occurrence of "would" back-shifted from "will," giving a future-in-the-past reading. Such is the case in the following true indirect speech example which describes Edward's preparations for the trip to Europe with Hattie and Indigo: "The superintendent was concerned over the child's rebellious behavior, but Edward assured him that they would be able to control the girl" (110). By the same token, FI sentences may likewise have instances of "would," as in the following example: "Too bad the sunflowers had to be sowed in June, but next season she would sow rows and rows of the giant sunflowers" (414). Here too one may note the typical FI occurrence of expressive forms, such as "too bad," or the quasi-direct speech article-less adverbial expressions of time "next season," hinting at a deictic communicative mode (Swan 219) that is closer to a direct utterance—as if linked to an imaginary "now" of the character—than would be the case with a narrator-mediated report. A similar phenomenon can be observed in the sentence cited earlier in the text, conveying Sister Salt's feelings: "She'd never go for a walk. . ." (343), where the contracted form 'd (would) signals, at one and the same time, the back-shifting that hints at a implicit higher-level past-tense verb of reporting, and an implicit orality, in that it is generally recognized that contracted forms belong more properly to the spoken language (Leech and Svartvik 207).

10. The role of the pluperfect as a reorienting device that induces a shift in perspective is mentioned, among others, by Lascarides (251), reinterpreting an example taken from Nakhimovsky: "The telephone rang. It was Mme Dupont. Her husband had eaten too many oysters for lunch. The

doctor recommended a change in lifestyle" (40), where the pluperfect signals a shift of control over the proposition from the narrator to the character Mme Dupont. Emmott likewise suggests that the pluperfect may signal reorientation rather than a straightforward time signal (*I*); Jahn, in a general survey of Narratology, notes that a tense switch is normally used to produce an effect of intensification or distancing (moving into/out of focus), change of perspective, etc. (*Narratology* 5.1.2).

11. For instance, the post-posed verbal auxiliary phrase "they had" is an expressive construction characteristic of a type of scornful sarcasm that is also found in oral contexts (especially in British English). Somewhat similar examples of this type are quoted in Zandvoort, where they are described as colloquial: "They're all alike, men are," "He never cared much for smoking, did your brother" (226).

12. Nor, of course, could it have featured the omission (rather than the repetition, as in endnote 11) of the pronominal subject and auxiliary before the verb "fled" that marks another characteristic of orality. This kind of omission is noted in Leech and Svartvik (117), citing casual and familiar speech forms such as "Want a drink?;" Zandvoort also mentions the ellipsis of the pronominal subject in familiar speech: "Don't think I'll be in time" (209).

13. Stative verbs do not necessarily follow the same pattern as eventive verbs (Declerck 26–27; Michaelis 235).

14. Back-shifted in this case not from a past tense but from a present perfect.

15. With its typically oral suppression of the copular phrase "it would be," which is not possible in true indirect speech, unless a parenthetical construction is used. Thus the putative rendering "She mused how ironic if the malaise were to return" is not a well-formed sentence, unlike the approximation "How ironic if the malaise were to return, she mused." On the close relation between parentheticals and FI, see Ehrlich, who attributes parenthetical verbal constructions to the narrator's point of view (110).

16. Similar phenomena are discussed by Vandelanotte (550) with reference to various types of text; Vandelanotte proposes an explanation in terms of a different typology of free indirect speech or thought representation which the author terms "Distancing," but the interpretation with regard to the interplay of narratorial and character voice is not completely dissimilar from that proposed here. Numerous analogous examples are found in Gardens, for ex. the mention of the name "Edward" rather than the pronominal form "him" or "himself" in "had arrived only hours before Edward," within a FI sentence that conveys Edward's own account of the situation (85). See also endnote 24.

17. As discussed in connection with endnote 29.

18. Jahn cites the following example: "'When do you leave?' she asked. 'Tomorrow night.' She said nothing more. Strangely enough, a tinge of melancholy had settled over her spirits. No doubt the proximity of the town was the cause of this" (Orczy, *The Scarlet Pimpernel*). Jahn's reasoning is that although there is indeed a contrast between the character's attitude and the reader's knowledge of the situation—in that the lady here thinks "the proximity of the town is the cause of my melancholy" whereas the reader and narrator know that this is just her counterfactual rationalizing and that the real cause of her state of mind is that her husband is leaving her—the question of FI is incidental, as the same ambivalence would arise if the reporting verbs were rendered explicit. Jahn also believes that the standard uses of FI are non-ironic and are more frequent than the ironic forms. ("Contextualizing" 356).

19. Thus the sentence "Before he graduated from college Joe published a book" may easily mean "Before he graduated from college, Joe had published a book," because the presence of the adverb "before" is sufficient to clarify the temporal sequence; the same point is made by Quirk and Greenbaum (45) with regard to *after*. In contrast, crucial disambiguation is required with a different

adverb of time: "When he graduated from college Joe published a book" does not mean the same as "When he graduated from college Joe had published a book," and it is the use of the pluperfect that acts as the discriminating element (Celce-Murcia, Tense and Aspect). An additional suggestion concerning the obsolescence of the pluperfect is put forward in the *American Heritage Book of English Usage* (§68) which quotes usage statistics on reported speech suggesting the pluperfect is falling out of use, with percentages varying between 23 and 41% allowing the simple past in sentences such as "He said the play opened (or: had opened) the week before."

20. The example cited by McGill from the Lancaster-Bergen Oslo corpus compiled by Leech and Johannson (1961) appeared in the British newspaper *The Guardian*, 15/11/1961: "Mr. Prys-Jones, prosecuting, said that on September 22nd Judge Evans's car collided with a stationary car at a cross-road at Howey." McGill also notes that the phenomenon is insufficiently addressed in English as a Foreign Language grammar books.

21. As noted by Celce-Murcia. It is interesting to cite one of Celce-Murcia's examples in full, in order to highlight the parallel with *Gardens* cited in the text: "The students sat in the bleachers of Pauley Pavilion watching the faculty enter in their caps and gowns. Dignitaries continued to arrive while the band played a festive melody for the onlookers. To the cheers of the crowd, President Clinton came in and took his assigned seat on the podium. UCLA's 75th anniversary celebration *had begun*" ("Tense and Aspect"). A similar observation is made by Emmott, a speaker of British English, who describes this use as "summarising the conversation" (5). In Kiparsky's terms (126), this can be seen as the resultative reading of the pluperfect, but Kiparsky stops short of interpreting it as a back-shifted form of the resultative present perfect.

22. It is also worth noting that according to the rules of English grammar the verb "tell" does not allow object complements composed of direct speech, in contrast to the verb "say;" "tell" requires a finite-verb subordinate clause, introduced not by a capital letter but, optionally, by the complementizer "that."

23. In the examples, expressions with a stative verb (e.g. the auxiliary 'be') or habitual forms are mainly disregarded, as also indicated in endnote 13.

24. Naturally, if one assumes a suppressed comment of this type, one also has to assume that the reporting verb 'explained' would be attributed to an intervention mediated by the narrator, thus momentarily overlaying Edward's own reflections with an external point of view and thereby creating a "dual voice" effect. In fact, such an intervention is indeed the case, for only the narrator can describe Edward's experiences with a mention of his name, whereas Edward's own flow of thoughts would have referred to himself by a pronominal form ('arrived only hours before me') which, in FI, would of course appear in the third person ('before him').

25. One of the examples cited by the Authors, albeit not illustrating FI, is: "Louise smiled. 'That's exactly what she used to say about you . . .'" (McDowell qtd. in Semino 31); an example of a similar kind from *Gardens*, but which does illustrate FI, is the fragment quoted earlier: "Aunt Bronwyn laughed merrily. Fled long ago, they had. . ." (264).

26. As an example, Ikeo cites the sentence "It was a lovely kitchen," which, if considered acontextually, would appear to be a simple case of narrator-based description, but if it appears in the middle of a text as a part of a character's memory, it can be interpreted as a free indirect form: "Her mother had once been photographed in the kitchen in a frilly apron, mixing a cake. The photographs were printed in a series of features about celebrities' wives and who they were and how they coped. It was a lovely kitchen. Their last meal in it should have been a kind of sacrament" (Angela Carter, *The Magic Toyshop* 54).

27. As noted by Jahn, a sentence such as "He took a day off with his wife and played golf," which may not at first glance look like represented speech or thought, yet in its actual context it is a back-

shifted version of a speech act of Dr. Holmes in *Mrs. Dalloway*. The reader derives this interpretation this from contextual features only; otherwise the sentence could also plausibly be interpreted as conveying the narrator's viewpoint ("Contextualizing" 352–53).

28. Emmott considers an example taken from Barbara Vine's *A Fatal Inversion* (194–95).

29. For instance, it fails to take into account that many occurrences of the pluperfect auxiliary "had" can be contracted to 'd or would automatically be understood as phonetically weak forms and therefore contribute little to any presumed awkwardness; furthermore, there is little evidence that any "cumbersome" problem affects other compound verbal forms in English, including complex modal constructions. But a comment by Nakhimovsky seems to appeal to an analogous awkwardness consideration when he states that "such a past perfect/simple past configuration is a must if one wants to go into a long multi-FS [flashback] digression, because there seems to be a strong limit on how long an embedded DS [Discourse Segment] can continue in the past perfect" (41). Similar recommendations are made by numerous aspiring writers' clubs (e.g. WritingClasses.com, Writersdigest.com), which advise authors that while flashbacks should begin and end with a few pluperfects, it is advisable to stop using the pluperfect too often once a flashback has been clearly established, because otherwise "the 'hads' weigh down the prose and suck the action out of the words" (Tritt tip11).

30. This is surely also the case in the example cited earlier from the Lancaster-Oslo-Bergen concordance, as well as those cited in the *American Heritage Book of English Usage*. Kiparsky (68) argues for the existence of an "independent past tense reading" in sentences such as "John knew the convict escaped," which he regards as acceptable "only on the reading on which the escape preceded the hearing," but although he discusses the Sequence of Tenses phenomenon and mentions free indirect speech, he does not consider the discourse-related alternation between simple past and pluperfect. Emmott likewise suggests the simple past might be regarded as a more immediate form, as if it were direct speech, but then goes on to associate this with avoidance of the cumbersome pluperfect, as in endnote 29.

31. Fitz notes that Silko's work seems to reveal a quest for a perfect language that is perhaps unrealizable in present forms of human language (6).

32. See also endnote 6.

33. On the concept of deictic center, see Nakhimovsky (37); on Deictic Shift Theory, see Vandelanotte (552), Ducham, Bruder and Hewitt (Ch. 1 and Ch. 6).

WORKS CITED

The American Heritage Book of English Usage. A practical and Authoritative Guide to Contemporary English. Boston: Houghton Mifflin, 1996. <bartleby.com/64/C001/068.html>.

Banfield, Ann. *Unspeakable Sentences: Narration and Representation in the Language of Fiction*. London: Routledge & Kegan Paul, 1982.

Celce-Murcia, Marianne. "Describing And Teaching English Grammar With Reference To Written Discourse." *Functional Approaches to Written Text. Section V- Approaches to Teaching Grammar*. Ed. Tom Miller. Washington, DC: USIS, 1997. US Department of State, Bureau of Educational and Cultural Affairs. <http://exchanges.state.gov/education/engteaching/pubs/BR/functionalsec5_13.htm>.

Coltelli, Laura, ed. *Native American Literatures*. Pisa, SEU Forum 4-5 (1992–93): 65–79.

Declerck, Renaat. *Tense in English: Its Structure and Use in Discourse*. London: Routledge, 1991.

Duchan, Judith F., Gail A. Bruder, and Lynne E. Hewitt, eds. *Deixis in Narrative: A Cognitive Science Perspective*. Hillsdale, NJ: Lawrence Erlbaum Assoc., 1995.

Ehrlich, Susan. *Point of View: A Linguistic Analysis of Literary Style*. London: Routledge, 1990.

Emmott, Catherine. "Real grammar in fictional contexts." *Glasgow Review* 4 (1996). STELLA, University of Glasgow. 13 Feb. 2006. <http://www.arts.gla.ac.uk/SESL/STELLA/COMET/glasgrev/issue4/contents.htm>.

Fitz, Brewster. *Silko: Writing Storyteller and Medicine Woman*. Norman: U of Oklahoma P, 2004.

Fludernik, Monika. *The Fictions of Language and the Languages of Fiction: The Linguistic Representation of Speech and Consciousness*. New York & London: Routledge, 1993.

Genette, Gérard. *Narrative Discourse*. Trans. Jane E. Lewin. Oxford: Blackwell, 1980.

Graesser Arthur C., and Cheryl A. Bowers. Rev. of *Deixis in Narrative: A Cognitive Science Perspective*. Ed. Judith F. Duchan, Gail A. Bruder, and Lynne E. Hewitt. *Minds and Machines* 6.3 (1996): 395–99.

Ikeo, Reiko. "Unambiguous Free Indirect Thought? An Approach From a Consideration of Ambiguous Cases." *PALA Papers: Prospect and Retrospect*. Proc. of 2004 International NYU Conference. Ed. Donald C. Freeman. Amsterdam & New York: Rodopi (forthcoming). New York University, Dept. of English. 4 Dec. 2005 <http://www.nyu.edu/gsas/dept/english/PALA2004/AcceptedAbstracts.html>.

Jahn, Manfred. "Contextualizing Represented Speech and Thought." *Journal of Pragmatics* 17 (1992): 347–67.

———. "More Aspects of Focalization: Refinements and Applications." Ed. John Pier. *GRAAT: Revue des Groupes de Recherches Anglo-Américaines de L'Université François Rabelais de Tours* 21 (1999): 85–110.

———. *Narratology: A Guide to the Theory of Narrative*. English Department, University of Cologne.

———. "Windows of Focalization: Deconstructing and Reconstructing a Narratological Concept." *Style* 30.2 (1996): 241–67.

Kiparsky, Paul. "Event Structure and the Perfect." *The Construction of Meaning*. Ed. David I. Beaver, Luis D. Casillas Martínez, Brady Z. Clark and Stefan Kaufmann. Stanford: CSLI Publ., 2002. 113–33.

Labov, William. *The Social Stratification of English in New York City*. Washington DC: Center for Applied Linguistics, 1982.

Lancaster-Oslo/Bergen (LOB) corpus. International Computer Archive of Modern English. Bergen, Norway, 1961.

Lascarides, Alex, and Nicholas Asher. "The Pluperfect in Narrative Discourse." *Proceedings of the 4th European Workshop on Semantics of Time, Space, and Movement and Spatio-Temporal Reasoning*. Ed. Michel Aurnague, A. Borillo, M. Borillo and M. Bras. Toulouse: Groupe "Langue, Raisonnement, Calcul," Université Paul Sabatier, 1992. 183–202.

Lawn, Jennifer. "Four Characters in Search of a Narrator: Focalization and the Representation of Consciousness in *Under the Volcano*." *Studies in Canadian Literature* 18.2 (1993): 11–31.

Leech, Geoffrey, and Jan Svartvik. *A Communicative Grammar of English*. Essex, England: Longman Group Ltd, 1975.

Leech, Geoffrey, and Mick Short. *Style in Fiction. A Linguistic Introduction to English Fictional Prose*. English Language Series 13. London: Longman, 1981.

McGill, Stephen. "Teaching your Grammar to Suck Eggs." *IH Journal* 18 (2005): 24–26.

Michaelis, Laura. "Tense in English." *The Handbook of English Linguistics, Part II*. Ed. B. Aarts and A. McMahon. Oxford: Blackwell, 2006. 220–43.

Nakhimovsky, Alexander. "Aspect, Aspectual Class, and the Temporal Structure of Narrative." *Computational Linguistics* 14.2 (1988): 29–43.

Pascal, Roy. *The Dual Voice: Free Indirect Speech and its Functioning in the Nineteenth Century European Novel*. Manchester: Manchester UP, 1977.

Ponzio, Augusto. "Hypertext and translation." Paper delivered at the International Conference, *Translating with Computer-Assisted Technology: Changes in Research, Teaching, Evaluation, and Practice*." University of Rome La Sapienza, Rome. 14–16 Apr. 2004. <http://www.augustoponzio.com/hypertext.htm>.

Quirk, Randolph, and Sidney Greenbaum. *A University Grammar of English*. Harlow: Longman Group UK Ltd, 1973.

Ryan, Marie-Laure. "On the Window Structure of Narrative Discourse." *Semiotica* 64.1–2 (1987): 59–81.

Semino, Elena, Mick Short and Jonathan Culpeper. "Using a Computer Corpus to Test a Model of Speech and Thought Presentation." *Poetics* 25 (1997): 17–43.

Silko, Leslie Marmon. *Gardens in the Dunes*. New York: Scribner, 2000.

Swan, Michael. *Basic English Usage*. Oxford: Oxford UP, 1984.

Tritt, Sandy. "Flashbacks and Foreshadowing." *Inspiration For Writers* (2004). <http://users.wirefire.com/tritt/tip11.html>.

Trotta, Joe. *Wh-Clauses in English: Aspects of Theory and Description*. Amsterdam/Atlanta: Rodopi, 2000.

Vandelanotte, Lieven. "From Representational to Scopal 'Distancing Indirect Speech or Thought': A Cline of Subjectification." *Text - Interdisciplinary Journal for the Study of Discourse* 24.4 (2004): 547–85.

Whorf, Benjamin Lee. *Language, Thought and Reality*. Ed. John Carroll. Cambridge: MIT P., 1956.

Wiebe, Janyce M. "References in Narrative Texts." *Deixis in Narrative*. Ed. Judith F. Duchan et al. Hillsdale: Erlbaum, 1995. 263–86.

———. "Tracking Point of View in Narrative." *Computational Linguistics* 20.2 (1994): 233–87.

Zandvoort, Reinard W. *A Handbook of English Grammar*. 7th ed. London: Longman Group Ltd., 1975.

CONTRIBUTORS

JAMES BARILLA is Assistant Professor of English at Lake Forest College, where he teaches creative writing and environmental literature courses. His research, which focuses on the intersections between ecological restoration and literature, has included helping to manage a 65 acre restoration site called the Experimental Ecosystem. He recently published the non-fiction essay "Aliens in the Garden," in *Writing the World: On Globalization* (MIT Press). He has also published non-fiction dealing with migration and ecology in *You Are Here: The Journal of Creative Geography*. His analysis of native and exotic identities in the work of J. M. Coetzee, Aldo Leopold and Leslie Marmon Silko will appear in *Coming Into Contact: Explorations in Ecocritical Theory and Practice* (U of Georgia P). His non-fiction book, *West With the Rise*, was published by the U of Virginia P in 2006. He is currently at work on a book about cultural and ecological restoration.

RACHEL BARRITT COSTA has a lifelong interest in language and linguistics, developed through language and literature studies at the University of Oxford, UK (B.A., St. Hilda's College) followed by in-depth studies of Linguistics in the USA (Ph.D., The University of Michigan). After beginning her academic career at Michigan State University, she moved to Italy, where she has taught English as a Foreign Language at the Department of English of the University of Pisa and Translation studies at the School for Interpreters and Translators of Pisa. She is currently teaching English at the Language Center of the University of Pisa, where she is coordinating a language certification project set up by the Language Center within the context of the European Common Frame of Reference for Languages. Her interests focus on the interface between linguistics-based text analysis and literary theory, seeking to determine the potential contribution not only of discourse analysis but also of grammatical phenomena such as verbal tense, pronouns and anaphora, and sentence structure to an insightful account of the literary work. She is also interested in contrastive and culturally diverse approaches to text-writing and their impact on translation and foreign-language composition, as well as the role that foreign language learning can play as a vital element in enhancing language awareness and language education in general. Rachel Barritt Costa lives in Pisa and in London.

LAURA COLTELLI is a professor of American Literature at the University of Pisa. She has written contributions on travel and colonial literature. She has subsequently pursued her research interests by focussing attention on American poetry and on multiculturalism, above all the literary production of contemporary American Indian writers. Her recent publications include *Winged Words. American Indian Writers Speak* (1990), *Voci dal Sudovest. Terra e identità negli scrittori indianoamericani* (2002), *Le radici della memoria. Meridel LeSueur e il radicalismo americano della fine degli Anni Trenta* (2002) and "Joy Harjo's Poetry: 'A Journey for Truth, for Justice'" in *The Cambridge Companion to Native American Literature* (2003). She has also edited the Italian translations of works by Leslie Marmon Silko, N. Scott Momaday, Joy Harjo, as well as an anthology of contemporary American Indian women writers. She is the general editor of the series "Crossroads" devoted to American writers, which was recently inaugurated with a volume of selected poems by Sherman Alexie and with *Men on the Moon* by Simon Ortiz.

MARY MAGOULICK is an Associate Professor of English and Interdisciplinary Studies at Georgia College & State University in Milledgeville, Georgia (the public liberal arts university for the state). She received an M.A. in English from the University of Virginia and a Ph.D. in folklore from Indiana University (in 2000). Her research interests focus on Native American studies (especially narratives and literature), women's studies, nature writing, mythology, folklore, and popular culture. She spent two years doing fieldwork among Ojibwe (or Nishnaabe) people in the Upper Peninsula of Michigan for her dissertation. While there, she taught at a tribal college and studied the Ojibwe language. Her published articles include "That Way We Should be Walking" (in Brian Swann's *Algonquian Spirit*, University of Nebraska Press, 2005) about an Ojibwe woman's oratory of cultural renewal; "'Hey! Get up! You got no relations here!'" on jokes in Ojibwe culture; and "Frustrating Female Heroism: Mixed Messages in *Xena, Nikita,* and *Buffy*." Her manuscript, *Coming to Life: Revitalizations of Culture and Identity in Michigan Ojibwe Communities* is under consideration at the University of Nebraska Press. She is currently researching a book on female heroism from a variety of cultures and contexts. Dr. Magoulick has traveled extensively as part of her on-going interest in cultural studies and cross-cultural contact. Some of her major foreign excursions include two years as a Peace Corps volunteer in Senegal, West Africa, a teaching stint for the Semester at Sea program, and a Fulbright grant to lecture in Croatia.

DEBORAH A. MIRANDA is a mixedblood woman of Esselen, Chumash, French and Jewish ancestry. She is enrolled with the Ohlone-Costanoan Esselen Nation of California. Deborah received her Ph.D in English from the University of Washington in 2001. Her first book of poetry, *Indian Cartography* (Greenfield Review P 1999) won the Diane Decorah First Book Award from the Native Writer's Circle of the Americas; her second collection is titled *The Zen of La Llorona* (Salt Publishing 2005). Deborah's other projects include a manuscript titled *"In My Subversive Country:" Searching for American Indian Women's Love Poetry and Erotica*, and a poetry collection in progress titled *The Uses of Anger and other Praise Poems*, as well as a collaborative project, *The Light from Carissa Plains*, that incorporates her grandfather's oral history of post-Mission Indian life in California from 1902–88. Currently, Deborah is Assistant Professor of English at Washington and Lee University, where she teaches Creative Writing (poetry), Composition, Women's Literatures and Native American Literatures.

DAVID L. MOORE is Associate Professor of English at the University of Montana. He teaches and publishes on Native American and American literatures, ecocriticism, and critical legal theory. Earning his MA in Literature from the University of South Dakota in 1980, he first taught in American Indian higher education there and then at Salish Kootenai College on the Flathead Reservation in western Montana. In 1994, he earned his PhD from the University of Washington and then taught at Cornell University until 1999, when he came back to Montana to live and work closer to certain Indian communities. Currently he is completing a contracted book manuscript, entitled "'That Dream Shall Have a Name': American Indians Rewriting America." He is working also on an ecocritical study of the Makah whaling controversy, as well as an edited collection of founding papers of the Pacifica Radio Foundation. Recent and forthcoming publications among his articles and chapters in the United States and Europe include "Ghost Dancing through History in Silko's Gardens in the Dunes and Almanac of the Dead;" "Cycles of Selfhood, Cycles of Nationhood: Authenticity, Identity, Community, Sovereignty;" "'The literature of this nation': LaVonne Ruoff and the Redefinition of American Literary Studies;" and "Return of the Buffalo: Cultural Representation as Cultural Property." His publishers include, among others, SAIL: Studies in American Indian Literatures; American Indian Quarterly; G.R.A.A.T.: Publication des Groupes de Recherches Anglo-Americaines de l'Universite Francois-Rabelais de Tours; the Dictionary of Literary Biography (Gale Research); Cambridge University Press; Smithsoni an Press; Prentice Hall; New Mexico University Press; and Nebraska University Press. He lives with his family in Missoula, Montana.

DAVID MURRAY is Professor of American Studies at the University of Nottingham, England, where he teaches modules on American Literature and culture, Native Peoples, and African American writing and music. He has published widely on American Indians, including *Forked Tongues: Speech, Writing and Representation in North American Indian Texts* (1992) *Indian Giving: Economies of Power in Early Indian-White Exchanges* (2000), and recent contributions to *The Columbia History of Native American Literature in the US Since 1945* (2006) and the *Cambridge Companion to Native American Literature* (2005). He has recently completed a comparative study of the representations of African American and Native American religion and magic, to be published in 2007, and has been director of a research project, funded by AHRC, *Criss Cross: Confluence and Influence in 20th Century African American Music, Visual Art and Literature.*

JOY PORTER is a lecturer in The Department of American Studies at the University of Wales, Swansea, U.K. where she teaches American and Native American history and literature. She gained her M.A. and Ph.D from The University of Nottingham, U.K. in 1990 and 1993 respectively. She is the author of *To Be Indian: The Life of Seneca-Iroquois Arthur Caswell Parker, 1881–1955* (U of Oklahoma P, 2002) and co-editor with Professor Kenneth Roemer (University of Texas, Arlington), of *The Cambridge Companion to Native American Literature* (U of Cambridge P, 2005). Her work on Indian themes can be found in a variety of books such as the *Cambridge Companion to Native American Literature* (2005); *First Nations of North America: Politics & Representation* (VU UP, 2005), *The State of U.S. History* (Berg, 2002) and in journals such as *New York History* and *Irish Studies Review*. She recently organised the British Academy-supported conference, "Place and American Indian History, Literature & Culture: 27th Meeting of the American Indian Workshop" whose keynote speakers included Simon Ortiz, David Treuer and Alan Trachtenberg. Her next books are an edited collection, *Place and Indian History, Literature & Culture* for Peter Lang (2007), a source book, *Fighting Words: Competing Voices From Native America* (Greenwood Press, 2008) and two new monographs, *The American Indian Poet of World War One: Modernism and the Indian Identity of Frank "Toronto" Prewett, 1893–1962 and Native American Freemasonry*, the research for which was supported by a Leverhulme Research Fellowship.

JOHN LLOYD PURDY is Professor of English at Western Washington University. His works include *Word Ways: The Novels of D'Arcy McNickle* and *The Legacy of D'Arcy McNickle: Writer, Historian, Activist,* which he edited. He has published poetry, fiction and creative nonfiction in national journals, and numerous articles on Native American authors, including James Welch, Leslie Marmon Silko, N. Scott Momaday, and Elizabeth Cook Lynn, as well as interviews with Sherman Alexie, Paula Gunn Allen, Simon Ortiz, Louis Owens, and Gerald Vizenor. He won Writer of the Year award from the Wordcraft Circle of Native American Writers and Storytellers for his anthology, *Nothing But the Truth: An Anthology of Native American Literatures.* He has taught courses on American Indian literatures in Germany and New Zealand, as well as on the Lummi and Warm Springs reservations in the Pacific Northwest. From 1994 to 2001, he was editor of *Studies in American Indian Literatures,* and from 2002 to 2005 he served on the Advisory Committee for the journal *Profession* for the Modern Language Association. Currently, he is on the Editorial Board: for the *Journal on Educational Controversy.*

BARBARA K. ROBINS is currently an Assistant Professor at the University of Nebraska at Omaha, Department of English. She teaches Native American Literature and composition courses, as well as introductory courses for the Native American Studies Program. She completed an interdisciplinary PhD in Native American literature and visual arts at the University of Oklahoma in 2001. Publications include book reviews for *American Indian Quarterly* and *Studies in American Indian Literature,* "Teaching Sherman Alexie's 'Every Little Hurricane'" in the *Eureka Studies in Teaching Short Fiction* and "Michael (Anthony) Dorris" for the *Dictionary of Native American Literature.* Her current research explores the roles of the arts in healing of trauma, particularly cultural and historical forms such as intergenerational trauma and the Native American response to the 9/11 terrorist attacks such as the series of Healing Poles created by Lummi totem pole carver Jewell James. She is also collaborating on an assessment and expansion of resources available to Native American studies scholars, teachers, and students at the University of Nebraska at Omaha. With research partner Linda Parker, she will be presenting on this project at the 2006 Joint Conference of Librarians of Color. In addition, Barbara is a painter and creative writer, currently focusing on playwriting and short fiction. She participates in both regional and national organizations promoting Native American visual arts, performing arts, and film and is a board member for TICOTA—The Indigenous Collective of Theatre and Arts, in Omaha, Nebraska.

KIMBERLY ROPPOLO, of Cherokee, Choctaw, and Creek descent, took her Ph.D. from Baylor University, specializing in Native American Literature, in May 2002. She is an Assistant Professor in the Native American Studies Department at The University of Lethbridge and is the Associate National Director of Wordcraft Circle of Native Writers and Storytellers. Recent publications of hers include "Morning Star Song" in *Studies in American Indian Literatures* 16.4; "Symbolic Racism, History, and Reality: The Real Problem with Indian Mascots," in editor MariJo Moore's *Genocide of the Mind: An Anthology of Urban Indians;* and "The Real Americana," in Editors Gloria E. Anzaldúa and AnaLouise Keating's *This Bridge We Call Home: Radical Visions for Transformation.* She received the Native Writers Circle of the Americas First Book Award for Prose for 2004 for her manuscript, *Back to the*

Blanket: Reading, Writing, and Resistance for American Indian Literary Critics. She resides in Lethbridge, Alberta with her husband and the two youngest of her three children. This past year, she was honored to participate in a playwrighting workshop led by noted First Nations writer Tomson Highway; subsequently, she has written two plays in progress with Blood Rez Productions. She is currently working on a biography of Eugene Blackbear, Sr., the oldest living Cheyenne Sun Dance priest.

A. LAVONNE BROWN RUOFF is professor emerita of English, University of Illinois at Chicago, and former interim director of the D'Arcy McNickle Center for American Indian History, Newberry Library. From 2001 to 2004, she was a member of the Executive Committee of the Consortium on American Indian Studies, Committee on Institutional Cooperation. Ruoff has served on the Modern Language Association's Executive Council (2002–05); the Committee on the Literatures of People of Color as member (1980–83, 1998–2001) and co-chair (2000–01); Delegate Assembly Organizing Committee (2004–05); the Language Map Advisory Committee (2005 to the present); and the Radio Committee (2006–09). In 2002, she received the MLA's Lifetime Scholarly Achievement Award. The MLA Division on American Indian Literatures and the Association on American Indian Literatures held a session in her honor (2002) and selected her as their first honoree (1993). In 1998 Ruoff received a Life-time-Achievement Award from the American Book Awards of the Before Columbus Foundation. She directed four National Endowment for the Humanities Summer Seminars for College Teachers on American Indian Literature and has received an NEH research grant and fellowship. General editor of the American Indian Lives Series for the University of Nebraska Press, Ruoff is the author of *American Indian Literatures* (1990), and with Jerry W. Ward, Jr., she edited *Redefining American Literary History* (1990). She has also published annotated editions of books by S. Alice Callahan (Muscogee-Creek), George Copway (Ojibwe), Charles Eastman (Dakota), and E. Pauline Johnson (Mohawk).

ANNETTE VAN DYKE is a Professor of English and Interdisciplinary Studies at the University of Illinois at Springfield. Her research interests include Native American women's literature and women's spirituality. In the fall of 2006, she will taking a sabbatical to Italy, Malta, Crete and Sicily to work on a comparison of Native American Iconography with ancient goddess sites. She is the author of *The Search for a Woman-Centered Spirituality*, (New York UP, 1992), which as a chapter on Leslie Marmon Silko and Paula Gunn Allen. Her most recent publications include: "Women Writers and Gender Issues," Cambridge Companion to Native American Literature, Kenneth Roemer and Joy Porter, editors, (Cambridge: Cambridge UP, 2005) and "Encounters with Deer Woman: Sexual Relations in Susan Power's The Grass Dancer and Louise Erdrich's *The Antelope Wife*," SAIL 15.3–4 (Fall 2003/Winter 2004): 168–88.

Finito di stampare nel mese di Marzo 2007
presso le Industrie Grafiche della Pacini Editore S.p.A.
Via A. Gherardesca - 56121 Ospedaletto - Pisa
Per conto di Edizioni PLUS - Università di Pisa